DOUBLE AGENT SNOW

ALSO BY JAMES HAYWARD

Shingle Street

The Bodies on the Beach

Myths and Legends of the First World War

Myths and Legends of the Second World War

Never Such Innocence Again

DOUBLE AGENT SNOW

The True Story of Arthur Owens, Hitler's Chief Spy in England

James Hayward

SIMON & SCHUSTER

London · New York · Sydney · Toronto · New Delhi

A CBS COMPANY

First published in Great Britain by Simon & Schuster UK Ltd, 2013
A CBS COMPANY

1 3 5 7 9 10 8 6 4 2

Simon & Schuster UK Ltd
1st Floor
222 Gray's Inn Road
London WC1X 8HB

www.simonandschuster.co.uk

Simon & Schuster Australia, Sydney
Simon & Schuster India, New Delhi

A CIP catalogue record for this book is available
from the British Library

Hardback ISBN: 978-1-47112-916-2
Ebook ISBN: 978-0-85720-857-6

Typeset in the UK by M Rules
Printed and bound by CPI Group (UK) Ltd, Croydon, CR0 4YY

'History with its flickering lamp stumbles along the trail of the past, trying to reconstruct its scenes, to revive its echoes . . .'

WINSTON CHURCHILL (November 1940)

CONTENTS

	Dramatis Personae	ix
	Prologue	xi
1	'Typical Underfed Cardiff Type'	1
2	Colonel Johnny	27
3	OIK Calling Hamburg	45
4	The Welsh Ring	63
5	Double Agent Dick	80
6	The Trawler Treff	101
7	Operation Lamp	116
8	Nazi Frightfulness in Surrey	136
9	Summer and Snow	162
10	The Executioners	177
11	Double Trouble	195
12	Working For Peace	213
13	Snow On Ice	234
14	Sins of the Father	255
	Epilogues	273
	Bibliography and Sources	279
	Acknowledgements	283
	Index	285
	A Note on the Author	304

DRAMATIS PERSONAE

Arthur Owens – the troublesome British double agent code-named SNOW by MI5, and JOHNNY by the German *Abwehr*. Hitler's chief spy in England between 1937 and 1941.

Captain Thomas Robertson – Snow's long-suffering case officer at MI5, informally known as Tommy or Tar.

Guy Liddell – Robertson's immediate superior at MI5, where he is head of B Division (counter-espionage).

Major Nikolaus Ritter – Snow's flamboyant German handler, based at Stelle X in Hamburg, aka Doctor Rantzau.

Lily Bade – Snow's beguiling mistress, of German descent and thirteen years his junior.

Bob Owens – Snow's eldest son, referred to as Snow Junior by MI5.

William Rolph – a former MI5 officer employed to supervise Snow between February and May of 1940.

Gwilym Williams – a former policeman from Swansea, hired by MI5 to help Snow run his imaginary 'Welsh ring' in 1939 (aka Agent G.W.).

Sam McCarthy – a dope smuggler of Canadian origin, and Snow's second MI5 sidekick in 1940 (aka Agent Biscuit).

Walter Dicketts – the veteran confidence trickster employed as sidekick #3 from late 1940 onwards (aka Agent Celery).

Wulf Schmidt – a German parachute agent and close personal friend of Ritter, turned by MI5 as Agent Tate.

Gösta Caroli – another German parachute agent, dropped into England in 1940 and turned as Agent Summer.

John Masterman – a colleague of Robertson and Liddell at MI5, later chairman of the so-called Twenty Committee charged with running Allied double agents.

PROLOGUE

On the night of Saturday, 19 April 1941, in lethal celebration of Adolf Hitler's fifty-second birthday, corpulent German air force chief Hermann Göring dispatched 700 bombers to London, intent on delivering his Führer a gift to remember. Flying in relays for seven hours, many crews managed to squeeze in two missions, with the keenest of the Luftwaffe bombardiers even notching up three. For the first time during the Blitz – and the last – the long tail of Heinkels, Junkers and Dorniers were able to drop 1,000 tonnes of high explosive on the beleaguered capital. Thanks to cloud overcast most of the raiders bombed blind, scattering their payloads wildly, killing 1,200 people and triggering more than a thousand major fires. The small price paid only added to mordant Nazi delight, *das Tausendtonnengeschenk* costing the Luftwaffe just four aircraft lost.

Major Thomas 'Tar' Robertson of B Division, MI5, drew back a corner of the heavy blackout curtain covering the office window at 54 Broadway. Beyond Green Park parachute mines and incendiaries rained down on Mayfair, demolishing banks, tailors and gentlemen's clubs. Searchlights, tracer and phosphorus dazzled; fire consumed. The war news from overseas was no more encouraging. Having routed the Yugoslavian army, victorious German troops had pushed back Allied forces in Greece and southern Albania, raising the possibility of yet another chaotic British evacuation by sea. On the other side of the Mediterranean the port of Tobruk was under determined siege by Rommel's Afrika Korps, while the recent destruction of several U-boats failed to disguise the fact that the tide of the Battle of the Atlantic was still running in Germany's favour.

That a mysterious female agent with 'good legs' had been observed stepping off the Lisbon plane at Whitchurch held a measure of promise for Robertson and Section B1A. All things considered, however, this trifling development was unlikely to bring about a swift Allied victory.

Besides, everything paled into insignificance beside the crisis of confidence which had lately enveloped Tar's star double agent. Codenamed SNOW by MI5, and JOHNNY by their opposite numbers in Germany, for the last five years the diminutive Welshman born Arthur Graham Owens had operated as Hitler's chief spy in England, masquerading as a nationalist traitor in return for an astronomic salary and a vanity rank. In truth Agent Snow was planting disinformation on the bungling German *Abwehr*, a bodyguard of lies by which Robertson's department hoped to reverse the disastrous flow of events since Dunkirk, making the so-called double-cross system one of the few effective weapons in a British armoury still desperately short of tangible hardware.

The flaw in this ingenious deception scheme was Snow himself. Even by the standards of the rogues' gallery of hustlers and shadowplayers run by B1A, Arthur Owens was more trouble than a barrel of Barbary apes. The little man had endeared himself to no one in the Service, a string of sceptical handlers noting a penchant for expensive motors, cheap women and flights of wild egotistical fancy that would shame Walter Mitty. 'In drink he is probably not completely aware on these occasions that what he is saying is a lie,' rued the latest glum case summary. 'Similar doubts have pervaded his motives in acting as an agent. At times in his complicated career Agent Snow has seen himself as a patriot doing dangerous and valuable work for his country; at other times, no less genuinely, as a daring spy, clever enough to outwit British Intelligence.'

Lisbon had been his nadir. Two months earlier, in February 1941, Owens had flown to Portugal to *treff* with his German handler, Herr Doktor Rantzau, only to return to London bearing a bullish peace proposal drafted by high-ranking Nazis. Worse still, Owens now insisted that he had been unmasked as a British double agent by the other side.

Fox shot, flush busted.

Instinct told Robertson that the vital double-cross secret was probably safe. After all, Snow had returned from Lisbon very much alive, his pockets bulging with sterling and dollars, and a veritable Woolwich arsenal of exploding pens. However, Owens appeared now to be a burnt-out case, pleading duodenal ulcers while at the same time sinking a bottle of brandy a day, and increasingly desperate to please Lily Bade, the high-maintenance floozy who had lately given birth to their child. Had the schizophrenic complexities of the disorientating double-cross realm become too much to bear? Or had Snow simply fabricated his tale of illness and exposure in Iberia in order to engineer a comfortable retirement with a foot in both camps?

The only certainty was that Owens had returned from Lisbon with a sexually transmitted disease. Louche, lazy and libidinous, everything Snow touched became corrupt or contaminated, like King Midas in reverse. True, since the end of the Phoney War in May 1940 he had achieved outstanding results for MI5, exposing several pre-war sleepers in Britain and luring a dozen hapless invasion spies who arrived by parachute and boat. Most had been captured with laughable ease, then dropped by the hangman after cursory trials. Better still, Robertson had managed to flip several of these incoming agents as fresh double-cross assets. Indeed, the Dane codenamed Tate had even been awarded an Iron Cross by his gullible German masters.

With the first stirrings of spring, however, Snow's credibility had melted clean away. The Lisbon fiasco aside, on April Fools' Day the body of a previously unknown German agent had been discovered in a shelter in Cambridge. Isolated, penniless and emaciated by hunger, the V-man had hastened his own demise by placing an Abwehr-issue 6.35 mm Mauser automatic to his temple and squeezing the trigger. Poorly forged papers identified him as Jan Willem Ter Braak, an unremarkable Dutch refugee, yet his pink ration book told a different story, while his ID card bore telltale sample serial numbers buzzed to Hamburg on Agent Snow's transmitter.

Ter Braak had been at large for six months, during which time Cambridge had suffered several damaging air raids. How many more Nazi spies might have bypassed Snow's illusory shadow network?

Back at his desk, Tar Robertson leafed again through page after page of muddled, contradictory transcripts and flimsies. Rogue Agent Snow was a riddle wrapped up in an enigma. The one glimmer of hope was that new Ultra decrypts from Bletchley Park confirmed that Germany was poised to invade the Soviet Union, perhaps even as early as May. Codenamed Barbarossa, the assault would commit Adolf Hitler to a war on two fronts that would eventually destroy his 'thousand year' Reich. Though far removed from the frozen steppes of Russia, Agent Snow too had a key role to play. The intricate lies put across in his name would one day step up from tactical to strategic, their deceptions determining the fate of tens of thousands, whether Bomber Command airmen high above the steel mills of the Ruhr, merchant navy sailors dodging U-boats in the freezing waters of the North Atlantic, or entire infantry divisions storming the beaches of Italy and France, opening up the second front, delivering Europe from evil.

Humdinger, as the little man himself was apt to say.

Bombs continued to fall thick and fast as the Führer's birthday Blitz entered its fourth violent hour, those dropping closest to Broadway causing the very foundations of the building to shake. Robertson could picture the scene at Homefields, the comfortable Surrey safehouse provided for Hitler's chief spy in England, two dozen miles from the mayhem surrounding SW1. Probably Owens was playing cards with his Intelligence Corps minder, pouring freely from a bottle of black-market brandy, conjuring fresh alibis and ailments, his fate dangling by the most slender of threads.

Snow.

Shabby, scapegrace little man Snow. Running with the hare while hunting with the hounds. Hiding in plain sight, always playing both ends against the middle.

Shrugging off a powerful sensation of déjà vu, Major Robertson reached for his green-handset scrambler phone and asked the girl on the switchboard for a Weybridge number.

The die was cast.

1

'Typical Underfed Cardiff Type'

By his own account, Arthur Owens' extraordinary career as a double-cross agent was triggered by Zeppelin shells. A quarter century before the Luftwaffe delivered the *Tausendtonnengeschenk* on London, marauding German airships were sent to harry the capital with pinprick raids, causing little material damage but confirming a Hunnish reputation as barbarians and 'baby killers'. Barely sixteen when the first Zepps arrived in 1915, and thus too young to take to the air in an Avro or Sopwith, or charge over the top from a trench, Owens would later lay claim to feelings of profound outrage.

Profound, yet wholly unpatriotic. By his own account, after his father's engineering firm devised a 'special shell' which brought down Zeppelins in droves the War Office denied the company any credit, resulting in the loss of hundreds of thousands of pounds. A more elaborate version of the same story found room for corrupt officials, titanic legal battles in the High Court and the confiscation of a private yacht by vindictive government agents. This, so the little Welshman said, had left him feeling 'very bitter' towards England.

Tall tales of political and personal betrayal provided the perfect backstory for Hitler's chief spy in England. That the Zeppelin shells story was entirely untrue also served to set the scene for Owens' picaresque rise as a secret agent, whose erratic moral compass and predilection for intrigue and fantasy would, by 1940, bring his country to the brink of disaster.

With his sharp features, beady eyes and nicotine-stained fingers, Arthur Graham Owens was nobody's idea of a gentleman spy. The youngest son of a master plumber, the future Agent Snow was born in the small Welsh industrial town of Pontardawe on 14 April 1899. His father, William Thomas Owens, had moved his business from Bristol to Glamorganshire fifteen years earlier, just as coal-rich Pontardawe began to boom and bloom as a micro 'tinopolis', exporting tinplate and galvanised steel to all four corners of the globe. Though his small engineering business was dwarfed by the forges and mills thrown up by the ironmasters, entrepreneurial William Owens expanded his company as the town grew, graduating from manufacturing humble plumbing supplies to cast-iron radiators and acetylene gas equipment, styling himself as an inventor and patentee.

In middle age William Owens took a second wife, Ada, who was some sixteen years his junior. Like William, Ada was a native of Somerset, making the Owens household at 224 Dyffryn Road culturally rather more English than Welsh, aspirant middle class, with a small complement of domestic staff. Their youngest son Arthur received a solid education at Pontardawe County School, where he showed a talent for sciences, and then served an apprenticeship with a firm of electrical engineers in nearby Clydach, no doubt with a view to bringing new skills to the family business. Short of stature, as well as social graces, the young scion was nevertheless talkative, quick witted and blessed with a keenly inventive mind. But for primogeniture, William Owens & Company would almost certainly have been his eventual inheritance.

However, these formative years were overshadowed by the outbreak of the First World War in August 1914. With his flair for mechanics, Arthur dreamed of joining the Royal Flying

Corps, the newest and most glamorous of the three armed services; later he would hint at having held a commission and flown fast Sopwith Camels. In truth Owens was too undersized for military service, and too highly strung. There were no pilot's wings, and no Zeppelin shells. Condemned to remain in dreary Pontardawe for the duration of the conflict, surrounded by collieries, mills and begrimed mundanity, the little man determined to escape and seek his fortune elsewhere.

With his half-brothers held in reserved occupations, the name Owens appears nowhere on the Pontardawe war memorial. Nevertheless, genuine tragedy touched the family in the summer of 1918 when Ada succumbed to a brain haemorrhage. Now an elderly widower, William sold up and took his money back to Bristol, where he purchased a comfortable town house in the affluent suburb of Clifton. Arthur moved too, describing himself as a 'manufacturing chemist' of independent means, and stepping out with a petite blonde from Knowle named Irene Ferrett. Possibly Irene fancied that Arthur had been a scout pilot; certainly her diminutive beau was inclined towards flights of fancy and magical thinking. The couple married in September 1919 and moved into the large town house at 23 Gordon Road, living an indolent, carefree lifestyle until the following January, when William Owens, master plumber turned gas magnifico, succumbed to chronic kidney disease.

Zeppelin shells or no, the profits from large wartime contracts meant that Owens Senior left his heirs a substantial estate. Rather than return to industrial Glamorgan, or further his career as a chemist or engineer, Arthur instead moved to Mumbles, a popular seaside resort near Swansea, where he hoped to cash in on the postwar holiday boom by setting up a confectionery business. While her husband honed his skills as a humbug merchant, Irene nursed their son, born Graham Robert in September 1920 but known always as Bob. For many entrepreneurs the tourism bonanza delivered easy money, yet

Owens was financially irresponsible and proved incapable of living within his means. In little more than a year the pretender from Pontardawe had managed to run through the bulk of his inheritance, and found himself fending off disgruntled creditors.

Never knowingly heroic, the little man cut and ran. Like tens of thousands of other Britons during this turbulent postwar period, Arthur Owens chose to make a new life in Canada, where English-speaking WASPs were once again being encouraged to 'fill up the vast waste spaces' after the war in Europe had forced a lull in westward immigration. The family sailed from Bristol in October 1921 and eventually settled in Ontario, where Arthur gained employment as a public utility engineer. In 1925 Irene gave birth to a daughter, Patricia. After five years the couple became naturalised Canadian subjects, and Owens entered into a business partnership with an Australian named John Mercer. Applying his inventive skills to battery technology Owens claimed to have perfected a new type of lead oxide paste for use in accumulators, which the pair registered as a potentially lucrative industrial patent.

Seeking to emulate his prosperous father, but with no real capital of his own, Owens required backing to bring his innovations to market. Unfortunately the North American economy was becalmed in the midst of the Great Depression, during which patents came to be perceived as monopolistic and harmful, and their efficacy eroded by antitrust laws. Fatefully, during 1933 Owens received expressions of interest from George Hamilton, a wealthy investment banker based in London, who preferred the more cosmopolitan sobriquet of G. C. Hans Hamilton. With a varied portfolio of business interests, Hamilton sat on the board of directors of The Expanded Metal Company, a large industrial concern with plant and laboratories in West Hartlepool and a smart Westminster office at Burwood House. Lightweight but durable, the company's patent metal mesh supported several iconic landmarks, notably the Eiffel

Tower, the Forth Road Bridge and the Kohl Building – one of the few structures left standing in San Francisco after the devastating earthquake of 1906.

The opportunities afforded by Expanded Metal beat tinpot Pontardawe hands down. In August of 1933, six months after Adolf Hitler gained power in Germany, Owens obtained a Canadian passport and sailed from Halifax to Southampton. Convinced that urbane George Hamilton might make him a millionaire, Owens signed on as a salaried consultant with Expanded Metal, which in turn would invest in a new company formed to exploit Owens' patents and restore the fortune shamefully squandered on novelty rock in Mumbles. Back in Ontario, the family sold up and broke their long journey home with a stay in New York. Father and son returned first, arriving in London at the beginning of January 1934. Irene and Pat followed six weeks later, travelling in style on board the *Berengaria*, the flagship liner of the Cunard fleet.

Back in Europe there were already worrying signs that the great inventor was reverting to type. In filling out her boarding card, Irene gave her London address as 112 Stratford Road, a modest terraced property in Plaistow occupied by an elder brother named Fred. Arthur, meanwhile, selected the Grosvenor House Hotel on Park Lane, impatient to return to the high-rolling lifestyle lost a dozen years earlier. By the time his wife and daughter reached London the aspirant tycoon had taken rooms in Sloane Avenue Mansions, a smart apartment block in Kensington. No matter that much of his work would involve extended spells in humdrum West Hartlepool, mixing and testing oxide pastes; to Arthur Owens Expanded Metal seemed a 'right hot' prospect, this being only one of the snappy transatlantic phrases that peppered his lively, energetic patter.

Humdinger.

Absolute jake.

One hundred per cent.

In order to better exploit his innovations, Hamilton and Owens set up Owens Battery Equipment Limited, a new company part-owned by Expanded Metal but operating from separate offices on Copthall Avenue in the heart of the City of London. Unfortunately this arrangement would go badly awry. According to Owens, and much against his advice, Hamilton attempted to combine oxide paste with an untried process involving expanded (rather than solid) lead sheets. Although the Admiralty expressed firm interest in fitting the new model accumulators in its submarines, the expanded plates proved too fragile. As a result Owens Battery Equipment lost this lucrative contract and was obliged instead to seek sales abroad.

This setback steered Owens into murky waters. While notionally a banker and company sponsor, George Hamilton had held a commission in the Manchester Regiment during the Great War and still retained certain links with the War Office. Through him Owens was introduced to the Deputy Director of Naval Intelligence, and over lunch at the Army and Navy Club found himself invited to furnish the Admiralty with any useful snippets of information ('dope') that he might pick up while on business trips to Germany. Seduced by the notion of secret agency, Owens' first mission took place in January 1936, when he returned with information of 'distinct value' on coastal motorboats operated by the German navy, lately rebranded the *Kriegsmarine* ('war navy') by the new Führer.

No record exists of the amount paid to Owens for this dangerous favour, though it is unlikely to have been more than a few pounds. Subsequently he was passed on to the Secret Intelligence Service (MI6), whose primary function was the collection of information abroad. SIS assigned Owens a starchy case officer named Edward Peal, who codenamed his latest asset SNOW, a partial anagram of his surname. Colonel Peal and MI6 had no reason to doubt that Owens was anything other than a promising freelance agent, whose corporate credentials gave him perfect cover for work inside Germany, once again a potential enemy. So far as the little man was concerned, the glamorous spy game satisfied his cravings to become a 'big nut', while at the same time keeping his sponsor Hans Hamilton sweet.

Agent Snow's first assignment for SIS was a trip to the Baltic port of Kiel, where he snapped several Kriegsmarine warships lying at anchor. Worryingly, however, this mission almost came unstuck on his return to Britain, when zealous customs officials seized his Leica camera – a high-end model, and German to boot. Owens blithely confessed to being a spy, then volunteered the telephone number of an MI6 office at Thames House on Millbank to prove his credentials. Plainly discretion was a weak point for garrulous Agent Snow.

So too was money. Displaying judgement just as poor as his insistence on expanded lead plates, Hamilton now introduced Owens to a chemical engineer named Erwin Pieper. German by birth, the elderly man whom Owens insisted on calling 'Peeper' carried an American passport and claimed to be fluent in nine languages. Once the two men were alone, Pieper offered to sell Owens details of an unspecified 'invention' devised by a serving German naval officer. Although this scheme came to nothing, the pair would soon meet again – this time in Germany.

'Pieper told me that he had several other propositions which he thought worth quite a little money,' Owens explained later. 'From that meeting we became quite friendly and confidential. I then mentioned that I would like him, if he saw his way clear, to get me information in Germany. He agreed to do this, and I paid him money for his expenses.'

This, at least, was the version Owens played back to Colonel Peal. In fact Pieper began to pump Owens for dope, at the same time promising that spying for Germany would offer greater rewards. This much was true, for between the wars the effectiveness of MI6 was badly undermined by a chronic lack of resources. In 1936 SIS consisted of just 200 staff worldwide, and struggled to run its overseas operations on a miserly annual budget of £200,000. Moreover, careers in MI6 were non-pensionable, so that overworked, underpaid personnel were at risk of corruption. At the end of the year an errant passport control officer in The Hague put a bullet through his head, having embezzled almost £3,000 from Jewish visa applicants desperate to leave Europe for the safe haven of Palestine. Worse still, a duplicitous source inside Germany stung SIS to the tune of £10,000 for a worthless Luftwaffe order of battle.

Humdinger.

Whether Owens ever saw spying as anything other than a lucrative financial opportunity seems doubtful. Questioned by sceptical British intelligence officers in 1938, the capable inventor maintained that he had 'seen right from the beginning exactly what has been in the wind', and had recognised the existential danger facing Western Europe. 'I was told that the first job would be to organise a system in Germany to get information out. Probably my system is different from yours, but I have always had one object in view and that was to help this country when I could.'

Others received a more candid explanation. In 1940, with Britain and Germany again at war, the Welshman born of English parents, who had spent much of his adult life in Canada, insisted that nationalities did not count. All that mattered, Agent Snow claimed, was to be on the winning side.

Moreover, times were hard. With Owens Battery Equipment struggling to win contracts and cover his outgoings, Owens was forced to move his family from smart Sloane Avenue to down-market Brixton. In February he met 'Peeper' again, greeting the veteran German spy off the Harwich boat train at Victoria, then adjourning to the nearby Eccleston Hotel, where the pair discussed pooling resources and profits. Afterwards Owens was introduced to a mysterious Canadian named Gorringer, 'busy getting through a thousand pounds' at the Strand Palace Hotel with the aid of a 'foreign princess', both provided by Pieper for services rendered. A vast sum of money in 1936, worth perhaps £50,000 today, Owens was powerless to resist such lavish financial inducements. The addition of glamorous, available women made the short, puny Welshman all the more easy to seduce and suborn.

Operation Legover.

Right hot.

It was a package that MI6 could hardly hope to match. In April Colonel Peal handed Owens just £20 towards the cost of travelling to Brussels to wheedle further information from Pieper. There, comfortably installed in the Hotel Metropole, Pieper introduced Owens to one 'Doctor Hoffman' – notionally a business colleague, but in fact a senior German intelligence officer named Hilmar Dierks. A professional spy since 1914, Dierks now ran the naval section at the Abwehr station in Hamburg known as Stelle X, whose wide-ranging brief included espionage operations against Britain. With its work somewhat complicated by the Anglo-German Naval Treaty of 1935, Stelle X used neutral territories such as Belgium and Holland as buffers and springboards for clandestine activity, building a network of shady front companies and dead-letter drops, and holding discreet meetings (*treffs*) in select hotels.

Sizing up the little man for the first time at the Metropole, Hilmar Dierks might have recognised something of himself. As a tyro agent during the First World War, Dierks had tried twice to infiltrate the British Isles on behalf of the Kaiser, and when broke in 1925 had even offered his services to MI6. Untroubled, therefore, by Owens' contact with MI6, and swallowing the plausible fiction of the Zeppelin shell fraud, Dierks divined promising agent material and moved their discussion across the border to Cologne. 'I was asked if I could give them certain information for which they were prepared to pay very well,'

Owens said later. 'All expenses to and from Germany, all travelling and hotel expenses in England, and any money I thought reasonable for bribes. I was given a list of the information required and methods of communication, and a government paper which enabled me to pass without questions at the frontier.'

Designated A.3504 by the Hamburg stelle, Owens returned to London determined to pursue a mercenary middle way by peddling low-grade information to the highest bidder. Since MI6 were starved of funds, his preferred employer would be Hitler's Abwehr, who promised generous expenses and a monthly stipend. This treasonous scheme allowed no room for Erwin Pieper, who had outlived his usefulness by introducing Owens to his controller, Hilmar Dierks. Just one flaw threatened this cynical masterplan: a distinct lack of hard intelligence. True, Hans Hamilton knew people, and MI6 might be prevailed upon to provide a light dusting of low-grade chickenfeed. For the most part, however, the material Owens had gathered for Stelle X during the spring of 1936 was of no real value, having been cobbled together from public domain sources such as newspapers and magazines, and obscure technical manuals from specialist suppliers.

'I am sending you today Sample Number One,' Owens wrote to Dierks disingenuously, a humbug merchant once more. *'The other samples will follow in rotation, so please be on the lookout. The cost of making up samples here is £9.18.6 to be exact, including trips etc, and I trust you will find it in order. It was very difficult to produce. I will bring all test papers and reports with me when I next come over.'*

Still believing Snow to be loyal to the Crown, Colonel Peal contributed £30 towards costs incurred on his next trip to Germany. Owens returned to Hamburg that summer, the Abwehr stoking his vanity with a room at the plush Hotel Vier Jahreszeiten. At this, their second treff, Dierks got down to brass tacks. 'I was shown maps of aerodromes, factories, stores and stations in England, and told that these must be kept up to date,' recalled Owens. 'As time progressed, they would supply me with names and addresses in England where information would be received and sent. In fact I was to act as a sort of central agency between Hamburg, Berlin and London.'

Precisely why Dierks set such store by A.3504 remains obscure. Nevertheless, having gained the confidence of Stelle X, Owens was passed up the line to Berlin, where his status as Hitler's chief spy in England was confirmed. Although a promised introduction to the Führer seems not to have materialised, Agent Snow was accommodated at the exclusive Hotel Excelsior, and no doubt supplied with a foreign princess. Things truly were, in his own curious parlance, 'on the up and up'. Despite being wholly unconcerned by politics, to Owens the Germans appeared 'good people', governed by a dynamic Little Man far more to his liking than the grey bureaucrats of an enfeebled National Government which had failed to pull Britain clear of an interminable economic slump.

Back in London Owens checked in with Colonel Peal. If MI6 and the Naval Intelligence Division had been expecting solid dope on U-boats in exchange for their £30, they were sorely disappointed. 'Owens brought back practically no information,' carped Peal. 'He told me that he had made a visit to Berlin but was unable to get any information, as his visit was too hurried.' The colonel began to grow increasingly suspicious. 'On making enquiries I have now ascertained that Owens still has his flat at Sloane Avenue Mansions, and is receiving letters there. He has not admitted this.'

The Metropolitan Police Special Branch already viewed Snow with particular disdain. 'Typical Welsh underfed "Cardiff" type,' read one unkind observation report. 'Very short and slight, rather thin and bony face, somewhat shifty look. Curious brown eyes set wide apart and slightly oblique. Small bony hands stained from cigarette smoking. Soft-spoken and lacks assurance in manner. Usually wears brown shoes or boots. General appearance that of an underfed rat.'

Contrary to popular belief, Arthur Owens was not the first double agent fielded by British intelligence against the Hitler regime. This accolade belonged instead to Major Christopher Draper, a Great War fighter ace turned film actor and stunt pilot, whose reckless penchant for flying under bridges had earned him a reputation as 'the Mad Major'. In 1932 Draper took part in a barnstorming 'Aces of the Air' tour around Europe, and in Munich was introduced to Adolf Hitler, whose ascent to power was almost complete. Since the Mad Major was well known as a vocal critic of Whitehall's treatment of war veterans, he was earmarked by the Abwehr as a potential asset, and approached by the London correspondent of *Der Angriff* to provide intelligence on the Royal Air Force.

Draper dutifully reported this contact to the Security Service, MI5, and was instructed to travel to Hamburg. His case officer was Colonel Edward Hinchley-Cooke, a veteran MI5 interrogator who was half German, and so fluent in his mother's tongue that he had worked successfully as a stool pigeon inside prison camps during the Great War. For the next three years Draper posted the Abwehr occasional snippets of disinformation, cunningly disguised as innocuous correspondence about stamp collecting. Over time, however, MI5 ran short of plausible falsehoods, and the Mad Major's contact with Stelle X began to wither on the vine.

One of the several addresses used by Draper and Dierks was Postbox 629, Hamburg 1. A Home Office interception warrant placed on mail sent to and from this box meant that MI5 were soon able to identify virtually all of the Abwehr's existing operatives in Britain. Crucially, one of the letters examined revealed that Dierks (masquerading as 'L. Sanders') was keen to meet with another of his British agents at the Minerva Hotel in Cologne on the morning of 24 September 1936.

The identity of this new Nazi agent came as something of a shock to British intelligence. For it was none other than Arthur Owens.

Instead of confronting errant Agent Snow immediately, Colonel Peal allowed the letter to proceed to its original destination, which just so happened to be the London office of Expanded Metal. A port watch subsequently confirmed that Owens had honoured his appointment with Dierks, travelling to Germany on 23 September, and remaining there for six days. Ominously, MI6 had received no advance warning, and no request for expenses. On his return, Peal summoned Snow to an SIS office on Victoria Street and demanded an explanation. Owens admitted that he had met Erwin Pieper a year earlier, when the elderly German had offered to sell secrets, but insisted that his own intention in stringing 'Peeper' along was to infiltrate the Abwehr.

'My duty at that time was to get all I could and be in a position to help this country,' Snow fibbed artfully, feigning grave indignation. 'I risked my life to get it to you. At least I deserve a little thanks. Understand that I am one hundred per cent with you, and if I make a slip over there I'm not coming back. I am pro-German completely. I have to be.'

But Peal was no fool. The little Welshman was clearly playing both ends against the middle, and in November learned that his services were no longer required by MI6. Peal also threatened Owens with prosecution under the Official Secrets Act, though his genuine dealings with British intelligence, including his successful reconnaissance of Kiel harbour, promised acute embarrassment in a court of law. True, Owens held a Canadian passport, and still owed allegiance to the Crown if it came to charges of treason. Nevertheless, criminal proceedings might prove a very tricky business indeed.

At the same time, Owens also aroused the displeasure of his Abwehr handler, Hilmar Dierks. Still writing as Herr Sanders from Box 629, yet straying from the language of philately, Dierks upbraided Owens over some decidedly outdated intelligence on British tanks. *'I'm sorry to say,'* he wrote in December, *'that the contents of your letter were not in the least new to me. The newspapers of your country are much quicker than your letters. Since a number of years I am also in possession of the magazine pictures you sent me, and you no doubt will understand that all this is rather disappointing. I don't own a museum, you know. Henceforth your letters will have to be a little more up to date.'*

The abrupt termination of double agent Snow by MI6 now threatened his lucrative, elevated status as Hitler's chief spy in England. Arthur Owens needed superior samples, and stronger dope. By sheer dumb luck, at the beginning of 1937 the embattled traitor would be assigned a brand new case officer, fresh to the Abwehr and Stelle X, whose vaulting ambition far outstripped his limited experience.

By his own account, Nikolaus Ritter had spent much of the First World War in the United States as a German spy, only narrowly evading capture by stealing an aeroplane and barnstorming across the border to Mexico. In truth these exploits were just so many Zeppelin shells. A garrulous Rhinelander born in 1899, Ritter served as an infantry soldier on the Western Front, and reached New York only in 1924, filling a dozen haphazard years as the foreman of a textile works, a brush importer and a loan shark. Though the FBI would later vouch that Ritter acted as a dangerous 'Gestapo agent' in America for an extended period, keeping tabs on the aviation industry, the reality was that Ritter, like Owens, was an unscrupulous opportunist, with a history of failed business ventures and profligate tastes.

Married with children by 1935, but stony broke, Ritter returned to the Fatherland to find his perfect English highly prized by the Abwehr, first in Bremen, then at air intelligence (*I Luft*) in Hamburg, a comfortable posting enhanced by a smart blue Luftwaffe uniform. However, the novice spymaster commonly known as 'Doctor Rantzau' was blithely dismissive of detail and overly fond of delegation. 'He has a very American attitude to life,' Owens remarked later, with evident approval. 'He has wonderful schemes one moment, then scraps them the next in favour of another.' Indeed, with his prominent gold tooth and fat cigars, and a broad American accent more appropriate to a Hollywood B-movie than Hitler's secret service, Hauptmann Nikolaus Ritter seemed all too often to be acting out a role.

For Owens, Doctor Rantzau's arrival at Stelle X in January 1937 was a timely development indeed. Choosing to ignore the doubts voiced by Dierks, Ritter set his sole English agent a simple test. Eschewing naval matters, A.3504 was asked to provide plans of the RAF aerodrome at Northolt, fifteen miles west of central London, together with details of a new munitions factory in the Midlands. With his livelihood on the line, Owens spied hard for the first time since Kiel. The results were sufficiently impressive to convince Ritter that he might exploit the diminutive Welshman more fully than had his predecessor, a fresh start deserving of a brand new codename: JOHNNY.

Sceptics at Stelle X came to prefer a more disparaging sobriquet: *Der Kleine*. The Little Man.

The pair met for the first time in the summer of 1937, when Owens travelled to Hamburg on the pretext of drumming up battery sales. Posing as his interpreter, Ritter quickly gained the measure of Johnny's peccadilloes, allowing Owens the run of Hamburg's finest hotels, as well as indulging his fondness for beer and brandy at nightspots such as the Nagel, Hofbräuhaus and Münchner Kindl. Often the pair were joined by Ritter's aristocratic secretary, Irmgard von Klitzing, who in turn provided a respectable blind date for Johnny – or a foreign princess, if all else failed.

Neither role was required at the exotic Valhalla Club, situated on the infamous Reeperbahn sin strip, whose unique selling point was a network of table telephones. 'Most of the tables were occupied by young single women,' Ritter recalled fondly. 'You simply dialled their number, and asked them to come over to your own table. Arthur didn't speak any German so he asked me to do it, and chose three.' Frustratingly for Owens, ice-cool Irmgard von Klitzing remained unavailable – and was soon embroiled in an affair with Ritter. His wife Mary Aurora Evans, a native of Clayton, Alabama, promptly sued for divorce.

His fortunes restored, back in London Owens moved Irene and the children into a luxury apartment at Pullman Court, an upmarket apartment complex atop Streatham Hill. Completed in 1936, the boutique development comprised nine dazzling white blocks designed by Frederick Gibberd, who tempered harsh modernist lines with roof gardens, swimming pools and landscaped grounds. Compact and bespoke, the flats within were intended to appeal to the young professional classes, and thus chimed with Agent Snow's self-image as an international man of affairs. Gibberd even designed a range of deco furniture for his tenants, although the sheer modernity of Pullman Court almost proved its downfall, with vocal locals initially fearful that the preponderance of single bedroom studio flats would encourage prostitution.

For Arthur Owens, the prospect of living cheek by jowl with the demi-monde was very much a plus. The downside was that the chic apartment commanded a steep annual rent of £130, for which he came to rely almost exclusively on the Abwehr. Ditto the payments on a sleek white Jaguar SS100 Roadster, which retailed at an eye-watering £295. During this period Owens admitted to receiving average monthly payments of £20, paid in cash on his regular visits to Hamburg, and often bumped up by lavish expenses. In return, 'Johnny' operated as a one-man London stelle, travelling far and wide to photograph airfields and factories, and developing a network of informants – some real, but most imagined. Owens Battery Equipment also forged links with an ostensibly legitimate German firm named Auerbach, based in the Wandsbek district of Hamburg. In reality the company was yet another Abwehr front, named in honour of the famous cellar restaurant in Leipzig, where Goethe placed Faust for his first treff with Mephistopheles, the Devil Incarnate.

Irony rooted in literature was entirely lost on Owens, who read books only to devise codes. 'As an agent Johnny was highly reliable,' averred Ritter. 'Always delivering his material in person, and always on time. At first none of it was particularly sensational, but enough of it was new, and the precision of his reports inspired confidence. Most of it was based on trips into the field, and a network of sub-agents that he built up slowly. One worked in the Air Ministry, a couple more at RAF depots. All of them were Welsh, just like Johnny.'

Absolute jake.

During this honeymoon period Owens' idiosyncratic methods alarmed Ritter only once, an event recorded in his circumspect postwar memoir. Arriving at the Auerbach office one day in 1937, Owens produced a small foil packet from his briefcase. Sealed inside the waterproof wrapping was a scrap of paper, covered in a jumble of spidery hieroglyphics.

'What's this?' demanded Ritter. 'Remember tradecraft, Johnny. A blind man could see that's a code.'

Owens shook his head, then tapped at his teeth with his forefinger. 'I keep all the good dope hidden up here.'

'Up where?'

Dropping his jaw, Owens removed his false teeth, stuck the packet to the crown with a lick of saliva, then deftly replaced the denture. Faintly appalled, Ritter warned him against repeating this unappealing trick in the field. Owens ignored him, and would later confess to spitting out secret material on several occasions during dicey frontier crossings.

As for Johnny's Welsh network, few if any of these sub-agents actually existed, though one genuine mole might have been his brother-in-law, Fred Ferrett, who worked at the Short Brothers aircraft factory at Rochester. The suborning of impecunious service personnel also remained a profitable pastime for Stelle X, though Owens fought shy of direct approaches, arguing that he was already too valuable to risk arrest. Apparently Berlin agreed. 'They have one hundred per cent confidence in me,' bragged Owens. 'I don't know why. They just have, that's all. I have not made any slips at all.'

Nor, so it seems, did Major Ritter. 'I was always very frugal with money,' he insisted. 'Besides which, our policy was to pay according to the value of the delivery. To begin with most of Johnny's material was rather ordinary, and he seldom received more than £50. It was also a security precaution. Too many agents had been caught out in the past, because they began to live suddenly and conspicuously above their means.'

In any event, high-rolling Johnny was already hopelessly ensnared. With payments from Expanded Metal now intermittent at best, rent arrears mounted on Pullman Court, attended by the threat of eviction. On 16 September 1937, Owens rang his former case officer at MI6, Colonel Edward Peal, and requested a meeting, hoping to resume his career as a double agent on a double income. Peal cautiously agreed, but also invited Colonel Edward Hinchley-Cooke of MI5, the veteran interrogator charged with running Mad Major Draper.

The man known as 'Hinch' to his closest colleagues took a strong and immediate dislike to the former Agent Snow, who seemed neither willing nor able to provide a coherent narrative of his dealings with the Abwehr. Referring obliquely to Rantzau and Auerbach, Owens hinted at 'very good contacts' in Germany in connection with U-boats, but bowled short on specifics and gave few straight answers. Profoundly irritated, Hinchley-Cooke told Owens that his dope was of 'no value' and warned him not to contact British military intelligence again. The frosty meeting lasted barely fifteen minutes, at the end of which the Little Man was instructed to sign a terse disclaimer, denying him compensation in case he 'got into difficulties' in his dealings with the Nazis.

In neat type printed above his signature, the former MI6 freelance meekly confirmed that *'I fully realise I am not employed and have not been employed since November 1936 by the British Intelligence Service.'*

Instead Owens found himself a marked man. 'They have a man watching me,' he complained soon after, considerably unnerved by the scrutiny of the Special Branch. 'I have been followed everywhere, my house has been broken into.' His son Bob, now aged eighteen, was questioned at his place of work by mysterious strangers. Come October, Hitler's chief spy in England felt sufficiently harassed to ask Ritter to allow Irene and their daughter Patricia to emigrate to Germany. Despite these travails, however, Owens could still travel freely on his Canadian passport, and therefore this subtle persecution did little to curtail his espionage work. As a result, MI5 was forced to acknowledge that 'substantially from the end of 1936 until the outbreak of war, Snow worked as a straightforward German agent, whose activities, though known to the authorities, were not interfered with in any important respect.'

In fact MI5 might have nudged the Inland Revenue, who threatened Owens with bankruptcy over tax arrears of £55 at the beginning of 1938. Patents had lapsed, the Owens Battery Equipment Company lay dormant, and overheads in Britain exceeded income from Germany. Finally evicted from upmarket Pullman Court, Owens and his family moved ten miles south to Morden, a dreary suburb at the bottom end of the Northern Line. There Owens rented a maisonette at 23 Grosvenor Court, a boxy block on a busy main road. Granted, his new accommodation was handy for RAF fighter aerodromes at Biggin Hill, Kenley and Northolt, and rather harder for the Branch to surveil. However, the Jaguar Roadster was long gone, and there could be no mistaking the fact that Snow's downward slide was fast becoming an avalanche.

In an effort to avoid letter intercepts, Owens set up shop in the visitors' writing room at Canada House. *'I would be very glad if you will send along payment by return,'* he wrote to Ritter, desperate for funds. *'The delay has been worrying me and my business people here. I am devoting nearly all my time and energy to this deal and am getting excellent results, and our business connection next year will be (as they say in US) a humdinger.'*

Frugal Doctor Rantzau was not so sure. *'As to the last battery, I must say that the price of £75 is rather high. As you wrote yourself that you were trying to get it a little cheaper, I hope that you have been able to convince your manufacturer that he has to revise his price. However, on account of such a price reduction there must not be any reduction in the quality.'*

Quality remained an intractable problem. In March, when Hitler annexed his Austrian homeland, Owens chanced yet another approach to British intelligence, this time through the Admiralty. Again he was rebuffed and escorted from the building. With Rantzau unwilling to pay over the odds for substandard samples, Johnny's London stelle badly needed to come up with a better pitch, and better product.

A humdinger, in fact.

Undertaken during the summer of 1938, Owens' next manoeuvre seemed calculated to appeal both to the Abwehr and MI5. Four years earlier the British Union of Fascists had boasted 40,000 members and enjoyed a brief flirtation with political respectability, buoyed by its charismatic founder Sir Oswald Mosley, and epitomised by an infamous headline in the *Daily Mail*: *Hurrah for the Blackshirts!* Although mainstream support tailed off following thuggish scenes at a mass indoor rally at Olympia, Owens now set about infiltrating the party, hoping to recruit gullible rank-and-file members as sub-agents and access sympathetic moles in the armed services. Since the Special Branch maintained a number of well-placed informers inside the BUF, Owens' conspicuous efforts were soon noticed, and fed back to MI5. 'Our friend Snow is on the warpath again,' noted Hinchley-Cooke with dismay. 'Some definite action is required to clip his wings.'

Even by the base standards of the BUF, Owens' pitch to the Blackshirts was remarkably crude. 'Snow spoke very freely about Thames House, St Ermin's Hotel, the St James's Park people and Colonel Peal,' noted Albert Canning, the man in charge at the Branch. 'He said that his work had revealed serious corruption in the British intelligence service, how it was run by Jews etc, and expressed his willingness to expose this "terrible racket".'

On the hackneyed pretext of working for peace, Owens warned that Jews were preparing an attack on Germany, hoping to trigger a 'criminal' war between England and the Reich. On the promise of funding from Hitler, he proposed setting up a chain of clandestine BUF radio stations to broadcast hate direct to a blinkered, complacent public who 'must be told what is going on'. Still more ambitious, Owens also hinted at a coup d'état. 'If the BUF had a reliable following who would "stick at nothing" to show the government how much they were in favour of Germany and detested the Jews, he could arrange for a cargo of arms for use in an attempt to seize power.'

Such blunt overtures betrayed surprising ignorance of far right nationalist politics. While virtually all Blackshirts were staunch admirers of the new European dictators (Hitler, Mussolini and more recently Franco), and most professed to loathe communists and Jews, far fewer were prepared to countenance acts of treason against King and Country. The moment Owens began to boast openly of being 'a direct personal agent of Hitler' and solicit military and industrial intelligence, doors began to close. It hardly helped that Oswald Mosley hoped to set up his own commercial radio station, funded with Nazi money.

'Owens is regarded with considerable suspicion by the few leading officials of the BUF cognisant with his approach,' Canning concluded. 'Some describe him as an agent-provocateur, and others as a knave or fool.'

The vexatious petty traitor was both, leading MI5 to again consider charges under the Official Secrets Act. Ultimately the Little Man was dismissed as an impostor: several clandestine assignations at the Regent Palace Hotel were found to entail the debriefing of gullible young women rather than ruthless Nazi spies, while a colourful sidekick named Hellfire Williams quickly vanished from the scene. Undoubtedly Owens boasted one or two genuine contacts on the fringes of the military, and perhaps even inside the Air Ministry itself, yet most were invented, like the fictive Welsh ring. Unfortunately even imaginary agents seemed inclined to let Johnny down. Poking around in a chandlery one day, Owens purchased an instrument described as a pressure gauge from a British submarine and in due course took it to Hamburg, fibbing that his source worked in an Admiralty dockyard. In fact, as Ritter soon discovered, this latest 'sample' was merely an obsolete inclinometer from a scrapped Great War biplane.

Owens laughed it off, excusing that he could hardly be held responsible for the honesty – or otherwise – of every contact. Ritter reminded Johnny that Stelle X still had no plans to open a museum.

Whether or not Irene Owens knew of her husband's undercover antics at the Regent Palace Hotel, or on the Hamburg Reeperbahn, their marriage of twenty years was rapidly turning sour. In July 1938 Owens took his family to Ostend, ostensibly to enjoy the long sandy beaches and cut-price casinos of the Belgian Riviera, then whisked Irene away to Germany, leaving Bob and Patricia in the care of the hotel manager. Owens' main objective in taking his wife to Hamburg was to introduce her to Doctor Rantzau and demonstrate that his frequent business trips were entirely legitimate. But Irene was not much impressed. 'It was clear to me straight away that there was little real affection between the two of them,' noted Ritter. 'They might have been similar in terms of physical appearance, but not in character. His wife hardly contributed to the conversation and seemed completely uninterested.'

According to Irene, the scenario played out in Belgium that summer was infinitely more sinister. In a self-serving statement made to the Branch the following year, Irene insisted that while she and Owens were away, a German agent arrived in Ostend and attempted to 'blackmail' the children. The visitor was none other than Erwin Pieper, the elderly Abwehr spy who had introduced Owens to Hilmar Dierks back in 1936. Fortunately the hotel manager intervened and threatened to have Pieper arrested. 'Peeper' promptly disappeared.

Owens told it differently, explaining that Pieper had attempted to bilk money from the hotel and was ejected from the lobby following a violent exchange. Whatever the truth behind events in Ostend, tension hung heavy in the air across Europe throughout the long, hot summer of 1938. This climate of fear was only heightened in September by the Munich Crisis, when events in Czechoslovakia prompted Owens to launch yet another bid to re-ingratiate himself with British intelligence.

This time the former Agent Snow found MI5 unexpectedly receptive. Whereas the annexation of Austria by Hitler was seen as little more than the occupation of his own backyard, the addition of Czechoslovakia to his lengthening territorial shopping list marked a first real grab at *Lebensraum*, the sinister geopolitical policy by which living space (or 'habitat') would be seized in Eastern Europe, thereby creating an enlarged Third Reich known as Greater Germany. On 12 September the dictator delivered a violently anti-Czechoslovak speech at Nuremberg, citing wrongs committed against ethnic Germans living in the Sudetenland frontier zone and threatening military action at the end of the month. A localised war seemed imminent, one likely to spread across Europe since both France and the Soviet Union had forged alliances with the Czechs that had far more bite than any protection offered by the young republic's membership of the toothless League of Nations.

As the beleaguered Czech government prepared to fight, and 38 million British civilians glimpsed the future through the mica eyepiece of flimsy rubber gas masks, issued free of charge by a failing government, Arthur Owens seized his chance. Presenting himself at Scotland Yard, Agent Snow offered up his most detailed statement to date. Besides admitting to acting as Hitler's chief spy in England, Owens also volunteered that he would soon take delivery of a short-wave wireless transmitter. 'It's very small and powerful,' the Little Man boasted, as if describing himself. 'It has a transmitting radius of 12,000 miles and takes practically no current.'

This disclosure burst like a bombshell at MI5, for at no time had Mad Major Draper been offered a secret radio. Despite remaining deeply suspicious of Owens, Colonel Hinchley-Cooke agreed to a meeting on 24 September, which lasted rather longer than fifteen minutes and was transcribed in full by a stenographer. For the most part Owens was typically evasive, though his rambling, tangential answers did include details of the Abwehr organisation in Hamburg, including cover addresses used by Doctor Rantzau, as well as the promised transmitter and wireless codes.

'It will be the first one in the country,' boasted Snow. 'The thing's so small you can take it up and work it in your hand.'

'Is your Morse up to speed?' asked Hinchley-Cooke.

'I was in the Boy Scouts, and they've had me practising all hours. Sixty letters a minute will be fine and dandy.'

'And they pay you?'

'Oh yes.'

'How much?'

'Thirty or forty pounds a month. It depends on the dope.'

'Tell me more about Doctor Rantzau.'

'Actually, there's five or six different people.'

'The more the merrier. Please give me their names.'

Owens sucked on his gums. 'Look – let's leave all that business aside. I've got to tread carefully, see. My life's not worth two hoots if there's any slip made.'

Hinch fixed Snow severely with a hard-eyed stare. 'The point you don't quite seem to realise is, you've been working against our instructions.'

'And you people don't seem to realise that I'm trying to work on the level!' Owens snapped back, his bile rising momentarily. 'I've always done everything I could for this country. Probably my methods are different from yours, but if you let me carry on I can bring in vital information.'

'Such as?'

'Where the first bombs will fall, for a start.'

Hinchley-Cooke began to listen very closely indeed. Fears that the Luftwaffe would raze Paris and London the moment war was declared had already reached MI5 from other sources, reviving nightmarish estimates of 3,000 tons of bombs on London in a single day, causing hundreds of thousands of casualties and a million cases of hysteria. Now, if Owens was to be believed, Hitler's spies had identified a zone south-east of London which was poorly defended by searchlights and anti-aircraft guns, providing the German air force with a safe corridor for a mass attack on London. The Abwehr, so he said, knew this dangerous gap as 'The Channel'.

In truth, Snow's dope was a barrage of Zeppelin shells. The Luftwaffe would be in no position to launch mass raids on the British mainland until 1940, when the fall of France delivered forward bases on the Channel coast. Even then, it would manage to deliver more than a thousand tons of bombs just once in five years, on which occasion the death toll was limited to just twelve hundred. However, none of this could be predicted by nervous appeasers in September 1938, and the possibility remains that Owens' tendentious warning was a masterful political bluff which helped serve to excuse the shameful Munich Agreement. Just five days later, on the eve of the German attack on Czechoslovakia, the governments of Britain, France and Italy sold this promising new democracy down the river, laying false claim to 'peace with honour' yet at the same time ceding the Sudetenland to Hitler, and surrendering additional territory to Poland and Hungary.

'When Chamberlain returned from Munich waving his piece of paper we all had an acute sense of shame,' admitted one serving MI5 officer, unwilling to read major victory into the betrayal of a minor country. 'We felt, too, some relief that we were not to be subjected to an immediate aerial bombardment.'

With grave misgivings, Hinchley-Cooke cautiously encouraged rogue Agent Snow to continue his work as an arm's-length freelance. The promise of a powerful short-wave wireless transmitter could hardly be ignored. Nor could the fact that MI5's alpha agent, Mad Major Christopher Draper, had recently been exposed as a 'Nazi spy' by the Fleet Street dailies and forced into hiding in Broadstairs.

As a result, Double Agent Snow now became the responsibility of another case officer at MI5, far younger than either Hinch or Colonel Peal, yet infinitely more shrewd. The Little Man's new handler was Captain Tommy 'Tar' Robertson, then in charge of a small sub-section within B Division specialising in wireless traffic but destined to become one of the greatest unsung heroes of the Second World War.

2

Colonel Johnny

Just as Arthur Owens was no ordinary spy, so Thomas Argyle Robertson was a far from orthodox soldier. Schooled at Charterhouse, and a graduate of the Royal Military Academy at Sandhurst, Robertson spent only two years with the Seaforth Highlanders before resigning his commission, followed by spells in the City and police work in Birmingham. In 1933 he transferred to the Security Service, still aged only twenty-four, and in no time at all established an enviable reputation as a counter-intelligence officer par excellence.

All that was required were a few rounds of drinks in a Mayfair saloon bar. Aside from Nazis, Blackshirts and the Irish Republican Army, during the last year of peace the long list of subversive organisations monitored by MI5 included the Communist Party of Great Britain, lately implicated in a spy ring at the huge Woolwich Arsenal. With the 'red menace' regarded as a clear and present danger, companionable Captain Tommy duped a suspect Foreign Office cipher clerk named John King over drinks at the Bunch of Grapes on Curzon Street. After King passed out drunk Robertson borrowed his keys, burglarised his office and recovered a batch of incriminating papers meant for dispatch to Moscow. Following a secret trial held in camera, the hapless mole was sent down for ten years.

A sobering experience indeed.

'Robertson was in no sense an intellectual,' recalled John Masterman, a wartime colleague at MI5. 'But he had certain qualities of a high order. A born leader, gifted with independent judgement, he had above all an extraordinary flair in all the intricate operations of his profession. Time and again he would prove to be right when others, following their intellectual assessments, proved to be wrong.' Widely known as 'Tar' on account of his initials, smitten female staff at MI5 preferred a more irreverent sobriquet, with 'Passion Pants' derived from his penchant for dress trousers cut from the colourful blue-green Mackenzie tartan of his parent regiment.

In the run-up to war diligent work by the Security Service led to the arrest of several low-level Abwehr operatives, including a hairdresser from Dundee named Jessie Jordan, and an Irish bricklayer, Joseph Kelly, who stole plans from a munitions factory near Chorley. Like thirsty communist mole John King, Kelly received a stiff ten-year sentence and Jordan four. MI5 were less fortunate with Walter Simon, a veteran spy also run by Nikolaus Ritter, who refused to crack under close interrogation and could only be deported.

'Don't come back,' Colonel Hinchley-Cooke warned the elderly spook on the dockside at Grimsby. 'You won't be so lucky next time.'

In contrast, fortune continued to smile on Hitler's chief spy in England. Now in effect a triple agent, on the first day of January 1939 Owens travelled from Dover to Hamburg by boat, notionally on battery business but in fact to collect his short-wave transmitter. The winter crossing was particularly rough, prompting Owens to scrawl Irene a cursory note from the Hotel Graf Moltke. *'There is quite a little snow here, although it is not very cold. Everything is very busy and business seems to be very fresh. There are a lot of batteries being sold. I hope your shoulder is better and the children behaving themselves OK. So cheerio, love to all.'*

Battery business was brisk indeed. After delivering appropriate samples to Stelle X, Ritter and a wireless specialist named Trautmann escorted Owens two hundred miles east to Stettin. There, at a spy school housed in a military barracks, Johnny clapped eyes on his first transmitter. Consisting of high-end component parts sourced in Germany, Holland and France, the set was small enough to fit inside an ordinary attaché case, making it easy to smuggle across borders, and came equipped with chargeable batteries for use in the field.

'They said it was portable and that I should travel as much as I could,' Owens told Tar some time later. 'I could hire a car, and if there were machines, munitions or guns on any of the aerodromes they wanted to know at once. All I had to do was run out two wires as an aerial. The set takes practically no current, and cannot be checked up as regards the click of the Morse key.'

In order to demonstrate home use a model apartment had been constructed at the Stettin school, with the long high-frequency aerial cunningly concealed behind the wallpaper. To Agent Snow, it must have seemed as though he had stumbled onto the set of the latest thriller by Alfred Hitchcock, and cast in the glamorous lead role. However, other aspects of his visit to the Baltic port impressed him rather less. His digs, for instance, at the Angel Pension, turned out to be a temperance hotel. For the thirsty Welshman this was almost as bad as Prohibition.

Owens returned to London on 6 January, though his British handlers would hear nothing for more than a week. Only on the morning of 14 January did he trouble to call his designated contact, a flinty Special Branch inspector named William Gagen, to arrange a meeting at a Lyons Cornerhouse in Westminster. Over tea he furnished brief details of his trip to Stettin and a copy of his wireless code. Owens also revealed that he expected to receive the transmitter in a matter of days. 'He said that he had not the time to explain its use then,' noted Gagen, 'but would soon be in a position to amplify his story.'

The pair met again two days later, this time at the offices of Expanded Metal at Burwood House, where Owens revealed that the transmitter was now available for collection from Victoria station. Instructing Gagen to follow him at a discreet distance, Owens took a cab to the busy rail terminus and retrieved a small brown attaché case from the left luggage office, then conducted a brief examination of his own before handing it over to the bemused detective.

'Owens stated his sole motive was to help this country,' Gagen revealed in a lengthy typed report. 'Messages from the transmitter will be picked up in Hamburg, Cologne and Stettin. It can be used with a 350 volt battery, or plugged into an ordinary lamp socket. He has arranged to send a trial transmission to Germany in the near future, and asks that the transmitter, code etc be returned to him on Saturday morning.'

With that Owens vanished, explaining that he was off to 'take some photographs' in the north of England. Well aware that he was being played, Bill Gagen took the attaché case straight to MI5, where it was received with alacrity by Tar Robertson and Hinchley-Cooke. On lifting the lid Robertson found a Morse key, several coloured leads and a compact transmitter unit measuring just 12" × 6" × 4", with two powerful Miniwatt Dario valves and variable frequency control. Grudgingly, the intelligence men were forced to concede that the German set looked rather more jazzy than any comparable gadgetry in British service.

The apparatus was subsequently examined in detail at the Post Office research laboratory in Dollis Hill. There a specialist from MI6 confirmed that it was far more sophisticated than any other previously encountered – and promptly broke it. One version holds that a resistor burned out; another that the set was dismantled too thoroughly to restore to working order. Whatever the truth, it was hardly an auspicious start. Then again, the boffins were unaware that the Abwehr's own disparaging term for these early short-wave sets was *klamotten*: junk.

Once it had been repaired, Gagen returned the transmitter to Agent Snow in the bar of a Morden pub. In return, Owens handed the detective a telephone number for Stelle X in Hamburg. Plainly Hitler's chief spy in England was engaged in writing his own insurance policy against prosecution, confident that no jury was likely to convict a notional traitor who was actively collaborating with the Security Service. This left Owens free to do largely as he pleased, and for the next nine months A.3504 was able to run rings around British intelligence, who had no prior experience of running a wireless agent, nor any detailed knowledge of the internal workings of the Abwehr.

Snow's stratagems even ran to an attempt to turn a profit from his new klamotten. Intrigued by claims that messages buzzed on the set were undetectable in England, Owens took it to George Hamilton, his erstwhile sponsor at Expanded Metal, hopeful that another joint venture company might be formed to exploit the Abwehr's cutting-edge short-wave technology. The set was subsequently examined by Hamilton's brother Noel, a wireless wizard who had served as a junior staff officer at the Air Ministry. Unlike his ambivalent sibling, Noel Hamilton viewed Owens as positively dangerous, and tipped off his former colleagues at Adastral House.

'Squadron Leader X (retired) is particularly anxious that he shall not be involved in any form of enquiry,' noted a subsequent intelligence report. 'Owens talks openly of his connection with a certain Colonel and Scotland Yard, and brags that he was partly responsible for the arrest of a woman in Aberdeen. Further, when "in his cups" he said that he worked on behalf of Germany as well, and that he held a secret service badge.'

In an effort to test Snow's mettle, Robertson and Hinch set him up with a stooge. Posing as a shady civil servant in need of quick money, a Special Branch detective took to drinking with

Owens and filed a damning report at the end of March. Rehearsing the Zeppelin shells story by way of credentials, Owens boasted of transmitting to Germany on a regular basis, and expressed keen interest in obtaining military manuals as well as any juicy scandal involving senior political figures for use in Nazi propaganda. 'Snow appears to have plenty of money and travels from place to place in taxi cabs. He makes no secret of the fact that he is paid by the Germans, and speaks very highly of them in every way.'

Crucially, Owens expressed particular interest in dope on recent 'secret experiments' aimed at bringing down hostile aircraft. This new technology, he claimed, was referred to by those in the know as 'the wireless cloud', research into which had lately reached a critical stage.

Here A.3504 was sniffing around radar, or radiolocation, at that time the most sensitive military secret in Britain. In 1935 the Air Ministry asked the scientist Robert Watson-Watt to investigate the feasibility of a 'death ray' that would utilise a powerful beam of electromagnetic waves to stop the engines of enemy aircraft, or boil the blood of the pilot. The Ministry even offered a standing prize of £1,000 to anyone able to demonstrate a ray weapon capable of killing a sheep at a thousand yards. Though this macabre bounty went unclaimed, Watson-Watt took note of the fact that aircraft in flight often interfered with wireless reception, and turned his thoughts from radio-destruction to radio-detection.

The result was the early warning system known as Chain Home. In 1937 work began on a string of twenty four CH stations positioned between the Tyne and Southampton, capable of detecting hostile aircraft at a range of 80 miles, at altitudes up to 15,000 feet. By Easter of 1939 the radar chain was fully operational, shielding Britain by means of the invisible 'wireless cloud' beamed from lofty steel pylons 350 feet tall. Since these masts were highly conspicuous, inquisitive Luftwaffe commanders brought the giant airship *Graf Zeppelin* out of mothballs to reconnoitre the English coastline at a leisurely pace, hoping to pick up telltale radio signals. On her second trip in August 1939 the lumbering gasbag was buzzed by a pair of ageing Hawker biplanes from 612 Squadron, so that for a few short minutes the Luftwaffe's stealthy investigation into future electronic warfare technology came to resemble an air-show restaging of a Great War dogfight.

To complicate matters, Germany was developing radar of her own. During an official visit to Britain at the end of 1937, Luftwaffe General Erhard Milch asked several pointed questions about radar over lunch at Fighter Command headquarters, at the same time dropping broad hints that scientists in the Reich were one step ahead. His boast held water on a technical level, but the tactical application of the 'wireless cloud' lagged far behind in Germany, where it was seen as little more than a highly accurate electronic gunsight.

In the midst of this snooping on radar, libidinous Agent Snow found himself zapped by an altogether different kind of ray.

For several years Owens had used the home of his brother-in-law at 112 Stratford Road in Plaistow as a cover address, often adopting the pseudonym 'Thomas Wilson'. The spy game, it seems, was a family affair. Fred Ferrett probably fed Owens dope gleaned from his job at the Short Brothers aircraft factory in Rochester, which produced the Sunderland flying boat, while Irene was obliged to stand by as 'Uncle Arthur' attempted to groom her niece Alice as an East End Mata Hari. Alas, in May 1939 Fred Ferrett died of tuberculosis, leaving Irene and her sister distraught. True to form, amoral Agent Snow chose this ticklish moment to fall head over heels for Alice's best friend, a shapely blonde seamstress named Lily Sophia Bade, who promised to be ideal sleeper material.

Born in West Ham in May 1912, Lily was blonde, blue-eyed

and curvaceously sexy – 'well built', according to an ungallant observer from the Special Branch – with a turned-up nose and unusually long fingernails. Youthful, lively and flirtatious, Lily Bade was a street-smart working-class girl on the make, keen to escape the confines of a large East End family and an overcrowded home. Owens in turn set about sweeping the 27-year-old dressmaker clean off her feet – if not quite literally, since Miss Bade was appreciably taller than Owens, and several stone heavier.

Owens turned 40 on 14 April and it is tempting to view his sudden infatuation with a younger woman as symptomatic of midlife crisis. Moreover, his mother Ada was sixteen years younger than her husband William, so perhaps Owens' vigorous pursuit of Lily owed something to learned behaviour. In any event, after twenty years of marriage to sullen Irene, vivacious Lily held the promise of a golden future, and seemed genuinely taken by the prospect of romance and intrigue at the side of Hitler's chief spy in England. Tellingly, Lily's mother Louisa Virgiels was of German extraction . . . In no time at all 'Mr Wilson' had added the Bade family home at 28 Caistor Park Road to his long list of dead-letter drops.

Irene Owens was not amused. Nor was their daughter Patricia, now aged fourteen, and dead set on a legitimate career as an actress. Thus were sown the seeds of Agent Snow's undoing.

Owens spent the last week of April 1939 in Hamburg, swapping notes with Ritter on airfields, rearmament and marital travails. 'Nikolaus was very fond of women,' recalled one of his female agents, without great affection, 'but naive in his relations with them.' Like long-suffering Irene Owens, Ritter's American wife Mary had recently found herself traded in for a younger model, namely Irmgard von Klitzing. Ritter's second marriage proved a lavish affair, after which the happy Abwehr couple honeymooned in Italy and Yugoslavia. However, Owens thought Irmgard a snob, and mean with it – unlike Ritter himself, who was generous to a fault with Nazi money.

On learning that Mary Aurora Evans wished to return to the United States, the wily Doctor exiled his ex-wife to Bremen and had her passport confiscated. The Alabama-born divorcée knew far more than was good for her about Rantzau's nefarious activities in New York. Soon so too would the Federal Bureau of Investigation.

Back in Morden, life at Grosvenor Court became increasingly intolerable. Owens now spent his evenings with Lily, haunting various bars and hotels around London, seeking fresh sources and sidekicks, and imbibing freely. Unfortunately reliable sub-agents were hard to find, and a scheme involving a lorry driver from Colliers Wood, whose long-haul routes promised excellent cover for trips with the portable transmitter, was dropped after MI5 raised objections. Consequently Owens kept quiet about Alexander Myner, an unemployed accounts clerk from Glasgow who specialised in procuring false passports, and his own son Bob, now aged nineteen and a trainee draughtsman. Following his father's dubious example, Snow Junior set about mapping several RAF fighter airfields dotted around London, chief among them Biggin Hill and Kenley. This handiwork he then posted direct to Auerbach in Hamburg, knowing full well that the battery company was an Abwehr front.

'He obtained the address from his father,' Robertson discovered much later. 'He addressed the packet to himself at one post office in London, collected it, and re-mailed it to Hamburg. He did so out of a sense of adventure, and received no payment. But a message was sent over to say that the Germans were very pleased with what had been done.'

The apple seldom falls far from the tree. Meanwhile, in March, Hitler occupied the remainder of Czechoslovakia, whose president Emil Hácha suffered a heart attack at the negotiating table, an ominous development followed in May by the so-called Pact of Steel, promising mutual assistance between Germany and Italy in the event of war. In Britain, civil defence organisations expanded rapidly, forcing regular blackout and respirator drills on an anxious public, once again raising the spectre of bombardment from the air and mass evacuation. In the race to rearm, all three services were freed from existing financial limitations, allowing the War Office to increase the size of the army to 32 divisions, and permitting the Air Ministry to order 700 new aircraft a month, the number of all-important Spitfire squadrons in Fighter Command rising from two to nine.

Having suborned his own son, in the middle of July Owens also wrote to Ritter. Terrified in equal measure by the prospect of air raids, detention and his enraged wife Irene, Snow proposed quitting Britain for Germany on a permanent basis, with his mistress Lily in tow. Unsurprisingly, Ritter declined: with Europe sliding inexorably towards war, Johnny's stelle was now the absolute cynosure of Abwehr activity in England.

In Morden, hostilities broke out on 29 July. As the IRA outraged Britons with explosions at King's Cross and Victoria, Owens dropped a bombshell of his own at Grosvenor Court by walking out on his wife and family. Irene's shrill threats to expose her feckless husband as a traitor prompted an ugly scene. 'Owens thoroughly searched the house, including her handbag,' noted a subsequent police report. 'He destroyed every possible scrap of evidence against himself before he left, and disposed of the wireless transmitting set. Owens has been drinking for some time past and has not been sober for weeks. He has threatened to shoot Mrs Owens and ruin her family should she give information about him.'

In truth, Agent Snow had no gun, much less the nerve to execute the mother of his children. Now homeless, and wary of London hotels, the adulterous double-crosser was obliged to beg a spare room from shady passport agent Alex Myner, who lived with his wife at 12 Parklands in the leafy south

London suburb of Surbiton. Lily joined him immediately, much enthused by the prospect of sharing life on the lam with a real live master spy. 'We became intimate,' she later revealed to Bill Gagen, the Special Branch inspector, choosing her words very carefully indeed. 'On about 3 August Arthur asked me to go for a holiday with him to Germany. I agreed. He said I would need a British passport and gave me the money to pay for it.'

Knowing full well that the trip was no mere summer vacation, Lily handed in her notice at Brownstones, the West End firm where she worked as a seamstress. These dubious holiday plans also found room for Alex Myner. 'I told him I was only in casual work,' explained the jobless clerk, short on money and scruples. 'He intimated that he would introduce me to some of his business friends in Hamburg, with a view to representing them in this country.'

This tale was as tall as Owens was short. Tellingly, Agent Snow gave MI5 no advance warning of his latest overseas excursion, and elected to travel by an unusual route at inconvenient hours. The trio gathered at Victoria coach station on the afternoon of 10 August and took a bus to Dover, then waited at the port for several hours before crossing by overnight boat to Ostend. Owens took care to keep a discreet distance from Lily and Myner, and as a result he alone was observed by the port authorities at Dover, neatly turned out in a light blue-grey suit, topped off by a brown felt hat with a snap brim.

From Ostend the party took a train to Hamburg, arriving on Friday night and checking into the Berliner Hof, where Owens and Lily masqueraded as husband and wife. Ritter appeared the following morning, accompanied by another Abwehr officer introduced as Herr Schneider. 'Rantzau spoke English fluently with a broad American accent,' noted Myner, 'but no business was discussed in my presence. Lily was handed a twenty Reichsmark note by Owens, who had received it from

Schneider, telling her that she should go for a walk with me – which we did.'

Left alone with Ritter and Schneider, Johnny was in for an unpleasant surprise. Demonstrating chilling sang-froid, Irene Owens had written two vengeful letters to the German spymaster known to her as Doctor Rantzau, each denouncing Arthur as a serving British spy. 'My old wife was giving me trouble,' Owens recalled later, in a rare example of understatement. 'Tried to give me away to the Germans. Rantzau had proof in black and white.'

Humdinger.

Keeping his wits about him, Owens laughed off Irene's accusations as absurd, pointing to the presence of his sexy young mistress in Hamburg as corroborating evidence. Hell had no fury like a woman scorned, and so forth.

This, at least, was the story played back to MI5. In fact, Ritter already knew of Johnny's contacts with British intelligence and approved of them to the extent that Owens remained a free agent, rather than operating under British control. 'Rantzau said to me, "You're in a very nice position",' Owens admitted two years later, under close interrogation by MI5. 'He seemed to think it was an ideal position from their standpoint. I had got a free hand to do more or less what I liked with the British organisation.'

Double-cross it, for example. Despite Irene's best efforts, Der Kleine's tenure as Hitler's chief spy in England remained secure. That same afternoon, Ritter entertained his British guests in a beer garden. 'Lily was blonde like Johnny's wife,' the doctor observed approvingly. 'But that was all they shared in common. Whereas Irene was small, quiet and mannered, his new friend Lily was large and robust, a whole head taller than Johnny, and several years younger. Gay, intelligent, and with a good deal of natural sex appeal. Johnny was clearly infatuated.'

Unlike Lily Bade, Alex Myner was introduced to Stelle X as

promising agent material, for whom Owens expected to receive a finder's fee. Following an initial interview with Ritter, on Sunday the impecunious Scot was introduced to a junior officer named Leitz and told to report to the Great Eastern Hotel at Liverpool Street four days hence. 'Leitz indicated that he would give me some business,' Myner explained in a subsequent statement, careful to avoid self-incrimination. 'Nothing further of interest happened. I returned to London on Monday night, leaving Owens and the girl behind.'

Owens and Lily stayed on in Hamburg for a week, during which Irmgard kept the pretty dressmaker amused while Ritter fettled Johnny as a wartime spy. Owens spent much of his time at the main Abwehr signals centre at Wohldorf, a short distance from Hamburg, where he got to grips with the new model Afu transmitter, technically superior and far more robust than the older klamotten, and brushed up on coding techniques. One such was based on the word CONGRATULATIONS and utilised simple numbers and squares; another made use of a best-selling novel by Alice Hobart, *Oil for the Lamps of China*. Photography and sabotage also featured on the curriculum, as well as instruction on basic meteorology. In the event that war broke out between Britain and Germany, A.3504 would buzz across daily weather reports, enabling the Luftwaffe to select optimum conditions for the destruction of London.

Still more sinister, Owens learned of new forms of chemical warfare, after a Nazi scientist with a double chin let slip details of 'a concentration of acid vapour' that was highly lethal. Owens, as Ritter well knew, possessed a degree of skill as a chemist, and for the right price might be persuaded to deploy a doomsday weapon. 'Being heavily concentrated this vapour hung around indefinitely, and had extraordinary corrosive powers which not only ate away the flesh of sheep in a very short time, but disintegrated metals.'

Right hot.

Blind to such frightfulness, Lily purchased a small blue hat with a veil. On 18 August, a Friday, the odd couple left Hamburg for Berlin, where Owens may have been formally presented at the Abwehr's central headquarters on the Tirpitzufer. 'Arthur was with me all the time in Berlin and nothing happened of particular interest,' his mistress fibbed later. 'Nothing happened in Hamburg which aroused my suspicions. I had no idea that he was engaged other than with business connected with the Expanded Metal Company Limited.'

Beguiling Lily Bade was hardly so naive. On Sunday the lovers left Berlin for a three-day break at Timmendorfer Strand, the fashionable spa resort on the Baltic coast near Lübeck, a token of appreciation from Stelle X. Despite darkening political storm clouds, the high summer of 1939 was among one of the hottest and driest on record, bringing Mediterranean temperatures as far north as Stockholm. Better still, Arthur Owens could also now bask in the warm glow of an honorary military rank: Colonel Johnny. Soon, come *Der Tag*, antagonists such as Hinchley-Cooke might even have to throw up an occasional salute.

No matter that his compulsive pursuit of high status and abundant wealth involved the betrayal of his country in shameful fashion. Countries, according to Owens, mattered not at all. For these few precious, balmy days on the beach with lovely Lily, it must have seemed to the Little Man that he was on the verge of a very big win indeed.

This tainted summer idyll was destined not to last. Not content with denouncing her husband to Doctor Rantzau, Irene now repeated the trick at Scotland Yard. She had, she insisted, intended to inform the police of 'this despicable business' for some time, but had held back for the sake of the children. As if to emphasise the point, Bob sat meekly beside her, tight lipped on the subject of his own excursions to sketch aerodromes at Kenley and Biggin Hill. Now that Owens had threatened to shoot her, and heap shame on the Ferrett family name, Irene demanded draconian punishment – and police protection to boot.

Her lengthy statement to a Special Branch inspector named Lansby read like bad vaudeville farce. 'Through a millionaire named Hamilton he met an American Jew named Pieper and joined the German secret service. Owens has a very good knowledge of many British aerodromes and a wireless transmitting set with a minimum radius of 60 miles. It is alleged he is very clever and carries code messages covered in tin foil in his mouth, or in the petrol cavity at the end of a cigarette lighter.'

Naturally enough, Irene was particularly piqued by his affair with sexy Lily Bade. 'Owens has made her extravagant promises of reward. He said he would take her to Germany and, as far as is known, they may be there at present, although Owens is supposed to be at the Golden Sands holiday camp, Great Yarmouth.'

In fact, Irene was no less devious than her husband, and no friend of MI5. Having informed the Branch that Snow ran a network of Nazi agents who worked to his orders, she found their names had slipped her mind. 'Mrs Snow has promised to communicate with me when she remembers them,' Lansby noted patiently. 'If she finds any correspondence or addresses which her husband may have been left behind.'

Time was running out – for Owens, and for Europe. On 23 August came news of the Nazi-Soviet Pact, a bogus non-aggression treaty dividing Eastern Europe into German and Soviet spheres of influence. That Poland would be the next chunk of *Lebensraum* seized by Hitler had long been abundantly clear, and already the troubled republic had secured firm guarantees from Britain and France to defend her territorial integrity with military support. Five months later, the totalitarian accord between Hitler and Stalin signalled that war must inevitably follow, making the dog days of August 1939 an uncertain time to enjoy sand, sea and sunshine on Timmendorfer Strand. From Copenhagen to Cannes to Casablanca, holidaymakers hurriedly packed their bags and scrambled for the ports, anxious to return home before the blue summer skies grew dark with bombers, perhaps eclipsing civilisation itself.

A driver from Stelle X collected Owens and Lily from their hotel and sped them to Flushing on the Dutch coast. From there the pair crossed the North Sea to Harwich on an overcrowded passenger ferry, though without the new Afu suitcase transmitter. Other fascist fellow travellers hastened in the opposite direction, notably William Joyce, the oily Blackshirt luminary soon to become infamous as radio propagandist 'Lord Haw-Haw'.

As Owens and Lily hastened home from the Baltic, Irene twisted the knife still further. 'Have received information that the two parties mentioned are now in Hamburg,' she told Scotland Yard in an unsigned letter. 'No doubt they will return via Ostend, the latter part of the week. I also have the address of the man who is able to get any kind of passport, which a certain party may be travelling on as man and wife . . . That is all for now. You will know who this is from.'

Among several enclosures was a visiting card for 'passport agent' Alex Myner, which confirmed his address as 12 Parklands, Surbiton. These details were noted, only to be overlooked in the chaotic run-up to war. On arriving in London the previous day Owens and Lily went directly to Parklands, certain that hotel registrations would now be monitored. Rogue Agent Snow could, and should, have been detained immediately by the Branch on behalf of MI5. Instead, at 04.30 on the morning of 28 August, his temperamental klamotten installed in the bathroom at Parklands, Colonel Johnny made his debut test transmission to Germany. Trautmann and Wein, the wireless operators ('*funkers*') assigned to A.3504, stood by at Wohldorf, paying close attention as this historic first signal buzzed in through the ether.

'Ein Glas Bier!'

A glass of beer.

With these few frivolous words the Abwehr's London stelle was finally on air. Ritter was ecstatic. 'These were the only German words that Johnny knew off by heart. On countless occasions Trautmann, Wein and myself had been amused to hear them uttered when drinking on the Reeperbahn, or in the Hofbräuhaus. Now the connection was established, and we were ready for the imminent European emergency.'

Fortunately Owens followed his drinks order with a meaty main course. *'Royal Navy reserve convoy leaving Portsmouth for Gibraltar today, seven-thirty.'*

CONGRATULATIONS indeed.

As Agent Snow opened the batting, MI5 dropped the ball. Guy Liddell, the Deputy Director of B Division, and a talented amateur cellist to boot, chose this moment to open a war diary, which over the next few weeks would swing unsteadily between paranoid fancy and languid inertia. With Hitler's chief spy in England still at large, and transmitting freely to Hamburg, Liddell's entries at the end of August seemed somewhat complacent: 'At the request of the Home Office we have agreed that nobody on our lists of Nazi Party members or suspects should be stopped at ports unless we have very special reasons for holding them.' Elsewhere, a supposedly credible source swore that Hitler had got the jitters. 'He even suggests that if the order were now given it is doubtful whether the Germans would march.'

Despite such woolly thinking, the Security Service hurriedly expanded onto a war footing. With space at a premium at their central London premises, however, large parts of MI5 had to be relocated four miles west to Wormwood Scrubs, a grim Victorian prison complex in the hinterlands of Hammersmith. Evacuation of the previous occupants took several days, resulting in chaos, overlap and no little bemusement. Several staff stumbled upon unemptied chamber pots in the malodorous cells now requisitioned as offices, while one Registry girl spotted her father's solicitor among the prisoners taking exercise in the yard. 'Don't go near them,' warned a vigilant warder. 'Some of them ain't seen no women for years.'

The steady stream of 'Mayfair types' heading through the imposing Gothic gateway each morning also attracted unwanted attention. On reaching the prison, several among the more waggish bus conductors took to calling out loudly: 'All change for MI5.'

As August gave way to September, others inside the Scrubs were also disinclined to view the prospect of war too seriously. The ageing Director-General of MI5, Sir Vernon Kell, in post for almost thirty years, suggested calling in Sir Oswald Mosley and Harry Pollitt for a cosy fireside chat, keen to know 'what their attitude is', and confident of obtaining their help in 'dealing with the Fascist and Communist problem.'

Adolf Hitler cared less. At dawn on Friday, 1 September, 1939, several small commando units from the Abwehr's elite Brandenburg battalion crossed the Polish border, followed by almost 2 million troops and 2,000 combat aircraft. Two weeks later Stalin's Red Army joined in the pillage from the east. Polish resistance was heroic and fierce, but would crumble in just four weeks.

The Second World War had begun.

3

OIK Calling Hamburg

On the morning of Saturday, 2 September 1939, again at 04.30, Colonel Johnny buzzed Wohldorf from the bathroom at Parklands, encrypting his message in CONGRATULATIONS code, and using a highly apposite call-sign: OIK. *'Situation in England extremely serious. Planes loaded Biggin Hill, Hornchurch. Blenheims. Will radio during day. Stand by day and night.'*

Wohldorf stood by, but no updates followed, and as the day developed the atmosphere grew increasingly sultry and oppressive, conveying to many a sense of impending doom. On Saturday night a series of violent thunderstorms swept the country, cutting power and communications, and causing panic in Portsmouth when four barrage balloons were struck by lightning, lighting up the night sky with clouds of eerie, floating flame. Quite literally, war was in the air. Although Sunday morning dawned bright and sunny, tension continued to mount as cathedrals and churches filled to overflowing, the nation hoping against hope for a miracle, some small retreat from the edge of the precipice.

As Arthur Owens fiddled nervously with his wayward klamotten most listeners tuned in to the BBC. The first news bulletin at 07.00 confirmed that Hitler had failed to respond to the Allied ultimatum issued two days earlier, and that German forces remained inside Poland. Finally, at 11.15, the Prime Minister addressed the nation. Now a frail old man of seventy, racked by terminal cancer, Neville Chamberlain's voice sounded weary, even sepulchral. Britain, he announced, was again at war with Germany. 'You can imagine what a bitter blow it is to me that all my long struggle to win peace has failed. It is evil things that we shall be fighting against – brute force, bad faith, injustice, oppression and persecution. And against them I am certain that right will prevail.'

Chamberlain's downbeat speech was followed by the national anthem, for which not every citizen stood. Eight numb minutes later came the dread sound of air raid sirens, a banshee wail that carried across London like a great cry of pain. Gas masks in hand, the population filed towards the shelters and 'bogey holes' in orderly fashion, some regarding the sky expectantly, others staring glumly at their feet. Three years earlier moviegoers had been horrified by scenes of urban apocalypse in *Things to Come*, glimpsing fact in science fiction. Now, with war a reality, most expected to emerge from underground to find their homes reduced to cinders and rubble, and the streets choked with corpses and poison gas.

Lazy Arthur Owens stayed tucked up in bed. Now that the BBC had pulled weather reports from the airwaves, the Luftwaffe would be reliant upon Colonel Johnny for accurate meteorological data. Already, however, there were rumours that MI5 had commandeered a fleet of Post Office mobile detector vans in order to hunt down enemy wireless spies. Fearful of betraying his location, Hitler's chief spy in England remained silent until early evening, then warmed his valves to buzz Ritter details of a brand new strategic fuel reserve depot, lately and discreetly cut into a hillside in Hampshire. *'Eastern side of long Winchester-Basingstoke railway line between Micheldever station and tunnel, 10 million gallons of aviation fuel in chalk cliff. Easiest to bomb from southern end.'*

Owens' jumpy paranoia increased tenfold when Bob called

to warn that the Branch had come calling at Grosvenor Court, anxious to detain his absent father under Defence Regulation 18B.

This was Plan Snuffbox, by which known enemy agents were to be rounded up as soon as war broke out. The select arrest list compiled by MI5 included Arthur Owens, whose own 18B Order was issued within hours of German troops crossing the Polish border. The Branch had missed him in Morden, while illicit transmissions were difficult to pinpoint, B1A having found that the balloon barrage now floating above London served to distort radio signals. Nonetheless, it seemed that it would be only a matter of time before the 'political cops' from Scotland Yard located Owens at the Surbiton bolt-hole thoughtfully provided by Alex Myner.

Everywhere events moved quickly. The governments of France, Australia, New Zealand and India joined Britain in declaring war on Germany, while Holland, Belgium, Denmark and Spain declared strict neutrality. Seeking to preserve his own non-aligned freedom, at noon on Monday Owens called Bill Gagen and arranged to meet him at Waterloo station at four o'clock. 'He stated he wished to offer his services to the British government,' the Special Branch inspector wrote, 'but declined to reveal his address.'

Snow knew full well that this meeting was a calculated risk. Travelling into central London with Lily, he told her to keep her distance on the crowded concourse at Waterloo, and warned what to do next if the Branch failed to greet their star double agent with chocolates and flowers. These fears proved well founded. After Owens again refused to confirm his address, Gagen placed the Little Man under arrest, then bundled him into a shiny Vauxhall saloon and sped him directly to Wandsworth gaol.

A grim Victorian complex south of the river, Wandsworth was the largest prison in London by some measure, able to accommodate more than fifteen hundred inmates and with a working gallows still in situ on E Wing. Gagen endorsed and served the 18B Order en route, whereupon Agent Snow became suddenly cooperative. 'Just before we entered the prison Owens gave his address as 12 Parklands, and added that a transmitting set would be found in his bathroom.'

Despite this belated admission, Owens soon found himself cooling his heels in a spartan cell. Fellow 18B detainees ranged from suspect German nationals to Percy Rapp, a thuggish fascist taxi driver whose regular visits to the German embassy had earned him a place on the Snuffbox list. For the most part, Mosley's Blackshirts remained at liberty. With no idea of Owens' whereabouts, Lily hurried back to Surbiton, reaching Myner's flat at around five o'clock. 'Three men have taken Arthur away,' she told the tyro sidekick. 'He told me to tell you to get rid of that parcel in the bathroom.'

Myner's version of events was the work of a practised liar. 'Although I was suspicious at the time, I buried the parcel in the corner of the garden. I now realise that my action was indiscreet, but thought I was doing him a good turn owing to his domestic troubles with his wife. I now understand it was a transmitting set belonging to Owens. I had seen him tinkering with it in the bathroom.'

'Alex said he would help Arthur for my sake,' agreed artful Lily, who helped Myner bury the set in a brown paper sack. 'Then I went out for a walk.'

Miss Bade was still absent when Gagen arrived at Parklands an hour later, accompanied by Tar Robertson and another MI5 officer, Colonel Adrian Simpson, the author of *Notes on the Detection of Illicit Wireless*. 'At first Myner and his wife denied all knowledge of Owens,' noted Gagen. 'Later they admitted he was living there as the husband of Lily Bade.' A thorough search of the flat failed to locate the transmitter, though a crude receiver, apparently constructed by Owens himself, was found in the bathroom cupboard. After a short, sharp interrogation, Myner broke down and led the intelligence men outside. 'He pointed out the spot where we found the transmitting set in a paper carrier. By this time Lily had returned to the house, and she and Myner were taken to Kingston police station, where statements were taken.'

With the war just one day old, the Abwehr's London stelle had collapsed like a house of cards. 'The Germans refer to Snow as their number one man in England,' Robertson remarked wryly. 'If this isn't a bluff – which seems likely – then they are pretty badly off!'

At Wandsworth, Owens languished in solitary confinement. Tuesday brought a visit from Robertson, Gagen and Lieutenant Colonel J. S. Yule, a coding expert attached to MI5, and the originator of the RAF motto *per ardua ad astra* ('through adversity to the stars'). After testing Snow's proficiency in Morse, judged by Yule to be limited, the discussion moved on to wireless procedures and the Abwehr organisation in Hamburg.

'There's a man called Theile,' Owens lied smoothly. 'He's in charge of their radio section. As for the transmitter, I'm to send over the dope at four in the morning, when everything's dead quiet. Wavelength 60 metres. The operator on watch speaks English, to give an immediate reply.'

'What dope do they want?' asked Robertson.

'Weather reports, like I told you people before. Visibility, wind speed, cloud cover and whatnot. Until I give the word there'll be no bombs on London.'

This bold assurance rang hollow, since wireless-equipped spies had suddenly become a matter of acute concern for Robertson and MI5. In the late afternoon of 4 September Bomber Command launched its first daylight bombing raid on Germany, sending a mixed force of Blenheims and Wellingtons to attack enemy warships in Wilhelmshaven and the Kiel Canal. The result was a disaster, with seven out of twenty-nine aircraft dispatched shot down, a crippling loss rate that nudged 25 per cent. Although determined pilots scored two hits on the German pocket battleship *Admiral Scheer*, both bombs failed to explode, while other crews mistakenly attacked friendly vessels in the North Sea. Bad weather compounded the debacle, with at least one Wellington missing Kiel by a hundred miles and unloading its bombs over neutral Denmark. Ironically, two of the air gunners from 9 Squadron who failed to return were members of the British Union of Fascists.

The chief cause of this calamity was radar. Germany's early warning system might not have been as complete or efficient as the British Chain Home, yet their Freya apparatus was technologically superior, and a mobile unit had tracked the raiders as they approached across the North Sea. None of this was known to British intelligence, who feared instead that the raid had been defeated by radiolocation of a different kind. In his diary Guy Liddell confided: 'Tar Robertson's section reports that warning signals by an enemy agent were intercepted before the raid on Kiel somewhere in the vicinity of Driffield, from which the raid started. This seems to call for some action to clear all areas in the vicinity of aerodromes and I am taking this up.'

More suspicious signals were detected at Driffield two nights later. Owens remained under lock and key in Wandsworth, with a watertight alibi, yet Tar remained convinced that the Welshman was holding back. 'There are inconsistencies in Snow's interpretation of various points in the transmission code, and it is my impression that he is not telling us by any means all he knows.'

MI5 now stood at the Rubicon. Owens could be detained indefinitely under Regulation 18B, or even put on trial, yet both options would render him useless as an intelligence asset. Pursuing a bolder agenda, the Little Man might yet become the Adam agent of a viable double-cross system, planting disinformation on the Abwehr and unravelling their British espionage network from within. Yet these were uncharted waters, stirred by uncertain tides. During the Great War each and every spy caught in Britain had been promptly dispatched by firing squad at the Tower of London, while Mad Major Draper, loyal and keen though he was, had achieved little of consequence. Then again, Draper had never been entrusted with a wireless transmitter, or been appointed Hitler's chief spy in England.

Nonetheless, the Security Service knew that a double-cross game could win actual battles. Late in August 1914 the War Office had sent 3,000 Royal Marines to Ostend in an effort to stiffen the crumbling Allied line, a force quickly transformed by wild rumour into 30,000 ferocious Russians, shipped via Archangel and Aberdeen 'with snow on their boots'. At the same time MI5 shadowed a German spy named Carl Lody, whose letters home were intercepted and read. One such informed his masters of the 'great masses of Russian soldiers' passing through Edinburgh 'on their way to London and France'. Lody put the number at 60,000, a fiction which MI5 saw no harm in allowing to reach Berlin. The Germans subsequently diverted precious reserves, and in consequence – some said – lost the Battle of the Marne.

Twenty-five years later – almost to the day – MI5 decided once more to steal a march on their German counterparts. With Snow on their boots.

There was no time to lose. On Friday afternoon Robertson transferred Snow's klamotten from the Scrubs to Wandsworth, where it was set up in an empty cell by a wireless expert from GCHQ named Meakin. At six o'clock that same evening Owens was invited to resume wireless contact with the Abwehr signals centre at Wohldorf. At short notice, a prison warder named Maurice Burton, who happened to be proficient in Morse, was briefed to listen in. His expert ear would ensure that the message buzzed by Owens corresponded to the text agreed by Robertson, and was clean of obvious cheats ('tells') which might alert Stelle X to the fact that Colonel Johnny was operating under control.

What happened next did little to assuage Tar's myriad doubts about Snow. 'Unfortunately, in looking over his set Owens pushed a switch which caused a fuse to blow. This ended our activities for the day, as we were unable to repair the set before the following morning.'

No signal, just noise.

Apprehension over Snow's bona fides only increased with the simultaneous arrival of a registered letter from Amsterdam containing four £5 notes, addressed to 'Mr Wilson' at 112 Stratford Road. Having sided with her forsaken sister-in-law Irene, Esther Ferrett took the incriminating package to West Ham police station. On returning to Wandsworth on Saturday morning, Tar initiated a robust exchange with Owens, during which he made it 'abundantly clear' that it was in his best interests to establish contact with Stelle X. 'Since our conversation it is now my impression that Snow is doing all he can to get in touch with Germany.'

Owens' change of heart owed less to a sense of patriotic duty than a desire for simple self-preservation. There was also Lily, his Achilles heel, now back with her parents in West Ham, exposed to the fury of the Ferretts, and perhaps even that of the public at large. His choice was no choice at all. By six o'clock on Saturday evening Meakin had managed to repair the faulty klamotten. With Owens on the key, his Morse signature slow and apprehensive, B1A's first double-cross signal flashed across the ether to Wohldorf: *'All ready. Have repaired radio. Send instructions. Now awaiting reply.'*

No convoys or Blenheims, no fuel dumps, no weather.

Not even *ein glas bier.*

And no reply.

A repeat transmission at 19.45 gave the same disappointing result. According to boffins at GCHQ the strength of both signals was poor, with no definite reply detected. Owens suggested buzzing the message for a third time at 04.00 on Sunday morning, when the funkers at Wohldorf would be listening in for Johnny. Again, however, the test proved negative. 'Unfortunately our transmission was reported as completely jammed by a powerful unidentified station,' Tar wrote ruefully. 'It is of course possible that the message might have been received in Germany, but no reply was picked up by GCHQ.'

Desperate to escape Wandsworth, Owens offered to contact Hamburg by letter, though Robertson demurred. Besides, there were now indications that the future security of London might not rest entirely on the feeble shoulders of Agent Snow. 'Klop Ustinov has reported,' wrote Liddell, 'that the reason for the German abstention from bombing England or France is that Hitler intends to destroy Poland, then offer to make peace on the grounds that he has taken no offensive action against the Allies.'

During this brief interregnum Arthur Owens and Tar Robertson struck an unprecedented deal. This bargain – more a Faustian pact – involved the provision of a new home for Snow in Kingston-upon-Thames, an upmarket suburb not far from Surbiton, together with false identity papers in the name of Thomas Wilson. In return for relative personal freedom, and a small monthly retainer, Owens would transmit controlled messages to the enemy, continue to treff with Rantzau on neutral territory, and maintain the fiction of a zealous Welsh sabotage ring. Best of all, Lily would also reside at the new London stelle.

The complexities were considerable, not least the small matter of housing Snow and his klamotten. 'Enemy agents in this country using radio transmitters would be operating under difficulties,' observed a specialist from the Radio Security Service. 'It was not easy for a man to take lodgings, put up an aerial and lock himself in his room for a period each day while he sent messages and received replies on equipment which, if it were seen by the landlady, would certainly cause her to call the police.'

MI5 might have preferred to keep Snow's priceless transmitter under lock and key at Wormwood Scrubs, yet there was always the risk that the Abwehr would triangulate his signals, and smell a rat. Verisimilitude therefore required that Owens actually broadcast from home, which in turn raised further complications, including the need for a live-in wireless operator and constant supervision by watchers from the Special Branch and Section B6. Since the high-frequency bands used by Wohldorf required an aerial thirty metres long, erected high in the air and free from obstructions, there was also the need for a large roof space, ideally situated above a top-floor flat.

Finally released from Wandsworth on the evening of Monday, 11 September, Owens spent his first night of liberty in a cell at Kingston police station, albeit as a 'special' prisoner. The following day was taken up with house-hunting, Robertson and Gagen eventually settling on a four-room apartment at 9 Norbiton Avenue. The house was a nondescript Edwardian villa a mere stone's throw from the nearest railway station, though, less conveniently the vacant flat was unfurnished. Meakin spent the rest of the day installing Snow's bothersome transmitter, concealing the lengthy dipole aerial in the attic, while Robertson carefully drafted Snow's next message to Doctor Rantzau. *'Must meet you in Holland at once. Bring weather code. Radio town and hotel. Wales ready.'*

With Tar at his shoulder, Owens keyed the signal at 11.30 that night. Yet again there was no reply. After waiting for several long hours, the message was repeated at 04.00 on Wednesday morning. This time the funkers at Wohldorf were wide awake. 'We immediately received a reply,' Tar noted. 'But their message was quite undecipherable. We asked for a repeat, whereupon the Germans replied that *they* wanted a repeat. After this last message we decided it was high time to give it up.'

Despite these frustrations, this fumbled exchange represented a significant breakthrough. 'There are dramatic moments in the history of most institutions,' vouched an internal history of MI5. 'This, in the record of double-cross activities, was one of them. For with Snow's first message the double-cross system was well and truly launched. He was in fact the *fons et origo* of all our activities for the next five years.'

Only now was the 18B Order served on Owens formally suspended, and Lily allowed to join him at Norbiton Avenue. Snow's pretty lover was driven down from West Ham by Bill Gagen and provided with funds to buy furniture. Quite correctly, Robertson surmised that wily Lily Bade was rather more than a mistress on the make and would need to be watched just as carefully as Agent Snow. Determined to take no chances, Owens' minders placed the klamotten in a locked room with the key retained by B1A.

For Snow to remain credible with 'Herr Doktor Rantzau' it was vital to resume some more meaningful contact without further delay. With deep misgivings, MI5 agreed to allow him to return to the Continent to treff with the Doctor in person, this time in Rotterdam. With the Netherlands still neutral, Owens could maintain his pre-war cover as a commercial traveller and simply call Stelle X by telephone once he arrived. Rantzau, Tar hoped, would hasten across the border to meet with Johnny, provide dope on other Nazi spies still at large in Britain, and perhaps even betray Hitler's military designs on Western Europe.

Colonel Johnny had other ideas. On Thursday, 14 September, Robertson returned to Kingston with a passport and exit permit made out in the name of Thomas Wilson, and briefed Owens to travel via Tilbury and Flushing the following day. Reverting to type, Owens asked Tar to conjure up a suitable Welsh sidekick, sufficiently well briefed to convince Rantzau that 'Wales ready' was no idle boast. Gagen proposed a Special Branch sergeant who spoke German and 'had the appearance of a Welshman', though his candidate was immediately vetoed. 'Snow said that the Germans do not understand Welsh as he had tried them out in the language. But they know what it sounds like and would not be easily taken in by an impostor.'

Owens had every reason to be cautious. Agent Snow was loyal to neither side, an imposture that even the thickest Special Branch sergeant was quite likely to detect. Besides, the disorientating, schizophrenic world of the double agent in wartime required nerves of steel, as well as the ability to contrive endless stories and subterfuges – some as Johnny, more as Snow. An amateur might easily crumble under pressure. Instead, Snow's ideal stooge should be the type of man described by MI5 as possessed of 'a natural predilection to live in that curious world of espionage and deceit, and who attach themselves with equal facility to one side or the other, so long as their craving for adventure of a rather macabre type is satisfied.'

That neither Tar Robertson nor Nikolaus Ritter could be entirely certain of what Owens got up to on the far side of the water made his dangerous game so much easier to play.

Snow finally departed from London on Friday, arriving in Rotterdam at six in the evening and checking into the Hotel Monopole, a fascist-friendly establishment. Having left a telephone message at the Auerbach office, Owens sat down to wait for the Doctor. Over the course of an eventful weekend there was much to occupy his mind. The Soviet Union invaded Poland from the east, causing the Mościcki government to flee to Romania, while U-29 torpedoed and sank the British aircraft carrier HMS *Courageous* in the Bristol Channel, causing the shocking loss of 518 men. With 50,000 troops of the British Expeditionary Force (BEF) already landed in France, the chances of a negotiated peace looked increasingly remote.

Ritter did not arrive until Monday, bringing with him a colleague named Kurtz and taking a suite at the Weimar, a luxurious waterfront establishment. 'He asked me what work I had done,' Owens recalled. 'I told him that my time had been occupied with getting a new address, and putting the radio in working order. Rantzau said he had £80 for me, and as much as I required in London. I complained of radio trouble. They said things were difficult but that they would get the new set to me by U-boat at the first opportunity.'

What actually transpired between Snow and Rantzau is difficult to gauge, since Owens' reports to British intelligence were highly selective and few Abwehr files would survive the war. By his own account to MI5, following detailed discussion of codes and transmission times the conversation turned to sabotage in Wales. Ritter identified heavy industry around Port Talbot and Briton Ferry as possible targets.

'I've got a contact in Swansea,' fibbed Owens. 'Just an ordinary sort of man, not very flush with money. He's in touch with the head of the Welsh Nationalist people, Plaid Cymru. Their leader lives somewhere up north.'

'Is this middleman reliable?' asked Ritter.

'One hundred per cent.'

'Then bring him to Brussels in a fortnight. We'll put him up at the Savoy, show him we mean business.'

'He'll be tickled to death.'

Ritter recharged their glasses, then asked Colonel Johnny to find a quiet spot on the Welsh coast suitable for landing arms and explosives. Owens cast his mind back eighteen years to his brief, unhappy interlude as a candy magnate in Mumbles. 'Oxwich Bay, perhaps. Maybe Rhossili.'

'Keep it coming, Arthur. Troop movements, tank units, any RAF squadrons transferring to France. And more on this wireless cloud business.'

'I can give you that now,' replied Owens, initiating an exchange recorded only in Abwehr files. 'There's a line of UHF radio stations running right the way down the east coast. They bounce electronic beams off aircraft. Wash out death rays and stalling engines, that's nothing but a stunt. These things are capable of tracking the approach of your bombers from miles away – range, altitude and numbers. The whole damn works.'

'This dope comes from where?'

'A Philips engineer, attached to the Air Ministry.'

'English?'

'Dutch. But he's on the level.'

The Doctor smiled broadly, his gold tooth flashing. Here, at last, was confirmation that the nests of puzzling masts dotted around the English coastline beamed out something more significant than marine navigation signals, or primitive television broadcasts. The workings of the British radar network was Johnny's best sample yet. Worth reporting to Admiral Canaris in person, in fact.

CONGRATULATIONS all round.

By way of a quid pro quo, Ritter offered Owens a strategic revelation of his own. 'Once the main part of the British army has left for France we intend to surround London with thousands of paratroops. Probably most of our *Fallschirmjäger* will die, but think of the effect on morale. Nazis with Tommy guns and flame throwers, running amok in the garden of England.'

'Your public water supply,' added Kurtz. 'Easily poisoned with deadly bacteria. And you're a chemist, I see.'

'*Schrecklichkeit*,' grinned Ritter, 'followed by swift surrender on favourable terms. There's no need for this unfortunate war to drag on, Arthur. We're all of us working for peace. And I see big things ahead for *Der Kleine*.'

From humbug merchant to mass poisoner in one fell swoop. Never mind the Hall of Fame at the Reichstag, Ritter's latest stunt promised immortality in the Chamber of Horrors at Madame Tussauds.

Next day Owens left Rotterdam £80 richer, albeit green with fright at the prospect of being torpedoed midway between

Flushing and Tilbury. There was also the prospect of Luftwaffe raids on the new Hawker Hurricane factory at Kingston, barely a mile from Norbiton Avenue. This, too, Ritter had predicted. Death from the air, and poison in the water. Perfidious Albion, so it seemed, held even greater perils than Nazi Germany.

The jumpy triple agent would have fretted even more had he known that MI5 were now in dialogue with the War Cabinet about mandatory capital punishment for enemy spies.

'The matter appears to have been overlooked in our Defence Regulations,' remarked Liddell. 'The Director of Public Prosecutions says that trial for high treason would be far too cumbersome and ineffective. All the high legal pundits agree that a law should be framed so that if a spy is convicted of espionage the judge has no alternative but to sentence him to death, on the same lines that he would sentence a murderer. It is always open to the king to whittle the sentence down to three weeks if he so desires.'

Indefinite detention without trial under Defence Regulation 18B would be condemned as 'in the highest degree odious' even by Winston Churchill. To captured spies, however, unlimited gaol time under draconian emergency powers beat a date with the hangman, or a firing squad.

Back in Blighty, Agent Snow was grilled by Robertson for several hours. Owens bluffed at length about Welsh Nationalists, Italian submarine parts and Russian oil, but mentioned nothing about selling out British radar, or loose-lipped sources at Philips. Instead, Robertson was struck hardest by the Little Man's animated chatter about terror raids and secret weapons. 'Snow impressed on me that Rantzau has lived a lot in America, and has acquired the American outlook of showmanship. Yet he has the greatest respect for Rantzau's brains and ability, and says that his power is quite extraordinary.'

So too was his timing. On the afternoon of Tuesday, 19 September, as Owens made his way back to Tilbury, Adolf

Hitler broadcast a speech from Danzig, triumphalist in tone, laced with hints of a secret weapon 'against which no defence would avail'. Suitably alarmed, British intelligence agencies scrambled to discover more about the fantastical doomsday device, said to be capable of blinding and deafening its victims. Public alarm spread like wildfire, fuelled by sensationalist newspaper coverage; some no doubt feared an atomic bomb, a weapon of mass destruction first mooted in public six months earlier. 'This terrible weapon is probably meant to intimidate,' wrote John Colville, a junior secretary at the Foreign Office. 'But it does give one a slight feeling of uneasiness, because even Hitler and his satellites usually have something on which to base statements of this kind.'

SIS turned to a gifted young Oxford scientist, R. V. Jones, who noted that the latest 'death ray' demonstrated to MI6 had shown remarkable properties only as a fruit preserver, and deduced that the weapon kited by Hitler in Danzig was merely the Luftwaffe. Nevertheless, in his final report Jones sounded a note of caution. Dismissing some of the more fantastic rumours, including 'machines for generating earthquakes' and 'gases which cause everyone within two miles to burst', the scientist warned that a number of Nazi projects deserved to be taken seriously. This prescient list included long-range rockets and pilotless aircraft, as well as two items brought back from Rotterdam by Agent Snow: bacteriological warfare, and poison gas.

Within days, irate freshwater anglers found vulnerable reservoirs suddenly closed to fishing. Meanwhile, by sinister coincidence, a virulent measles epidemic tore through MI5. Quietly grateful, Tar Robertson and his team were allowed to return to central London, quitting Wormwood Scrubs for the more convivial surrounds of 58 St James's Street, a short walk from Piccadilly.

Reunited with Lily at Norbiton Avenue, Owens set about

discouraging the Luftwaffe from bombing the Kingston area by transmitting unfavourable weather reports. *'22.07 hours, September 23. Cloud base 350 metres. Westerly wind, Force 3. Sky totally overcast.'*

Visiting Snow three days later, MI5 fell prey to paranoia of a different kind. That evening Tar Robertson's new assistant, a former banker named Richman Stopford, drove down to Kingston to supervise the evening transmission. He was joined on the journey by another B Division officer, Michael Ryde, recently appointed as Regional Security Liaison Officer for Surrey. Mindful of tradecraft, the pair parked near Norbiton station and completed their journey on foot. As they walked through the subway, Stopford's gaze was drawn to a loitering girl. 'She was fairly thickset, short, aged about 25 to 30, wearing a dark blue felt hat and dark coat in some tweed material. In the darkness of the subway I could not be certain of the colour of her hair, although I passed very close to her. My impression was that it was dark.'

On turning the corner into Norbiton Avenue the intelligence men watched as an expensive-looking car drew up outside number 9, disgorging Owens and Lily, along with two unidentified men. Electing to telephone Robertson, Stopford retraced his steps to the station, only to find that he was being followed by a third unidentified male. Moreover, the dark, dumpy girl still stood guard at the mouth of the subway.

Happily the mystery was soon dispelled. The men in the car were Bill Gagen and his sergeant, and the tail behind Stopford one of the Special Branch watchers detailed to keep tabs on Owens, plainly good at his job. But who was the mysterious female in the blue felt hat? 'I told Owens that we were suspicious someone had been watching us, possibly a girl,' warned Stopford. 'This news made him somewhat nervous, so much so that I had to code most of his messages myself.'

Stopford took security very seriously indeed, and poured

scorn on the amateurish conduct of their rival spooks from Scotland Yard. 'The fact that neither Mr Ryde nor I were aware that Inspector Gagen was intending to appear at Snow's flat very nearly resulted in a major calamity. It is essential that the minimum number of people should be seen to enter and leave, and it is taking a quite unnecessary risk to allow Gagen, in a large and shiny car, which he parked outside the door, to go in and out as he chooses. The good lady in the flat opposite did in fact put her head out of the door to see who all the people were going up and down her back stairs.'

Thanks to these various misadventures, Owens only just managed to transmit on schedule at 22.00. Numbering his message #13, OIK informed Wohldorf that he was now: *'Leaving for Wales. Will radio Friday night at 12. Seeing Williams. Please reply.'*

After requesting a repeat, Wohldorf replied: *'Need military and general news urgently daily.'*

Ignoring this plea, Owens buzzed over a mundane weather report, reception of which was confirmed after two repeats. *'Visibility 900 metres. Cloud base 400-500 metres. North-easterly wind, Force 2. Temperature 50 Fahrenheit.'*

Apparently happy, the distant Abwehr operator signed off with some light-hearted banter: *'Good night, old boy.'*

Seldom had war seemed more phoney.

4

The Welsh Ring

Unreliable Special Branch officers aside, worried Agent Snow had not long to wait before uninvited guests began to darken the door of the new London stelle. Responding to a knock on the morning of Tuesday, 3 October, Owens found himself face to face with a tall, thin, bespectacled man whose voice when he spoke carried the faintest hint of an American accent.

The stranger asked whether Owens knew 'the Doctor', and asked for a telephone number. Owens hedged artfully. What with the war situation, he said, the Post Office would take at least a week to connect a line. The sinister American promised to return. Closing the door in his face, Owens called Major Ryde to demand increased protection. 'We must assume,' Tar remarked, 'that from now on Snow will probably be followed by someone from the other side.'

Even if the thin man really existed, the Security Service stood no chance of tracking him down. Despite having doubled in size since the outbreak of war MI5 found itself swamped by a rip tide of urgent requests, all of which competed for top priority. For Liddell and Robertson in B Division, the investigation of innocent foreign nationals and suspected Fifth Columnists took up fully three-quarters of their time, an absurd state of affairs epitomised by a report from a clergyman's daughter in

Winchester, who confidently denounced a lodger as 'un-English' for failing to flush a lavatory.

This left B1A with insufficient resources for proper counter-espionage work, such as identifying Snow's mystery visitor, and investigating reports of clandestine signalling from Land's End to John O'Groats. Much of this technical toil was undertaken by the Radio Security Service, in truth little more than a collection of pre-war radio hams. 'Tar tells me that our DF organisation is virtually no organisation at all,' Liddell fretted. 'We require 60 experts at least. At the moment we have 27 amateurs twiddling knobs. In the meantime another station has been located in Belfast. This is interesting as Owens had already told us of its existence. There seems no reason to doubt his loyalty at the moment, but he is under close supervision. When things begin to warm up we hope to do useful work by sending misleading messages.'

For the moment, the war refused to come to the boil. With the RAF dropping more leaflets than bombs on Germany, Hitler remained confident that peace would prevail, offering broad hints in speeches from the Reichstag and putting out feelers via neutral diplomats and the Vatican. The Phoney War was real only at sea, where U-47 penetrated the Grand Fleet anchorage at Scapa Flow to sink the battleship *Royal Oak*, killing 800 sailors and triggering panic over Scottish sleeper spies and secret submarine bases in Ireland. Time and again, British intelligence failed to see the wood for the trees. After Hitler ordered his generals to attack Belgium, Holland and France in the middle of November, a staunchly anti-Hitler Abwehr officer named Hans Oster leaked details and dates to his opposite number in the Netherlands, Colonel Gijsbertus Sas. Yet Sas was ignored, and even dismissed by some as a German mole.

Already there were dark mutterings that MI5 and MI6 were punching well below their weight. 'A suggestion has come through that we might scatter dud banknotes in millions over

Germany,' mused Guy Liddell. 'But it hardly fits with the high moral tone of the war. Perhaps when things have deteriorated through the use of poison gas, bacteria etc a suitable occasion may arise for a venture of this sort.'

Blitzkrieg had given way to Sitzkrieg, a veritable Bore War. With no sign of the airborne mayhem promised by Rantzau in Rotterdam, Colonel Johnny bided his time and sent daily weather reports laced with scraps of anodyne chicken feed authorised by MI5. *'At the moment very few troop movements around London,'* Owens buzzed innocuously at the beginning of October. *'Same news received from other centres.'*

Meanwhile Robertson scrambled to activate Snow's fictional Welsh sabotage ring ahead of the next treff in Brussels. Through Maxwell Knight, a Secret Service veteran whose autonomous sub-section B5B specialised in infiltrating radical political groups, Tar located a retired police inspector from Swansea named Gwilym Williams. Lately employed as a court interpreter, Williams spoke several dialects and languages, German included, and ran a sideline as a legal-enquiry agent. A big man – six foot two, and eighteen stone – he had served in the Royal Garrison Artillery during the previous war, and despite a career record marked by a fondness for beer and fisticuffs, seemed likely to convince as an ardent Welsh Nationalist and man of action. Following a preliminary vetting session conducted in Swansea, the burly ex-policeman travelled up to London on 16 October, a Monday. There he reported to Knight's flat-cum-office in Dolphin Square, the luxurious Pimlico development where recent near neighbours had included Sir Oswald Mosley and William Joyce, the latter now broadcasting from Germany as Lord Haw-Haw.

'I asked Williams whether he was willing to undertake the work which we hoped to assign to him,' wrote Knight, a past master of intrigue. 'He said, "Yes, sir, I will go and I will do my best".' Following detailed discussion of ways and means, it was agreed that those involved in the case would use the password 'Crowhurst', answerable by 'Ginger'.

With Agent Snow due in Brussels as early as Wednesday there was no time to lose. Hastily codenamed G.W., at midday Gwilym Williams was introduced to Owens at the Bonnington Hotel on Southampton Row. Here the pair spent three hours discussing the imminent mission to Belgium, during which Snow instructed G.W. to keep his distance on the journey over, but to maintain visual contact at all times, and tell inquisitive officials that he was travelling to Rotterdam to meet a Canadian friend.

A subsequent Crowhurst–Ginger call from Knight to Robertson confirmed that this initial meeting had gone well. 'Williams very sensibly suggested that his occupation should be what it actually is – an enquiry agent willing to act in cases of injury caused by road accident. Owens has invited him to Kingston tonight. As Williams is quite new to the whole of this business, the opportunity of discussing it again with Owens – who has a keen mind – will probably be of considerable benefit.'

During the afternoon Williams was issued with an exit permit and £25 to cover expenses. Regrettably, stealth and tradecraft were nowhere in evidence when Agent Snow turned up to collect his latest sidekick from the Bonnington in a hired Daimler limousine, complete with uniformed chauffeur.

'Don't be surprised if I'm addressed as "Colonel" over there,' Owens announced grandiloquently as they pulled away. 'That's the rank I hold in the German army. In fact, I outrank Captain Robertson.'

'That can't be easy,' joked Williams. 'Seeing as you don't speak the lingo.'

'I'm their big nut over here. There's £50,000 on the table if I can bribe an RAF pilot to steal a Spitfire and take it over to Germany. Job for life for the flyboy, too.'

It seemed not to matter that the man behind the wheel of the

Daimler heard each and every word. As his conspicuous staff car circled Green Park, recently scarred with air-raid trenches, Colonel Johnny handed Williams a sheaf of Welsh Nationalist literature.

'When you meet the Doctor, tell him you get about Wales a good deal as a private detective. That you've seen for yourself the condition of the working man, how the people are oppressed and exploited by laws handed down by a government made up of Englishmen.'

'That hardly makes me a Nazi.'

'Then say some nice things about Hitler and Germany too. That they're a fine race of people who get things done.'

Williams frowned. It was hard to tell where the British double agent ended and his German *doppelgänger* began. At Norbiton Avenue Owens introduced Williams to Lily, then ushered him through to the small back room. Waving aside Burton, the former prison warder seconded as his operator, Snow fiddled with the klamotten until the sound of rapid Morse became audible.

'Direct from Berlin,' he announced proudly.

'Can you understand it?'

'One hundred per cent. Mind you, they slow right down for my benefit.'

At six o'clock Owens, Williams and Lily rode the Daimler into Richmond for drinks at the Castle Hotel, picking up a lively young couple on the way, and then trawling round several more pubs. Williams danced with a girl named Maude, and was pronounced a 'grand man' by Lily. The former policeman noted that Snow imbibed heavily throughout the evening, mixing whisky and beer, yet remained remarkably clear-headed. Back at the flat, he looked on as Owens and Burton transmitted a suitably inaccurate weather report. Finally Williams returned to the Bonnington, having arranged to meet Owens on Trafalgar Square at ten o'clock the following morning.

'Williams' first impressions of Owens are that he is very alert and highly strung,' noted Robertson. 'He does not rest much, has tremendous willpower, and is a fairly heavy drinker. In the latter capacity Williams confesses he cannot compete.'

Snow and G.W. finally left London on Thursday, crossing to Belgium from Folkestone, and profoundly apprehensive now that the German navy had promised to sink passenger ships sailing in convoys, or without lights. On reaching Brussels the pair checked into the Savoy as instructed. 'Owens was exceedingly nervous,' observed Williams. 'He expressed constant fear that a German contact might have seen the police visiting his house and sent word over, which would mean the end of us both.'

The histrionics increased with each hour that passed. 'Brussels is infested with German secret service men,' Williams learned. 'They can do exactly as they please.' Claiming to be a crack shot, Owens decided to buy a pistol, and asked Williams to help him fill out the necessary forms at the Commissaire de Police. The bizarre claim that he needed a gun 'to shoot rats in Canada' was accepted without question, and endorsed on his permit. A local gunsmith happily supplied a suitable automatic, and threw in 25 rounds of ammunition.

Perhaps Owens was enacting a charade for the benefit of Williams. Possibly he feared being double-crossed himself. Whatever the truth, on Friday afternoon an Abwehr emissary appeared to fix a meeting with Ritter the following day. Still Owens remained on edge, fretting now because the Doctor wished him to meet with a female agent who was being trained for a mission to England. 'Snow was much upset,' noted Williams, 'because he considers it dangerous to work with women.'

Or wives, at any rate.

On Saturday Ritter and his assistant arrived at the Savoy fully three hours late. The party of four left immediately, and at the

Gare du Nord boarded a train for Antwerp, the strategic port city famously described by Napoleon as a pistol pointed at the heart of England. From the ornate central station they took a cab to an undistinguished office building on the waterfront. Glancing around, Owens recognised the liner moored on the Canadian Pacific wharf as the SS *Pennland*, on which he had crossed the Atlantic almost six years earlier.

Following his gaze, Ritter complained that Canada was far too busy producing tanks, aircraft and Bren guns from Long Branch. 'I can find work for you over there, Arthur, should you wish.'

Inside the building an elevator conveyed them to the third floor. Owens and Williams were ushered into a spacious board room, where Ritter introduced to them two men known as the Commander and Doctor Kiess. These aliases disguised Leutnant Lothar Witzke, a 'stiff Bavarian type' in charge of sabotage operations against England, and Hauptmann Brasser, a specialist in aviation intelligence.

'How many men do you have at your disposal, Mr Williams?' asked Witzke, taking charge straight away.

'In South Wales, about thirty.'

'And are they willing to commit acts of sabotage on behalf of the Reich?'

'Where our interests coincide.'

Evidently satisfied, Witzke went on to suggest that supplies for the Welsh ring might best be delivered by U-boat. The explosives would be landed in bulk but broken down into smaller parcels, concealed in bottles, canned goods and so forth. This made storage easier and prevented deterioration.

'Dynamite?' asked Williams. 'TNT?'

Witzke shook his head. 'You'll be mixing the ingredients yourselves. Three parts potassium chlorate to one part sugar, detonated by sulphuric acid.'

Williams glanced at Owens. 'He's the chemist, not me.'

'I've laid on some basic instruction tomorrow. Then, in a month or so, you can come over to Germany for a more comprehensive sabotage course. And collect a wireless too, if you want one.'

'Wash that out,' snapped Owens, keen to protect his own patch. 'All signals traffic between England and Germany goes through me.'

Ritter raised a calming hand, then reached into his pocket and slid a buff manila envelope across the table towards Williams. Peering inside, Williams counted £50 in Bank of England notes. The former policeman hesitated, torn between the demands of his novel new role as a double-cross asset and his relatively law-abiding past.

'Take it!' urged Ritter, his gold tooth flashing. 'Only fools and fanatics work for free. Whenever you need more, simply call on Johnny.'

Arthur Owens bit his lip, after which Ritter derived further amusement by booking his Welsh Nationalist cadre into the Hotel London. The next day Leutnant Witzke took the pair to a flat in the centre of Antwerp, where a Flemish Nazi instructed them in the art of mixing explosives, laced with elementary tips on arson. At the end of the session Owens was handed a number of detonators concealed in a block of wood. The would-be saboteurs then retired to the Taverne Sonia, where Witzke was evidently a regular, and soon became exceedingly drunk.

The next day, while Witzke nursed his hangover, Owens conferred in private with Ritter and Brasser. As played back to MI5, at his second wartime treff Agent Snow discussed only trivia, including troop movements, petrol rationing and the 'jitterbug' effect of propaganda broadcasts by captured RAF aircrew. In fact Owens delivered up solid intelligence on the strength of fighter squadrons at Northolt and Croydon, Short Sunderland flying boats based at Pembroke Dock and the embarkation of 80 tanks at Avonmouth, bound for France. The location of several key war factories was also revealed, including a Rolls-Royce aero engine store in Didcot and a synthetic fuel plant at Methyr.

None of these disclosures stood approved by Tar Robertson or the newly formed Wireless Committee. By way of reward, for these revelations and his betrayal of British radar secrets a month earlier, Owens received an extravagant cash payment of £470 – the price of a modest house in 1939.

Henceforth, explained Ritter, Owens should expect regular payments through a woman in Bournemouth. Another sleeper agent in Manchester named Charles Eschborn was able to process tiny microdot photographs. 'He's entirely reliable,' vouched the Doctor. 'Besides which, the Gestapo are holding one of his brothers in Dachau.'

Next Ritter handed Owens a postage stamp. 'Your new questionnaire in microdot form,' he explained. 'A little on the sticky side, you might say. But much easier to smuggle across frontiers than paper or film.'

'I've just the place,' grinned Owens, reaching to remove his false teeth.

Ritter looked quickly away.

Their business concluded, agents Snow and G.W. returned to Brussels, checked back into the Savoy, and boarded a ferry at Ostend on Wednesday. The two men found British newspapers full of scorn for a speech delivered by Joachim von Ribbentrop, the German foreign minister, holding England responsible for the outbreak of a second Great War and portraying the Reich as the injured party. On disembarkation at Folkestone Owens was tailed discreetly by a Special Branch detective, who reported an emotional reunion with Lily on the platform at Victoria but failed to spot Williams at all.

Exhausted, Gwilym Williams went directly to Swansea, where he was debriefed at home by Richman Stopford. 'G.W.

still looks rather tired,' remarked Tar's assistant, 'but his report, attached, is excellent. Everyone is very friendly with Snow, and he is apparently trusted by them all. They refer to him as their number one man in England. So far as Williams can judge, the whole affair is a genuine effort on the part of the Germans, and he sees no sign of wool being drawn over his eyes. But then, he might not.'

In fact, Williams understood the case – and the man – all too well. 'He thinks that Snow's object is to get all he can out of the Germans, yet do enough to keep on the right side of us.'

Whether G.W. was prepared to risk going into Germany for sabotage training was another matter entirely. After seeking assurances that his wife and daughter would be looked after should he fail to return, Williams pointed out that his private enquiry business would slide in his absence and demanded a salary. 'I congratulated him warmly,' hedged Stopford, 'and said that his services would not be overlooked. He has spent £30 and been too rushed to keep accounts. Taking into account the German money he is still £45 to the good.'

However, £45 hardly compared to the £470 flaunted by Agent Snow. Already something of Owens' mercenary approach to the spy racket had rubbed off on the dubious ex-copper from Swansea.

Colonel Johnny nursed doubts of his own. Williams gave every appearance of incorruptibility, like a lily-white G-man from the FBI, and as such was of no value as an Abwehr stooge. Debriefed by Robertson, Owens set about devaluing G.W. as a double-cross asset, claiming that Doctor Rantzau had found him 'too nervous' in Antwerp and wanted Johnny to take personal control of sabotage operations in Wales. With G.W. in charge, fibbed Snow, there would be no U-boat, no explosives – and no cash payment of £30,000.

Owens obscured his own treachery by fibbing that the Abwehr had informants inside the Air Ministry and the

Admiralty, and that new V-men (*vertrauens*, or 'trusted') were on their way to London. 'Snow has returned from Brussels and is to receive instructions regarding the appointment of agents,' Guy Liddell wrote with unwarranted confidence. 'He also mentioned that they are anxious for him to go to Canada sometime in the near future, possibly with the object of organising a similar show for them out there.'

For all of a fortnight the going seemed good at B1A. At the beginning of November Snow travelled to Manchester to meet Charles Eschborn, standing back as the hapless photographer was quietly lifted by the Branch and flipped as double agent CHARLIE. Unfortunately for MI5 Eschborn was small fry, besides which Owens ignored protocol by co-opting Lily for his northern mission. By the middle of the month Tar found his patience worn perilously thin. 'I told Owens we were not at all satisfied with the way things were developing, and taxed him on the fact that we had been at war for over two months, yet so far he had not been contacted by anybody, he had not received the promised wireless set, and we had not received a list of contacts.'

Ironically, Tar also took Snow to task over his reliance on facts and chicken feed provided by British intelligence, rather than obtaining dope of his own. No one, it seems, perceived any vice in Owens worse than laziness, or gave serious consideration to the notion that the Little Man might actually be working for Germany and double-crossing MI5.

Humdinger.

Like Alice en route to Wonderland, the British secret service found itself locked in an endless downward spiral. At the beginning of November the veteran director of MI6, Admiral Hugh 'Quex' Sinclair, died after sixteen years in post, creating a power vacuum at the heart of the intelligence establishment. Just five days later, a humiliating debacle in Holland laid bare the dangers inherent in allowing unreliable amateurs to operate abroad. On 9 November German agents snatched two MI6 officers from a Dutch frontier post at Venlo, at the same time killing a Dutch intelligence officer. One of the men abducted was Major Richard Stevens, who ran the MI6 station in The Hague, the other a flamboyant expatriate businessman named Sigismund Payne Best, part of a sketchy SIS shadow network known as Z. The pair fancied they had established contact with a group of highly placed German patriots, who offered to fly a like-minded general to London for secret peace talks. The endgame, so they thought, was a military coup in Berlin and the arrest of Adolf Hitler. MI6 even provided the conspirators with a wireless transmitter, unaware that they were in fact negotiating with double-cross agents from the *Sicherheitsdienst* – a sister agency of the Gestapo, and sworn rivals of the Abwehr.

The violent denouement saw Best and Stevens abducted in broad daylight and hustled across the border into Germany, a humiliating coup that grabbed headlines worldwide as 'The Venlo Incident'. Both men cracked under interrogation, and were forced to endure the grinding miseries of Sachsenhausen and Dachau. 'With memories of past cowardice in a dentists' chair,' Best admitted, 'my estimate of my fortitude under torture was modest in the extreme.'

Inevitably, British intelligence agencies now viewed all German initiatives with deep suspicion, and Gwilym Williams' proposed trip to a spy school inside Germany was put on hold. 'Venlo will be a great blow to SIS and also ourselves,' Liddell commented. 'It seems not unlikely that a member of the Dutch general staff, Colonel Sas, previously reported as a German agent, was responsible for giving the whole show away.'

Sas was innocent, and the blundering continued apace. Towards the end of November MI6 received a mystery package from Oslo containing detailed intelligence on German electronic warfare technology, including guided missiles, navigational beams and even rocket research on an obscure

Baltic island called Peenemünde. This astonishing windfall also confirmed that enemy radar had been responsible for bouncing the disastrous Bomber Command raid on Wilhelmshaven on 4 September. 'It was probably the best single report received from any source during the war,' lamented SIS scientist R. V. Jones. 'But the leading doubter implied that the whole thing was a plant. All I could do was to keep my own copy, and in the few dull moments of the war I used to look it up to see what should be coming along next.'

Meanwhile, as Arthur Owens continued to buzz humdrum weather reports from rented rooms in Kingston, undermining MI5 at every turn, Richman Stopford found himself inexorably drawn towards the ladies' underwear department at Selfridges.

The upmarket Oxford Street department store became an unwitting battlefield in the secret war after Owens received his salary for November. Three of the four £5 notes posted from Bournemouth were found to be marked with a telltale rubber stamp, 'S & Co Ltd', which Lily recognised as belonging to Selfridges. After checking with the chief cashier, Stopford, a former banker, ascertained that the notes in question had crossed the counter on 14 November, when staff recalled serving a woman aged about sixty, said to be well spoken and possessed of a charming manner. During a subsequent case conference at MI5 the mystery customer was provisionally identified as Mathilde Krafft, a housekeeper employed by a naval officer living near Southampton, whose own bank records were found to match payments recently made to Snow.

Mail intercepts suggested that Krafft planned a return trip to London on 7 December. Accompanied by two counter girls from Selfridges, Stopford staked out platform 13 at Waterloo, then followed Krafft to a 'somewhat suspect' travel agency at Moorgate, where a firm identification was obtained. 'She was dressed in a very dark fur coat and wore a bunch of violets,' said Stopford. 'Moderately well dressed for an elderly lady, with a typical German *hausfrau* appearance, and a rather active look in her eyes.'

Krafft's biography was somewhat bizarre. German by birth, she had married a wealthy English coconut planter in Fiji but was now a widow with British nationality, and an adopted daughter named Editha Dargel. Even after Editha was deported on account of pro-Nazi agitation, Krafft continued to distribute Abwehr funds wired from the Sparkasse Bank in Hamburg, unaware that her cover now hung in shreds. Rather than have her arrested, Tar Robertson decided to keep the coconut widow under careful observation.

Despite having sacrificed Eschborn and Krafft to burnish his own reputation with MI5, a stunt not likely to have been authorised by Ritter, rogue Agent Snow still managed to blot his copybook, dispatching Lily to Manchester to liaise with Charlie while holding back funds earmarked for new microphotography equipment. Once again, Robertson was obliged to read Owens parts of the riot act. 'I pointed out that as Snowy was the head of their organisation in this country it was up to him to get the thing going. In order to keep him up to the mark, I said I would speak to him every evening and ask how he had got on. I also took Owens through his accounts. From what I can see he has done England for as much money as he can possibly get.'

Money, and a mansion to rival Sloane Avenue or Pullman Court. Tired of cramped conditions at Norbiton Avenue, and still fearful of raids on the Hawker aircraft factory, Owens and Lily moved three miles north to Richmond, taking the lease on a substantial four-storey property at 14 Marlborough Road. Aside from the fact that the leafy suburb was more upmarket than nondescript Norbiton, the proximity of Richmond Park also facilitated clandestine meetings, thus avoiding the steady flow of visitors that made the first safehouse untenable. At the fancy new London stelle on Marlborough Road Snow's B6 watchers occupied the lower floors, while Owens and Lily seized Lebensraum on the second and third. Once again the wireless aerial was concealed in the attic. Unbeknownst to Snow and his mistress, Robertson also installed a bugging device in the dining room.

Determined to see a return on his investment, Tar also convinced his superiors to allow limited disclosure of genuine military intelligence via Snow, subject to careful vetting by the Wireless Committee. 'We must not give the enemy information so valuable that it would be likely to outweigh any subsequent benefits,' warned a colleague. 'A nice assessment of profit and loss has to be made in every case.' Nevertheless, in order to put over the Big Lie, which might influence the outcome of entire battles and campaigns, it was also acknowledged that 'a long period of truthful reporting is usually a necessary preliminary.'

Forsaking trivial buzzings about food rationing and barrage balloons, Owens was allowed to reconnoitre RAF stations at Croydon, Kenley and Farnborough, all of them home-defence airfields for Hurricanes and Spitfires of Fighter Command. In addition Wohldorf received worrisome details of the Short Stirling, a new four-engined heavy bomber poised to enter squadron service and with sufficient range and lifting power to carry 3,500 pounds of high explosive to Berlin. Göring, the corpulent commander-in-chief of the Luftwaffe, had already sworn that no enemy aircraft would be allowed to overfly Germany, let alone the capital. 'If one enemy bomber reaches the Ruhr, my name is not Göring. You may call me Meyer.'

Meyer it would be.

At the same time Snow deliberately sabotaged his next treff in Belgium. Developing an earlier lie, he now warned Robertson that Williams appeared genuinely sympathetic to the German cause. 'In Antwerp, G.W. said confidentially to Snow that he thought they were very fine fellows, that the Nazi party had done a tremendous lot for German working people, and that Williams did not feel he was quite playing the game.' More credibly, Owens also argued that G.W. was a novice, liable to 'give the whole show away' if snatched in a Venlo sequel. Indeed, the two MI6 officers, Stevens and Best, were now reported by the press to be 'detained at the headquarters of the Nazi Black Guards in the Prinz Albrecht Strasse in Berlin'.

Evidently MI5 agreed, for on Friday, 15 December just one British spy boarded the Sabena DC3 carrying passengers to Brussels from the small, deco-styled civilian airport at Shoreham in Kent.

Duplicitous double agent Snow.

Once again, Owens met Ritter in Antwerp, and over a bottle of fine brandy at the Hotel Suisse handed over a wealth of 'samples' not cleared by the Wireless Committee: shadow war factories in the Midlands, bulk storage of aviation fuel at West Bromwich, shipping movements, improved torpedoes. There was but one black mark: Ritter had been recalled to Berlin to explain why weather reports from the London stelle were so innacurate. Seldom if ever did these tally with the bulletins received from Holland and Ireland.

The explanation concocted was simplicity itself. It was, Owens argued, quite impossible to furnish accurate weather reports after dark, let alone in the blackout. Patiently, Ritter instructed Johnny to assess the weather over London in daylight, then broadcast as usual at night.

By way of exchange Ritter handed over £215, with the promise of a regular monthly salary of £250 and better wireless equipment. The Doctor also told Owens to expect a delivery of time-fused firebombs disguised as packets of Swedish bread, to be smuggled on board Allied merchant shipping berthed at Liverpool. In addition, Hitler's chief spy in England was tasked with bribing a 'reliable fisherman' to rendezvous with a U-boat in the North Sea, this in order to take advantage of 'the ease with which smuggling is carried out on the east coast of England'.

Agent Snow flew back to Shoreham on Tuesday. Flush with money, he immediately splashed out on a Ford Model 10 – hardly the equal of the sleek white Jaguar SS100, but effective enough when it came to shaking off Special Branch tails on forays away from Marlborough Road. With less than a week to go before Christmas, however, there were no gifts for B1A, merely baubles and trinkets. Robertson learned only of fire-bombs which 'looked something like Ryvita', a revised weather code and vague details of a man 'influential in high military circles' known as Llanloch, who had sold secrets to Germany and now intended to stand for Parliament.

It was hardly the Oslo Report. Tar's frustration only increased after Owens and Lily grew wise to the bug installed in the dining room. 'Its usefulness has been impaired by the fact that most of the conversation is carried on in the kitchenette. Further, since it was installed Owens has bought a radiogram, which is turned on to the full extent when they indulge in any lengthy exchange. I am unable to resist the conclusion that it is done with the purpose of drowning the conversation.'

Worse was to follow in less than a week. Following Stopford's positive identification of Mathilde Krafft, the Selfridges coconut widow, Guy Liddell asked MI6 to make discreet enquiries of her adopted daughter, Editha Dargel, now living in exile in Copenhagen. Unhelpfully, the Danes interrogated Dargel in blunt fashion, in the process letting slip that British intelligence knew her mother was distributing Nazi money in England. The result, candidly described as 'a bad slip-up' by Liddell, saw Krafft warned off further activity, and a worrying wireless flash sent from Wohldorf to Richmond.

When it rained in London, so an old saying ran, the people of Hamburg opened up their umbrellas.

Until further notice, the London stelle was being shut down.

Kein glas bier.

5

Double Agent Dick

Across Europe the winter of 1939/40 was one of the coldest on record. As a relentless cold front blew from east to west, the Baltic iced over from shore to shore for the first time since 1883, while in Lapland Finnish and Russian troops froze solid like statues, fighting to the death in temperatures as low as minus 43. In Britain, birds froze in trees, mercury in thermometers and beer in mugs. Snowfall at sea solidified incoming waves at Folkestone, Southampton and Bognor, and in Cirencester a vicious ice storm lasted two whole days, flailing streets and houses with super-cooled raindrops that froze on impact. Large swathes of the Home Counties lay buried under impassable snowdrifts, some rising as high as fifteen feet, paralysing roads and railways for days on end, delaying deliveries of food and fuel, and prolonging the agonising cold. Frostbite gnawed, hypothermia dispatched.

In Richmond the frozen Thames enabled festive skaters to flit gaily from bank to bank. On the upside, with Snow on ice, the freeze in wireless traffic between London and Wohldorf meant that Arthur Owens was able to spend most of his time lounging in bed with his sexy mistress Lily Bade.

On the downside, Lily fell pregnant.

Humdinger.

At least the harsh arctic weather slowed the march of the Red

Army through Finland, and temporarily foiled Hitler's Blitzkrieg assault on the Low Countries. On 10 January a Luftwaffe liaison aircraft became lost in fog and crash landed on the wrong side of the Belgian border. Among the classified documents recovered was a complete set of plans for the attack, a catastrophic slip which forced the German High Command to postpone *Fall Gelb* (Plan Yellow) until spring, at the same time shifting the main thrust to Sedan on the French frontier. A lackadaisical diary entry from Guy Liddell betrayed muddled thinking within British intelligence: 'A German aeroplane came down in Belgium the other day with certain papers indicating an attack on Belgium and Holland. It looks rather as if this may have been part of the scheme for the war of nerves.'

Wartime reporting restrictions meant that many people in Britain failed to appreciate the extent and severity of the big freeze. Tar Robertson therefore pressed ahead with plans to dispatch Agent Snow on a reconnaissance tour of the North-East of England, this with the object of ticking boxes on Rantzau's latest microdot questionnaire. 'A double agent should, as far as possible, actually live the life and go through all the motions of a genuine agent,' decreed MI5. 'As a result his messages appeared to be true, and he did not trip over details of topographical or local observation. A lie when it is needed will only be believed if it rests on a firm foundation of previous truth.'

Like a diminutive Captain Scott, Owens left Richmond on 15 January, armed with coupons sufficient for thirty gallons of petrol, but precious little idea of the hazards ahead. Heading north along the A1 in his draughty Ford 10 Snow turned slowly to ice, and gamely struggled as far as Harrogate before finally being forced to turn back. Thawing out at the George Hotel in Grantham, he claimed to have watched a woman in a fur coat pump a group of RAF officers for information, fanning fears that the enemy were using 'Mata Hari methods' to glean military intelligence. 'Tar told me of another case of a prostitute who seems to be intimate with a number of RAF officers,' wrote Liddell, eyebrow raised. 'Cases of this sort seem to be on the increase.'

Forcing a passage to Newcastle next day, Owens attempted to infiltrate the headquarters of 13 Group, the fighter wing charged with defending the North-East. On Wednesday Snow attempted to reach the port towns of Hull and Grimsby but found each and every road blocked by his namesake, and once again crawled back to Grantham. A reconnaissance of Wattisham airfield in Suffolk on Thursday was more successful, with Owens able to drive straight up to the guardroom and swap small talk with a loose-lipped flight sergeant. 'He was told that recently an officer in RAF uniform had been all round the aerodrome, and not until after he had left was it realised that he was bogus. Owens said there was nothing to prevent anybody going all over the aerodrome without being in any way disturbed.'

After spending his fifth night away in Ipswich, Owens returned home on Saturday virtually empty-handed. Extreme weather had thwarted his efforts to reach Grimsby or Lowestoft to seek out a pliable boat-owning smuggler, and also stymied the collection of any worthwhile dope from Bomber Command stations across Lincolnshire and Yorkshire. *'No Handley Page bombers at Dishforth but Wellingtons instead,'* he buzzed ineffectually. *'Numbers etc unknown because everything covered in heavy snow.'*

Still Wohldorf was reluctant to communicate, and in response to a nudge informed A.3504 that Llanloch, the corrupt and doubtless imaginary politician, would not now be getting in touch. 'There is,' Liddell wrote ruefully, 'a slight impression that something may have gone wrong.' The thaw came only in February, when Rantzau suddenly requested another treff in Antwerp. Agent Snow set off for the tiny civilian airport at Lympne near Hythe on 7 February, hopeful of reaching Brussels despite the continuing bad weather, and again travelling alone.

But not for long.

At Victoria station, as Owens took his seat in the first-class compartment, he became aware of a mysterious stranger regarding him intently from the end of the corridor. Soon after the watcher sat down opposite and struck up a conversation. This was Samuel Stewart, a shady Glaswegian shipping broker whom MI5 already suspected of gunrunning for the IRA. By a strange coincidence – which was no coincidence at all – Stewart was also en route to Antwerp, with a seat on the very same flight. When bad weather grounded the Sabena DC3 at Lympne, the new best friends elected to repair to a hotel in Folkestone.

Owens and Stewart returned to the airport on Friday morning, at which point the Scot came slightly unstuck. 'He had a number of papers taken off him when passing through the controls,' Owens recalled. 'But not the passport he was taking over for a girl in Belgium to enable her to get into the United Kingdom.' Pressed by Robertson, Snow teased him by saying that he had glimpsed the passport too briefly to note any particulars. Indeed, he had 'deliberately trained his memory to forget everything, as a good memory for names, faces and information was dangerous.'

In Antwerp, Stewart further impressed Owens by picking up the tab for a lavish evening meal. 'Snow is firmly convinced that Stewart is supplying particulars of ships sailing from this country and Ireland,' Tar noted with approval, at long last sensing a breakthrough. 'And that he is a very large cog in the German espionage machine.'

Keen to crack bigger nuts than Charles Eschborn and Mathilde Krafft, Tar had briefed Agent Snow to complain to Ritter of being badly overstretched as a one-man stelle, and in sore need of help. When they met next day Ritter agreed, promising to send over a South African agent who spoke perfect English, and handing Owens a letter to post to one Eugene Horsfall, a sleeper residing on the Sussex coast where he posed as an examinations tutor. Ritter also gave Owens £650 in dollars and Bank of England notes to open a London office as a convincing front for international trade. More ominously, Herr Doktor Rantzau remained 'very anxious' to obtain particulars of the water supply to Birmingham, Liverpool and Newcastle, and promised that the 'real war' would start in the middle of April.

Whether the wireless shutdown in January was a genuine response to the Krafft fiasco, or a ruse to confound MI5, is unclear. Whatever the truth, back in London Tar Robertson judged Snow's fourth wartime mission 'highly successful'. To his great relief, the Abwehr had again confirmed Owens as a trusted agent worthy of considerable financial investment, and at long last disclosed the identities of several more Nazi spies who could now be discreetly surveilled. Indeed excitement over the unmasking of Sam Stewart, who appeared to connect the Abwehr with the IRA, served to eclipse a far more significant intelligence coup, namely Ritter's frank disclosure that the Phoney War would turn 'real' midway through April.

Hoping to learn more about the Dublin connection, Robertson instructed Owens to cultivate his new acquaintance, at the same time warning the Little Man to exercise caution. 'Stewart is a big fellow, and very fly. I instructed Snow not to ask too many questions but to keep his eyes and ears open.' The following week Owens visited Stewart at his office in Bevis Marks House near Aldgate, where he was 'treated like a millionaire and plied with cigarettes'. Brandy and bonhomie aside, however, Owens inevitably regarded Stewart as a rival, and thus a potential threat.

By curious coincidence, two days later the IRA detonated a string of bombs in the West End, the worst of which injured twelve people on Oxford Street. Ironically, no German bombs would fall on London for another seven months, and with Hitler still on a Phoney War footing the Abwehr censured the

Republicans for targeting civilians. Ultimately the Emerald Isle proved a veritable mare's nest for the German intelligence service. In an effort to re-establish wireless links with the IRA, one Ernst Weber-Drohl was dispatched with a new transmitter and $14,000. An improbable agent – as a younger man he had toured Irish fairgrounds as a wrestler-cum-weightlifter, but spoke with a thick Austrian accent and was now over sixty – Weber-Drohl dropped his klamotten in the Irish Sea while landing in the midst of a violent gale. Having struggled ashore in County Sligo, he was swiftly arrested for illegal entry and interned for the duration.

Neither Sam Stewart nor the circus strongman proved useful to MI5. Determined to remain neutral, the Irish government denied British intelligence officers access to Weber-Drohl at Mountjoy prison. Meanwhile Owens failed to provide any useful dope on Stewart, and over the course of several weeks a microphone placed in his Aldgate office failed to pick up any incriminating conversations. In all likelihood, Owens had tipped his fellow traitor the wink.

Blissfully unaware of Snow's duplicity, MI5 lavished time and money on setting up a London office for the Abwehr. In order to monitor activities there, Robertson found Owens a 'business partner' in the form of William Rolph, a retired MI5 officer of Swiss origin, lately employed as manager of Hatchett's, a popular restaurant on Piccadilly famed for its excellent breakfasts. Rolph duly incorporated Aeroplastics, a firm notionally engaged in battery exports to Belgium, and rented basement premises on Sackville Street, a smart Georgian thoroughfare behind Regent Street, and convenient for the MI5 office at St James's. Rent was thirty shillings a week; Rolph, somewhat down on his luck, received a pound a day.

Additional funds were earmarked for redecoration, verisimilitude dictating that Aeroplastics should appear to be a genuine trading company and turning a profit. Owens was tickled to death. As well as paying the rent at Marlborough Road, British intelligence would now foot the bill for his new London stelle.

Dandy.

Fortunately, plans to install the short-wave transmitter at Sackville Street were postponed after Snow again cast doubt on his own reliability. On 8 March, a Friday, Robertson received a call from his troublesome star agent and agreed to a meeting in Richmond that evening. Accompanied by his young wife Joan, Tar drove down by car, arriving at a pub called The Barn at six-thirty. Still dressed in uniform, he sent Joan inside to fetch Snow and Lily. Ten minutes later Owens emerged with the women and agreed to follow Robertson to a rendezvous point closer to Richmond.

'I drove slowly in the direction of Richmond waiting for Snow to catch me up,' Tar reported afterwards. 'I noticed a car following me, the number of which unfortunately I did not take. I stopped, and the car which was following me stopped immediately behind. The young man driving it got out and went round to the back of the car, ostensibly to look at the petrol tank, but it was quite obvious that he was looking at my car through the back window. In order to get rid of him I decided to go on, and accordingly went up Richmond Hill and into Richmond Park. The car did not follow.'

Owens had clocked the same man inside The Barn, seated by a window. Joan, too, noticed the mysterious stranger. 'During the time that my wife was in there, this young man kept a steady watch on the car park and the road, and left some little time before Snow and Lily and my wife, leaving about two inches of beer in the bottom of his glass. This struck my wife as being most curious.'

After discussing the incident with Guy Liddell and a Special Branch officer, Robertson concluded that the entire episode was yet another stunt, intended to demonstrate that sinister enemy agents were at large in London. 'Snow's reaction to the whole affair was one of complete calm, which made me wonder at the time if he was not double-crossing me.'

Kein glas bier.

A week later, another busy Richmond hostelry provided the venue for a far more significant contact. Situated on Friars Stile Road, The Marlborough was a large, popular pub a convenient stone's throw from Agent Snow's comfortable town house, and afforded the twin advantages of a sizeable beer garden and incognitious crowds. There, on the afternoon of 16 March, Owens fell into conversation with a happy-go-lucky commercial traveller named Dick Moreton. Somewhat taller than Snow, with slicked-back hair, large eyes and a dimpled chin, Moreton seemed every inch the gregarious bon vivant, conversing in loud, extrovert tones, and professing to drink nothing but gin fizz.

For his part, Owens passed himself off as Thomas Wilson, a wealthy businessman dealing in gold, diamonds and general investment capital. 'I had a few drinks with him, for which he refused to let me pay,' Moreton recollected. 'After a few minutes' conversation he said to me, "I can see you have travelled a great deal." He then discussed at some length the countries in which I had travelled, and he himself appeared to know intimately, including America, Canada and Germany.'

Cosmopolitan men of the world, the two discovered a shared love of exotic cuisine such as chilli con carne. What with all the gratis gin fizz, Dick Moreton omitted to mention that his real name was Walter Dicketts, and that his broad experience on the international circuit included jail time for fraud in France and Austria, as well as a crook's tour of America, where his collar had been felt in Chattanooga and Detroit.

Born in 1899, the son of a city stockbroker's clerk, Dicketts had obtained a junior commission in the Royal Naval Air Service towards the end of the Great War, followed by a period in an air-intelligence department (AI1), sifting material gathered for the Paris Peace Conference. Next, in 1919, came an undercover assignment for MI6 in Holland. Acting on personal instructions from Sir Mansfield Cumming, Dicketts shadowed the illicit resurrection of the Fokker aircraft company and was successful in locating a large cache of aero engines near Amsterdam. Or so he said. 'He often talks of his decorations and of a bad crash,' noted one authority, 'of which there is no record.'

Very much a temporary gentleman, back on civvy street Sub-Lieutenant Dicketts fell prey to hard times and bad habits. Still masquerading as a serving officer, in 1921 he was convicted of defrauding a car-hire company and was soon back in court after bouncing a cheque on Bond Street jewellers Mappin & Webb. Subsequently Dicketts served the first of several prison terms, punctuated by spells bilking widows and tourists on the Continent and a succession of shady escapades in America. Judged to be an expert and 'very plausible' travelling criminal by British detectives, his career touched bottom at Hampshire Assizes in November 1931, when the former spy received eighteen months' hard labour on thirty-one counts of larceny and fraud. This remarkable spree ranged from blagging 500 gallons of aviation spirit for a motorboat on the Norfolk Broads to relieving a Manchester landlord of several gramophone records and a brand new suit: plum-coloured, single-breasted, with permanent turn-up trousers.

To this sorry catalogue the *Police Gazette* could add two failed marriages, and a string of aliases including Richard Blake, Christopher Welfare and Squadron Leader G. A. Norman. In short, Walter Dicketts was an incorrigible rogue with an unfortunate knack for getting caught. Indeed, by the time 'Dick Moreton' attached himself to Owens at The Marlborough in March 1940 he was again on the run from the law, having bounced a £10 cheque on a Birmingham hotel and nimbly skipped bail.

Each man immediately set about inveigling the other. In Dicketts, Owens discerned a potential new sidekick, in financial low water and ripe for exploitation. For the seasoned confidence trickster, 'Thomas Wilson' was just another mark. 'When he asked me what I did I replied that I was living on my very small means, and that I had proposed a patent for ready-made mustard in containers similar to toothpaste. Owens immediately said, "That's an excellent idea, and if my partner agrees I'll finance it."'

Squeezable mustard.

Right hot.

Dicketts and his patent held such promise for Owens that the pair reconvened at The Marlborough in the evening, this time joined by their wives. In truth, Kay Dicketts was no more married than was Lily. She had 'chorus girl' looks and a criminal record for shoplifting in Wolverhampton. Despite all these secrets and lies, the quartet became fast friends quite literally overnight. For the moment, however, Owens was content to remain Thomas Wilson, and revealed nothing of his double life as a top Nazi spy.

'We spent the evening together at The Marlborough,' said Dicketts of the wealthy dealer in diamonds and gold, 'and at ten o'clock he invited us to play darts at his flat. We stayed until one o'clock the next morning, during which time we consumed a considerable amount of liquor.'

Sober next morning, yet still crazy for squeezable mustard, Owens advanced Dicketts £25 and told Rolph to apply for a patent. Since emergency legislation now prohibited the importation of batteries from abroad, forcing a swift revision of the Aeroplastics business plan, the mustard idea made sense of a sort. The scheme also chimed with Owens' long-held ambition of living off patent royalties without lifting a finger.

Better still, Walter Dicketts just happened to own a seaworthy boat, conveniently berthed in the harbour at Dartmouth.

Though B1A were able to monitor something of the pair's developing 'intimacy' via hidden microphones at Marlborough Road, Robertson failed to pick up on the fact that mustard-keen newcomer Moreton might be able to connect Owens with U-boats in the Bristol Channel and the North Sea.

Within days of meeting the two couples took off in the Ford 10 for a long weekend in the West Country, cruising on Dick's motor launch safe from eavesdropping microphones and living high on the hog at hotels in Bournemouth and Brixham. Everywhere, it seemed, wealthy Mr Wilson was more than happy to pick up the tab. Explained Dicketts: 'He gave me the impression that he was so overburdened with worry, work and responsibility that he had to have a confidant. Taking a liking to me, he tried me out for a fortnight and then started confiding in me.'

While this charade was enacted, the unwanted arrival of 'Dick Moreton' into Snow's irregular orbit paled beside yet another astonishing gaffe, which now threatened to bring down the entire double-cross system.

Four months earlier MI5 had moved quickly to spike an article proposed by the *Sunday Graphic*, which threatened to reveal that enemy spies might be turned and exploited as double agents. Inconveniently, the system of wartime censorship in Britain was voluntary, and on 18 March the *Daily Herald* broke ranks to splash a more or less identical story across its back page. Beneath the arresting headline *SPIES ALLOWED TO BROADCAST FROM BRITAIN – "NEWS" TO MISLEAD ENEMY PUT IN THEIR WAY*, the tabloid's unnamed 'radio correspondent' laid bare the secret that *'radio stations operated by enemy agents are still working in this country – by permission of the British Secret Service.'*

The *Herald*'s astonishing scoop left MI5 wondering where the Fourth Estate ended and the Fifth Column began. *'Britain's secret radio squad has tracked down dozens of short-wave broadcasting stations*

worked by spies – but not all of them have been silenced. It pays to let them go on sending out their messages. The efforts of British wireless engineers and technicians have revealed many German secrets – spies and disaffected persons have been allowed to continue their activities until they have implicated their friends. Members of the radio squad tune in not to German propaganda broadcasts, such as those of Lord Haw-Haw, but to unregistered short-wave stations which transmit in Morse code.'

The article might as well have mentioned Owens by name and printed a picture of the London stelle at 14 Marlborough Road. Ironically, the leak almost certainly stemmed from the Special Branch, where a number of officers felt deeply aggrieved that the sudden wartime expansion of MI5 had only found room for detectives from Scotland Yard. One of those snubbed was Inspector Bill Gagen, who still maintained regular contact with Snow despite having been removed from the case.

In a perfect world, all those involved in the murky *Herald* exclusive would have been given a taste of Regulation 18B. However, since recalling unsold copies would serve only to confirm the truth of the story, the editor received instead a rap on the knuckles from the chief press censor, Rear Admiral George Thomson.

Dicketts, too, suffered a professional setback. Returning from their long weekend in the West Country, Agent Snow arranged to see his new lieutenant at Sackville Street, only to learn from William Rolph that Colman's of Norwich already sold mustard in a squeezable tube. 'Rolph said that it was impossible to proceed with the mustard patent as it was already on the market,' carped Dicketts. 'I was very upset, but Owens assured me that I had nothing to worry about as he could use me in other directions and money was no object.'

If Dicketts is to be believed, Owens chose this moment to reveal his role as a 'key man' in the British secret service. It is more likely, though, that this occurred in Dartmouth, and Owens already knew of Dick's past in AI1 and MI6. Be that as it may, Snow now showed Dick his wireless transmitter and disclosed that he was acting as a double agent. Anxious not to be outdone, Dicketts laid claim to a photographic memory. 'He asked me what money I required to work for him, and said his last man had his nerve wrecked after a long third degree by the Gestapo. He instructed me to carry on normal business under his direction as a cover. I was told not to alter my style of living, not to say a word to anyone, and not to move to any better address than Montague Road.'

For Dicketts, business as usual meant black marketeering and long firm fraud. With mustard off the menu, he now proposed buying up bulk stocks of cheap gin and whisky, then relabelling the bottles and passing them off at inflated prices. Using Rolph's contacts in the West End hospitality trade, Dicketts would take care of sales and distribution for £10 a week plus expenses. Much enthused by the scam, and unaware that he was himself the ultimate mark, Owens gave Dicketts £50 to pay off personal debts and a further £97 to buy cut-price spirits. Sensing easy pickings, Dick also sought to persuade Owens to invest in The Rialto, a shabby nightclub next to the Café de Paris.

On the last Sunday in March Owens and Lily drove Dick and Kay to Brighton for a spirited joint anniversary bash. Feeling the love, or the pressure, Agent Snow grew tired and emotional. 'The very great amount of drink he had consumed somewhat overcame him,' said Dicketts. 'He said that the British air successes reported are chiefly lies, our machines not nearly so successful or as fast as the Germans'. RAF casualty lists show an appalling roll of dead and wounded. Pilots are refusing to go up, and several officers had been court-martialled and shot.'

Hitting his stride, Owens added that dissatisfaction was rife among BEF troops sent to France, and that wealthy British citizens were moving their money abroad with indecent haste. 'Hitler has Germany solidly behind him, and the British public are being consistently fooled. He then spoke out for peace and said that nationalities did not count.'

As if to emphasise the point, Owens announced that he would be travelling to Germany on 4 April. 'He told me Germany was certain to win the war and that he and Lily were going there to live as soon as his work was complete in England.' Owens added that as chief of the German secret service in Britain he could call on two million pounds. 'He said, be loyal to me and you'll be on the winning side, generously provided for all your life. I said I didn't want to do anything against the British Empire.'

Dicketts may or may not have been genuinely conflicted. Too old to join up, and reduced to living hand-to-mouth in a shabby furnished room, the impecunious fraudster found himself torn between a frayed sense of patriotic duty and a pressing need to make money. Reporting Owens to the authorities might count for something at the Air Ministry, might even lead to gainful employment with restitution of rank. Then again, turning the Little Man in was complicated by the small matter of an outstanding arrest warrant in Birmingham.

Dick felt squeezed, like mustard in a tube. Deciding to infiltrate Snow's Nazi spy gang deeper still, the con artist became a supremely untrustworthy V-man. With Owens due to fly out to Brussels on Thursday – apparently en route to Berlin – the next few days would surely prove highly revealing. Indeed, detailed notes kept by Dicketts offer up a unique insight into a day in the life of a low-level spy in wartime London.

On Wednesday morning Dick collected the Little Man from Marlborough Road and drove into central London. 'At the office he told me to take a taxi and arrange the whisky and gin. Rolph was arranging with a printer to print new labels for the bottles. Whilst walking down Sackville Street I noticed one and then a second taxi draw out slowly. I therefore went into the Yorkshire Grey Hotel in Piccadilly, ordered a drink, came out, and jumped into another taxi. Watching carefully through the back window I saw the two taxis, following at intervals. To see if I could get a view of the occupants I told my taxi to stop at the Phoenix in Palace Street. As he pulled up he said, "You are being tailed, guvnor." I thanked him and said I was on government service.'

Electing to return to Sackville Street, Dick warned Owens that he had been followed. Owens disposed of the problem with a call to the Branch. The two men then drove to Euston, where Owens was to meet Charles Eschborn off the train from Manchester. 'The agent was introduced to me as Charlie,' continued Dicketts. 'He was obviously a German and appeared to be very scared. We went back to the office and I was asked to leave the room for ten minutes, which I did. On my return I saw on the table a large pile of photographic enlargements of docks, airports and buildings such as factories. On the top of the photos was a minute roll of film. The photographs were put away, and Owens remarked that they were very good.'

While Dicketts copied out a list of shipping movements, Charlie told Snow that he needed a new enlarger. 'Owens took a roll of notes from his pocket, gave the requisite money to Charlie, and told me to take him to a large photographic shop in Bond Street. On the way Charlie was very frightened, and asked if we were being followed. While he was in the store a tall man in a Burberry mackintosh was standing at the counter near the entrance, focusing cameras in our direction, and I am of the opinion that he was photographing us.'

Eschborn's raw nerves owed something to the fact that he was also scamming Snow by securing the enlarger on part-exchange. After returning Charlie to Euston, Dicketts reported this duplicity to his employer. Agent Snow merely shrugged. 'Well, he's got away with an easy £50.'

Towards the end of the afternoon the pair were joined by Lily and Kay and strolled half a mile to Charing Cross Road, where

Owens spent £4 on expensive aviation books at Foyles. Back in Richmond, after an eventful day as an enemy of the state, Dick watched with interest as the Little Man grew increasingly anxious about his mission to Belgium, refusing even to play darts, and foregoing their customary nightcap. 'Later he warned me again of secrecy, and instructed me to call the following morning and go with him to Victoria to see him off on the 9.45 to Shoreham aerodrome.' By way of a bonus, Owens pressed on Dicketts a full bottle of genuine Mountain Dew whisky. 'I protested that he had been generous enough, and he replied, "You are having this with the Führer. Enjoy it, and don't worry about anything."'

Unbeknown to Hitler's chief spy in England, for the last twelve hours Dick had been playing his own double game. That morning, instead of keeping his appointment with a drinks supplier in Hammersmith, Dick stopped off at 151 Victoria Street, a security-service office since 1909. There he asked to speak to Air Commodore Archie Boyle, the newly appointed Director of Air Intelligence, with whom he had served two decades earlier. Boyle declined to see him, so Dicketts gave his statement to an aide, claiming that he had penetrated 'the heart of the German secret service in this country.'

This wholly unexpected development finally allowed Tar Robertson to identify Dick Moreton as Walter Dicketts. For B1A, the unauthorised admission of a career criminal into Snow's inner circle was yet another worrisome security breach. 'Owens is a stupid little man who is given to doing silly things at odd moments,' Tar fulminated. 'At this stage there must be a large number of people in this country and elsewhere who are quite au fait with what he is doing. If possible, we could in some way make arrangements to frighten Snow in order to prevent him from doing this sort of thing again.'

On Thursday morning Dicketts drove Owens to Victoria station. Less than a mile away, Neville Chamberlain prepared to tell a meeting of Conservatives at Central Hall that Hitler had 'missed the bus' by failing to deliver a knockout blow against Britain and France. Colonel Johnny saw things very differently indeed. Boarding the train to Shoreham airport, his parting shot to Dicketts was typically opaque. 'After Owens told me to stay with my wife at Marlborough Road and look after Lily, his last words were: "If I am successful I shall be able to do anything I like."'

This vaulting claim was no idle boast. Back in Antwerp, Owens kept his complex triple-cross game in play with fresh dope on the so-called wireless cloud, detailing a string of new radar stations between Grimsby and Southend, far smaller than the Chain Home sites but, like them, able to detect the approach of hostile aircraft by means of UHF radio waves. This latest innovation was Chain Home Low, able to track raiders down to 500 feet, and only just operational. There was even a detailed description of the CHL installation at Hopton, halfway between Yarmouth and Lowestoft, including the wooden tower and aerial array. 'The whole area was strongly guarded and I had to pass through at high speed,' Owens boasted. 'It's impossible to get close to the towers but I hope to get details from other sources. Do all you can to jam these signals, or knock out the power source.'

Plainly the Little Man had accomplished more in Suffolk in January than digging his Ford out of snowdrifts. To Ritter, dope of such potent strength served to excuse the clodhopping Krafft–Dargel fiasco in Denmark, and calamitous exposés in the *Daily Herald*.

Owens also promised to deliver up a suitable agent for sabotage training in Germany as early as May. Three months earlier Gwilym Williams, the former police inspector from Swansea, had been put forward for this high risk-assignment, only to fall victim to an outbreak of cold feet following the Venlo incident. Now Owens proposed a far better candidate: tall, aged about forty, knew his way around boats. Had knocked around the world a bit, too.

Walter Dicketts was absolute jake.

Unfortunately MI5 took a dimmer view of the *Police Gazette* regular as agent material. On Saturday morning, as Snow sold out Chain Home Low to the Abwehr in Antwerp, the telephone tap at Marlborough Road revealed that Dicketts proposed to meet Lily and Kay at noon on the platform at Putney station. Calling on Scotland Yard rather than the Branch, Robertson arranged for CID officers to arrest Dick on the Birmingham warrant, and reserved a cell for him at Richmond police station. Britain's least wanted was duly lifted without fuss, his enforced departure passing unseen by Lily and Kay.

Behind bars once again, Dicketts was quick to volunteer that he had 'valuable information' about a dangerous Nazi spy ring. After a lengthy interview, Robertson supervised a search of his room at Montague Road but found nothing incriminating. 'I am quite certain in my own mind that Dicketts is not a Gestapo agent,' he concluded with relief. 'He tried to report the facts of the case, and actually paid a visit to the Air Ministry. Although he is a rogue from a financial point of view, he is loyal towards this country, his one motive being to try to get some sort of job in the air force. He saw his chance when he stumbled by luck across Owens and his nest of German agents.'

Faced with the prospect of being taken to Birmingham under escort, Dicketts put through a call to Kay, explaining that he had 'got into some wretched business' with a quarrelsome family member, the whole amounting to 'rather a bother'. He was, he said, at his lawyer's office, and had no choice but to head north to put things right. 'I told her not to worry, or discuss it with anybody. I would tell Lily and Snow when I saw them, and wire when I was returning.'

On Sunday Robertson telephoned the Deputy Chief Constable of Birmingham and briefed William Clarence

Johnson on a tricky situation. 'I said that I was keen, if possible, to get rid of Dicketts for some time, and prevent him from saying anything in the witness box in connection with the Snow case, which he might easily do in a plea for leniency.' Since Dicketts had made much the same play before Hampshire Assizes nine years earlier, Johnson promised to do what he could to ensure that the recidivist crook swindler received another long stretch behind bars.

Owens flew back to Shoreham on Sunday. With £1,000 concealed in his false-bottomed suitcase, and complete freedom of action in Britain, Colonel Johnny breezed confidently through Customs and Immigration. Annoyingly, however, there was no sign of his sidekick-chauffeur outside the terminal building. Back at Marlborough Road, Agent Snow's displeasure increased tenfold on learning that Dicketts had been unmasked, and was therefore unavailable for sabotage training in Germany. 'I told him to cut adrift from his new friend and his business as soon as possible,' insisted Robertson. 'So far as his connection with Snow was concerned, Dicketts was trying to obtain as much money from him as possible in a long firm fraud.'

Dicketts faced the music at Birmingham Police Court on Tuesday, 9 April, where he was let off lightly with a £5 fine. At dawn that same morning 'real war' broke out as German forces invaded Denmark and Norway, seizing key ports and airfields with the aid of paratroops and local Nazi sympathisers – seismic events which put petty crooks and rubber cheques in their proper perspective. Scarcely able to believe his luck, Dicketts hastened back to Richmond that same afternoon, intending to collect Kay from Marlborough Road. On arrival, however, a 'tremendous row' blew up, with Owens berating Dick over his no-show at Shoreham and abandoning their wives to the mercy of enemies on either side.

'I heard later in the evening that they had become good friends again,' Tar noted drily, having received word from

Burton. 'I took steps to ring Snow's flat and insist that Dicketts remove himself at once and never return. Dicketts, fortunately, is under the impression that we assisted him considerably in letting him off with a fine. He has also been very strongly warned that he must not on any account mention the information about Owens in his possession.'

Robertson offered a carrot as well as a stick, and promised to try to find Dicketts a job. 'I don't mind what branch of the service I go into,' begged Dick three weeks later, writing from new lodgings in Kilburn. 'Field force, intelligence, clerical or stores. I am just forty years of age and in a fairly fit condition, with the exception of a certain personal nervousness engendered by my past of eleven years ago. I can drive any kind of car, handle any small boat, and don't mind risk or danger.' Unfortunately the Air Ministry knew Dicketts of old, and refused point-blank to consider reinstatement.

Having lost a sidekick far more promising than Alex Myner or Gwilym Williams, Owens played back little of value from Antwerp to MI5. The Doctor, he claimed, had advised him to change his code on a daily basis, and provided two copies of *The Dead Don't Care* by Jonathan Latimer, published by Methuen at sixpence. It was hoped that the pair might treff again in May. Owens also warned that the *City of Sydney,* a cargo steamer en route to Mauritius, was carrying two time-fused firebombs in her hold, smuggled on board by Abwehr saboteurs in Amsterdam.

'From our personal talk,' deduced Robertson, 'I am very much inclined to think that Snow is entirely trustworthy, and quite straightforward in the things which he gives me and the answers to my questions.'

Having invested rather less in the Little Man, Guy Liddell sounded a note of caution. 'These bombs may well be a plant, and I am advising that we take no action. The Director-General and Jasper Harker agree.'

In fact the Ryvita bombs were all too real, but of inferior design, and failed to explode before the ship reached Port Louis seven weeks later. Robertson was wrong to trust Owens, no doubt hoping against hope that money, comfortable lodgings and 18B bought loyalty of a sort. Harder to comprehend is the fact that MI5 seemed to miss the significance of Owens' next treff with Rantzau, proposed for May by the mysterious Doctor – on board a fishing trawler, in the middle of the cold North Sea.

Agent Snow had forecast 'real war' for the middle of April, a prediction borne out by the German invasion of Denmark and Norway. Now the trawler treff surely tended to suggest an absence of neutral dry land in Western Europe by the end of May. No Netherlands, no Belgium, not even a Duchy of Luxembourg.

Yet again, MI5 were in danger of missing the boat.

6

The Trawler Treff

In a fit of uncommon bravado, the British Foreign Secretary, Lord Halifax, denounced the German invasion of Norway on 9 April as the act of 'a homicidal lunatic or mad dog'. In fact, precisely the opposite was true. In moving to 'protect' Norway against 'Franco-British aggression' Hitler not only obtained sheltered bases for U-boats and surface raiders to harass Allied shipping in the North Atlantic but also secured vital shipments of iron ore from Sweden, Norway's close Scandinavian neighbour. There was also the small matter of the Norsk Hydro plant in Telemark, the only facility in Europe capable of producing heavy water for nuclear fission.

Right hot.

Parachute troops (*Fallschirmjäger*) dropped from the skies over Oslo to seize key harbours and airfields, in the process revealing a novel military innovation already flagged as a threat to London by Agent Snow. With no airborne arm of their own, Britain and France hurriedly embarked an amphibious force for Norway, though the troops boasted little in the way of specialist training and looked certain to face opposed landings at ports such as Narvik and Trondheim. Plainly some form of deception would greatly increase their chances of success, and perhaps repeat the trick of the 'Russians in England' in 1914, whose phantom presence delivered victory at the Battle of the Marne.

Thus, as a scratch Allied force was hastily assembled in northern ports, MI5 laid plans for the vanguard to land with Snow on their boots.

'French and Canadian troops sailing from Scotland to Norway,' Owens buzzed Wohldorf, sticking to a script dictated by the Wireless Committee. *'Information difficult to obtain. Very secret.'*

Adopting a somewhat bolder stance, on 19 April the Joint Intelligence Committee agreed that Agent Snow should try to convince the enemy that the main Allied effort would fall on Bergen. A scheme was devised whereby Owens would put across to the Germans that the War Office had issued an urgent call for photographs of Bergen. 'This information should be brought to Snow through Charlie, who is in a first-class position to hear of such requirements. On sending this over by radio, it is hoped that the Allies will be able to make a fairly easy landing at Trondheim.'

The stunt became all the more urgent after several British, French and Polish brigades landed at Narvik, only to encounter determined counter-attacks and raging blizzards. Inevitably, Snow's Bergen deception fell apart just as shamefully as did the entire Norwegian campaign. Charlie inexplicably failed to call Snow as arranged on the morning of Saturday, 20 April, after which Owens set off on a lengthy reconnaissance tour of the West Country, leaving William Rolph in charge at Sackville Street. Eschborn finally telephoned on Tuesday, but made no mention of Bergen and spoke only of Trondheim – where landings had already begun, flagged loudly in advance by the Fleet Street press.

The result was another inglorious debacle. Allied forces failed to gain a viable foothold anywhere in Norway and by the end of the month were being evacuated, with Quislings and a phantom Fifth Column widely held to blame. 'The place was full of spies,' complained one Scots soldier of the Trondheim expedition. 'Every move we made was known to the Germans almost as soon as we made it. A Norwegian radio operator signalled directions to German aeroplanes which were carrying out raids. The Norwegians shot him.'

Spies, so it seemed, lurked on every corner. The day after Owens set off on his field trip, Rolph received an exotic visitor at Sackville Street. Sporting a blue suit and an impressive black fez (but a limited command of English), an Indian seaman dropped off a package containing two brand-new wireless valves. In a rare display of efficiency Rolph tailed the dapper courier back to the *City of Simla*, a freighter berthed at the Albert Dock following a round trip from Tilbury to Antwerp. The Lascar was quickly identified as Mohideen Coonjee, almost certainly hired by Obed Hussein, a disaffected Indian national based in Antwerp, who had already attempted to sabotage British shipping using the port. Fortunately his efforts were no more effective than the dud firebombs placed on the *City of Sydney*.

MI5 remained at sea throughout April. While Snow toured aerodromes and ports around Exeter and Bristol, Robertson turned his mind to the intricacies of the proposed trawler treff. Although chartering a worthy vessel was relatively straightforward, hiring a civilian crew threw up significant security risks. Looking further ahead, Tar also recognised that it would not be enough to simply land the explosives on the east coast. 'Suitable factories must be picked in various parts of the country,' he advised Liddell. 'Naturally it will be necessary to have an actual explosion in order to instil confidence into the enemy. This should be followed by a necessary amount of publicity in the press.'

There was also the vexed question of a suitable sidekick. Walter Dicketts' lengthy criminal record kept him out of the frame, besides which he already knew far too much about Snow and the double-cross system to be allowed to travel into Germany. Gwilym Williams, too, was unsuited to the task, having been unable even to penetrate Plaid Cymru, let alone raise a functioning Welsh Fifth Column. 'I filled in the form but I received no reply,' the retired inspector informed Tar in a discouraging letter. 'With great respect, I wish to point out that my activities might be construed as being contrary to the provisions of the Police Pensions Act 1921, Section 15.'

Ironically, the candidate put forward by Maxwell Knight of Section B5B was a dead ringer for Dicketts. Sam McCarthy was an occasional MI5 informant who had 'knocked around the world a good deal' as a dope addict, smuggler, petty thief and jailbird, and had recently completed a mission in Holland linked to a fascist named Heath, now interned under 18B. Canadian by birth, and variously known as 'Frank' or 'Mac', B1A now saddled Knight's rough diamond agent with a puzzling new cryptonym: BISCUIT.

'He is to be put on Snow in such a way as to preclude the possibility of Owens realising that he is one of ours,' proposed Liddell. 'Snow is to see him and let things develop in the ordinary way.'

Owens returned home on the last day in April. Despite having spent more than a week in the field, however, the dope buzzed from Richmond to Wohldorf remained dangerously low-grade. *'Westland Aircraft producing new machines, Supermarine production 50 Spitfires monthly. Bristol Aircraft making new twin engined fighter . . . Cirencester aerodrome 30 machines + Airspeed Oxford, Hawker Fury and Hawker Harts.'*

Demanding rather more than he troubled to deliver, Johnny signed off: *'Urgently send me bombs.'*

On Monday, 6 May, two more Indian seamen called at Sackville Street, checking on the valves but dropping nothing explosive. The pair were traced to a cargo ship at Greenwich and allowed to remain at large, but failed to lead to other Nazi agents in London. Rolph, it was noted, appeared to be growing too close to Owens, yet MI5 failed to appreciate that these several visits by Lascar seamen indicated a private communication channel between Agent Snow and the Abwehr organisation in Antwerp.

The following day Robertson briefed Sam McCarthy at his London club. 'I asked him to go down to The Marlborough some time round about 6 pm tonight. I gave him a description of Snow, and suggested he should approach him from the Canadian aspect.' Mac would explain that he was thinking of moving to Richmond, and was short of funds. Tar advanced the hard-drinking former dope fiend a pound by way of beer money, and asked him to report on progress the next morning. 'I gave him a rough outline of Snow's character and pointed out that he was a tremendous talker.'

As Biscuit moved on Snow, speculation mounted that Germany was poised to invade Holland and Belgium. Dutch forces mobilised on 7 May, prompting an urgent signal from the London stelle to Wohldorf. *'Have secret documents + RAF reports. Applied for exit permit. When can I meet you?'*

Answer came there none. At dawn on Friday, 10 May, Hitler launched Operation *Sichelschnitt*, a broad 'sickle stroke' in which seventy-six German divisions steamrollered Holland, Belgium and Luxembourg, at the same time penetrating into Northern France through the thick forests of the Ardennes. The Sitzkrieg was over. German paratroops again dropped from the sky to seize key bridges and airfields around The Hague and Rotterdam, while just eighty men in gliders neutralised the giant Belgian fortress at Eben-Emael near Liège. Galvanised at last, the British Expeditionary Force advanced into Belgium to meet the enemy head on, repeating a strategy adopted in August 1914. By the end of the day ailing Neville Chamberlain had resigned as Prime Minister, to be replaced by a far more robust war leader in the form of Winston Churchill who famously offered the British people 'blood, toil, tears and sweat'.

Electing to govern by virtual decree, Britain's new premier

immediately stepped up the internment of aliens and hostiles under Regulation 18B. The success of enemy paratroops in Holland inevitably heightened paranoia about the Fifth Column, flooding the press with lurid tales of fanatical Nazis dressed as priests, postmen and – bizarrely – nuns. Paradoxically, Agent Snow welcomed these alarmist developments. A clean sweep of rival agents under 18B meant that Hamburg would become wholly reliant on the London stelle, and reduced the risk of visits by sinister sleepers. Moreover, the onset of Blitzkrieg in Western Europe might bring the war to a rapid conclusion, with Colonel Johnny a feted hero on the winning side.

Because countries didn't count.

Excepting Holland, where Ritter found himself arrested and detained on the eve of the German assault. As a result Wohldorf resumed radio contact with Owens only on 14 May, fully four days into the *Sichelschnitt* campaign. For MI5, the good news was that Doctor Rantzau wished to meet Johnny the following week. The bad news was that the centre of Rotterdam was razed by the Luftwaffe on the very same day, a blunt demonstration of air power that killed a thousand civilians and forced the Dutch government to capitulate. With Holland neutralised rather than neutral, the trawler treff was impossible to avoid.

By meeting Rantzau in the North Sea, Agent Snow stood to discover whether German paratroopers were set to ransack the Home Counties, or if a seaborne invasion was more likely. On 15 May Robertson and Richman Stopford hastened to the busy east coast port of Grimsby, where they met with Mr Leach of the Board of Agriculture and Fisheries to discuss chartering a suitable boat. 'We explained that we wanted to arrange for a trawler to go to a certain rendezvous in the North Sea, taking one or two people from our side who would meet a German submarine, or seaplane or trawler.' Leach was told nothing about the Snow case, or the reason for the rendezvous, learning only that 'there would be a short conversation, and possibly one or two from our side would not return.'

Leach recommended Sir Thomas Robinson & Son (Grimsby) Ltd, who readily agreed to lend MI5 a large fishing trawler named the *Barbados*. Built in 1905 and displacing 130 tons, the *Barbados* carried a crew of nine and was skippered by Captain Walker. 'He is entirely trustworthy,' noted Robertson. 'He is going to tell the crew that they will be seeing funny things on this trip, but whatever they see will not be what they think it is.' Tar also promised to pass Walker the German recognition signal as soon as it was known, having come to appreciate that 'it would not be safe to rely on believing Snow once the voyage has begun.'

So far as the crew of the *Barbados* were concerned, the two strangers were 'special observers' from a government department. As with Owens, financial reward was the principal driver. 'It is said they value money above most things. Each man will be promised a bonus of £5, the mate £10, and the skipper £20 – if the trip is satisfactorily carried out.'

After consulting with Leach and Walker, the treff was fixed for a point 120 miles due east of Grimsby, precisely midway between England and Holland and slightly south of the Dogger Bank. 'We decided on this position because fishing any considerable distance outside the permitted grounds would arouse suspicion, and might lead to action against the ship on the part of our own aircraft. The trawlers generally fish in company, or at any rate not far from each other. The skipper will have to detach the ship from any company she may be in discreetly and if possible after dark.'

Owens buzzed the details to Wohldorf next day. *'Name of ship Barbados. Meet me 53 degrees 40 minutes north 3 degrees 10 minutes east, 26 fathoms – midnight Tuesday 21st or Wednesday 29th May.'*

As yet, it was still unclear whether Biscuit would even join Snow, let alone risk his skin by going on into Germany. On

Saturday afternoon, as German armoured columns thrust ever deeper into France and the sound of distant gunfire rattled windows in Kent, Robertson met Owens and McCarthy in Richmond Park. Double-crossing his own double agent, Tar treated Mac as though he were a stranger and helped the pair concoct a shared past history in Canada. Afterwards he took Owens aside for a quiet solo briefing, taking care to stroke the Little Man's vanity.

'How's McCarthy?'

'On the level, seems to me.'

'Should we send him into Germany?'

'I reckon so. It's just as well that he's a greenhorn at this type of work. The less he knows, the safer he'll be.'

'I trust you've given him some money to settle his affairs.'

'Settle them yourself,' replied Owens, shrugging his shoulders. 'He's your agent now. Besides, I'm down to my last five quid.'

Robertson frowned. Owens received £250 each month from the Abwehr, bumped up by generous expenses; Lily Bade, now visibly pregnant, even had her own maid. As a British army captain with a regular commission Tar's own monthly pay packet barely amounted to £25. 'Snow said he was very short of money. Yet I had seen his notecase, which was quite half an inch thick.'

Robertson left the park with McCarthy, telling Owens that MI5 needed to vet his latest sidekick, but promising to return to Richmond as soon as Wohldorf buzzed over final instructions. As they drove into London McCarthy filled Tar in on his several conversations with the diminutive master spy.

'I'll go into Germany,' Mac promised. 'He told me not to worry because the Jerries will look after me, that they're all fine people. The way Owens tells it, he's working on squeezing as much dough as he can from your office. He keeps on saying, "Why shouldn't Robbie pay?"'

'Verisimilitude.'

'Come again?'

'For the sake of appearances your money has to come from Snow.'

Mac shook his head. 'He reckons *you*'re on the take. Swears blind *you*'ve skimmed off £5,000 meant for him. And he's definitely pro-Nazi. Says you and quite a few more at the office are due for the chop once the invasion kicks off.'

This was ironic indeed. Already there was talk at the Scrubs of bumping off double-cross agents come *Der Tag*. Ultimately all of them were disposable – McCarthy included.

'There's more,' Mac continued, unaware of the danger. 'He wants to introduce me to the Doctor as a British agent, and said I should mention your name. I told him it sounded pretty risky. Not to worry, he says, because Rantzau knows all about his connections with Captain Robertson and MI5.'

Robertson considered this for a moment. Not half an hour earlier he had allowed himself a rare moment of self-congratulation on successfully double-crossing Owens with McCarthy. Now, even if the Little Man was merely running off at the mouth, that confidence seemed horribly misplaced. Suppressing his annoyance, Tar told the driver to proceed directly to Hood House on Dolphin Square.

At Flat 308 the name on the doorbell was Captain King, a preferred pseudonym of Maxwell Knight. 'McCarthy and I went straight to Mr Knight's flat and discussed the whole affair with him,' noted Tar. 'Mac was very anxious for us to allow him to go on with the scheme and go into Germany, but Knight and I both agreed that it would be far too dangerous to take this course. In any event, by doing so we should get no further with the case.'

Instead, the *Barbados* would set course for a false rendezvous. 'This will make it appear to Snow that everything is going according to plan, but that Rantzau was unable to keep the rendezvous.' Only Mac and Captain Walker would be wise to this deception.

Robertson apprised Guy Liddell, whose response was reliably complacent. 'McCarthy has now made it clear that Snow is double-crossing us. Personally I think Snow just regards the whole business as a money-making concern and gives a little to both sides. Probably neither side really trusts him. He has not been in a position to give the Germans very much from this country, except information which we have planted on him.'

Nothing much save for the radar secret, along with unadulterated dope on key fighter aerodromes, war factories and the RAF's strategic fuel reserve.

At seven o'clock, by prior arrangement, McCarthy called Owens at Marlborough Road and made a show of disparaging MI5. 'Biscuit told Snow that he had only been given £2 by Robertson, whom he thought was a pretty revolting sort of bloke. Snow agreed.'

Soon the feeling would be mutual.

As Mac and Tar left Dolphin Square, Owens and Lily pitched up at Sackville Street, where William Rolph showed Lily an ornamental birdcage, and offered Colonel Johnny a priceless nest egg. With Panzer columns sweeping through France towards the Channel coast, and the Low Countries largely overrun, a swift German victory appeared not only possible but likely. Rolph was of Swiss origin, and like Owens untroubled by issues of national loyalty. Keen to curry favour with the winning side – and keep his creditors at bay – Rolph now offered Snow secret papers from MI5 in exchange for £2,000. The main document itself seemed unremarkable enough, being a menu card for a dinner held by the IP Club at Grosvenor House in May 1939. In the wrong hands, however, the card was priceless. For IP stood for 'Intelligence People', and the seating plan amounted to a veritable *Who's Who* of MI5 and SIS, including

Guy Liddell, Jasper Harker and the Director-General, Sir Vernon Kell.

And Thomas Argyle Robertson. Should the card fall into the hands of the Abwehr, let alone the Gestapo, the names of each and every diner would be added to a *Sonderfahndungsliste*, or special arrest list. At best, this would mean years in a concentration camp; at worst, being measured for a necktie fashioned from piano wire.

As yet, MI5 were unaware that Rolph had been corrupted. On Saturday evening, nursing deep misgivings, Robertson drove back to Richmond to issue Owens with final instructions. These included items of doctored intelligence based on Ritter's last microdot questionnaire, as well as £100 in used notes for Captain Walker. With the treff fixed for midnight on Tuesday, Snow and Biscuit would leave from King's Cross on Sunday morning and make their way to Grimsby by train. 'I told Snow the whole trip was very problematical as we had no indication as to what type of vessel Rantzau would actually come in,' Tar noted. 'Therefore it is difficult to say whether the meeting will take place on board our trawler, or in Rantzau's transport.'

Next day, Owens perfected his own deception. Breaking his journey to King's Cross station he stopped off at the buffet at Charing Cross, where Rolph handed over the all-important IP menu card and upped the ante by offering to supply certain 'blueprints' of MI5. The pair travelled onwards by taxi, Rolph insistent that the Abwehr pay over the £2,000 in dollar bills, perhaps with an eye on escape to America. They parted company only at Russell Square, fearful of being spotted by Robertson, or watchers from B6.

Maintaining a discreet distance, Robertson watched as Snow and Biscuit pulled out of King's Cross on the 11.10 to Peterborough, departing on a journey without maps and with no certain destination. The troubled head of B1A then returned to his office with the germ of a bright idea.

As the train steamed north through Hatfield and Huntingdon, Biscuit studied Snow with a critical eye. 'Owens told me how pleased he was that we were on our way. He said it would not be long before he would be able to get his own back, scandalising Captain Robertson and two others who he said would soon be making swastikas. He then brought out a book and a dinner card marked IP Club, and said: "I'll show you the damned names" and "Here's another son of a bitch, a high man at MI5."'

According to Owens, Robertson could expect to embezzle as much as £500 from the trawler treff. 'They are all like that,' he confided to Mac. 'A mean lot of lousy, grafting bastards. My people pay well, they don't bleed people and use them for mugs, no. But what mugs these wrongly-called intelligence people are.'

Snow then alluded to mystery blueprints. 'He said he would be glad when the advance guard got here, and that they would know who to get and where to get them. Then he put the book away and told me, "I'm having you trained in sabotage and espionage. You will be brought back here without MI5 knowing, and you will have a big part. We'll have a happy time when things start to happen."'

At Peterborough the two agents changed trains for Grimsby. With time to kill, Owens set to prowling the platforms and soon spied a large wooden barrow loaded with crates of ammunition. Fearful and fascinated in equal measure, McCarthy watched as the Little Man scribbled down the destination address on a scrap of paper that he stuffed quickly into his pocket. Fears of Fifth Column infiltrators had lately reached fever pitch, stoked by sensational warnings from the Ministry of Information about fake refugees with machine guns, and 'hairy-handed' nuns. Yet here was an apparently genuine Nazi agent, behaving like a vaudeville spy but attracting nothing so much as a raised eyebrow.

Back in London, Robertson and Liddell took a bold decision

to play for higher stakes. Hoping to capture – or kill – the elusive Doctor Rantzau, MI5 elected to stage a reverse Venlo. 'Snow and Biscuit are to go out on the trawler and hang about the fishing ground until dusk,' proposed Liddell. 'Instead of going to the rendezvous the captain will sail to some other point and bring the boat home. This will keep Snow out of harm's way and ensure that he does not get wind of any impending action. Meanwhile a submarine will play about in the vicinity, and if a U-boat turns up it will be torpedoed. If a trawler, it will be captured – we hope with Rantzau on board.'

CONGRATULATIONS indeed.

Such a sting would undoubtedly render Owens redundant as a viable double-cross asset, but the Little Man's loyalties were in any case suspect and Rantzau would surely be a useful prize. With Snow and Biscuit already en route to Grimsby there was no time to lose. Full of enthusiasm for the audacious Venlo-payback scheme, Tar hastened over to the Admiralty, weighing the odds on the Senior Service lending him a spare submarine.

As the slow Grimsby train rattled through the flatlands of Lincolnshire Owens continued to behave conspicuously, noting down details of airfields, power stations and navigational landmarks. All, he promised McCarthy, would be handed over to the Doctor at midnight on Tuesday. At length they alighted at Cleethorpes, a seaside resort five miles from Grimsby. Here Owens met with Mr Leach and Captain Walker, confirmed that the *Barbados* was ready to sail, and handed over the charter fee. Walker instructed the 'special observers' to be ready to sail from the fish dock at dawn. Their business done, the pair checked in at the Dolphin Hotel on Market Street and ate a hearty meal. Or Mac did, at least. Snow, as usual, grew increasingly tense, as though he were eating the last supper of a condemned man.

Afterwards Owens adjourned to the writing room to compose a letter to Lily, six months pregnant with her first child, and instructed McCarthy to wait in the bar. Ignoring this injunction, Mac slipped out and telephoned Robertson from another hotel nearby.

'Biscuit rang me,' wrote Tar, 'and said that all the way up on the train Owens had been running down me and other officers in MI5, and saying what a rotten organisation it was. He also said that Owens had been making copious notes of everything he saw from the carriage window.' Though disquieting enough, these disclosures were as nothing compared to Mac's next revelation. 'Apart from the information and photographs I had given him, Owens had on him an IP Club list.'

Robertson guessed immediately that the list had come from Rolph. While there was a certain bitter irony in a restaurateur attempting to sell a menu card to the enemy, confirmation that rogue Agent Snow intended to betray the names of half the intelligence establishment in Britain came as another devastating blow.

Phantom sleepers, blown fuses and unregulated treffs abroad. Daimler limousines and fancy town houses in Richmond. Maids for Lily Bade.

Squeezable mustard and Zeppelin shells.

It was now abundantly clear that Arthur Owens had spent two years inveigling the British secret service into a fraudulent triple-cross, trotting gaily from one mare's nest to the next. 'Snowy was double-crossing us,' Tar conceded glumly, his heart made all the more heavy by a keen sense of personal betrayal. 'He was pro-German in outlook, was acting for the Germans, and had told them everything that he was doing with us.'

Only by capturing Rantzau could MI5 hope to snatch victory from the jaws of defeat. With the two spies due to sail at dawn, Robertson decided to roll the dice. 'Biscuit was instructed to go on with the scheme and to act as though nothing had happened.'

Arriving back at the Dolphin, McCarthy learned from the porter that Owens had fallen into a blue funk and was hunting high and low for his missing companion. Happy to prolong his agony, Mac repaired to a pub on the seafront, where Owens located him ten minutes later. 'He thought I had taken a run-out powder at the last minute and was plainly relieved,' Mac noted coolly. The pair then set about imbibing a week's worth of drink. 'It was nearly midnight before we retired. In the hotel lobby was a coat rack, two naval coats hung there. Owens searched through the pockets – though I didn't see him get anything.'

The whiff of farce grew more pungent upstairs. Bidding McCarthy goodnight on the landing, Owens threw up a pantomime Nazi salute, topped off with a whispered 'Heil Hitler'.

With these unsober gestures Colonel Johnny's fate was sealed.

7

Operation Lamp

On the evening of 20 May 1940 a reconnaissance unit from the 2nd Panzer Division reached the French coast at Noyelles-sur-Mer, little more than a stone's throw from the historic battlefield at Crécy, where Englishmen with longbows had routed an entire French army during the Hundred Years' War. Having advanced almost sixty miles in a single day, the black-clad tank men were justly proud of their achievement. Standing on top of their turrets to gaze out across the English Channel, lungs filled with tangy salt air, the exhaustion of ten consecutive days of Blitzkrieg was momentarily displaced by the ecstatic realisation that the Allied armies were now divided in two.

That same Monday morning at 06.35 Agents Snow and Biscuit left dry land behind them, slipping out quietly from Grimsby on board the *Barbados*. Owens was wired with nervous energy, pumping the crew for information about convoys and flash lamps, and keen to establish whether the trawler still carried its single antiquated Lewis machine gun. With the coast still in sight the boat lay up for several hours off the Humber Lightship, then cautiously proceeded through the East Coast mine barrier. Owens remained in the wheelhouse with Captain Walker throughout the long day, occasionally descending below decks to gulp down cups of strong tea in the galley but never staying long enough to remove his overcoat, thus thwarting McCarthy's desire to run through his pockets.

'His entire behaviour all day was consistent with him expecting an early contact to be made,' Mac reported afterwards, the previous night's *Sieg Heiling* still fixed in his memory. 'I told the skipper that if it became necessary we would tie him up on Thursday night.'

The tension on board the *Barbados* increased tenfold at a quarter past five, when the trawler was buzzed by an inquisitive aircraft. 'A plane with English markings on the tail circled around us,' wrote Captain Walker. 'It then proceeded west, from which direction he had come.' The skipper was alone on the bridge at the time, and soon after was alarmed by the sound of distant explosions. Creeping paranoia began to envelop the trawler, permeating a message sent below decks to McCarthy. 'Walker said that the monoplane had RAF markings but in the wrong place – on his tail, not under his wings. The skipper was sure it was a Jerry.'

Peeved at having missed the mystery fly-past, Owens stayed on watch in the wheelhouse until midnight, flagging only when *Barbados* shot her nets on the western edge of the Dogger Bank, still forty miles and three days from the specified rendezvous. As the noisy winding gear dropped the net on the shallow fisheries Owens surrendered to fatigue and joined Mac in the galley, lying down on a bench and attempting to sleep, his overcoat still buttoned up tight.

For Walker and McCarthy, Snow's decision to retire for the night came not a moment too soon. Ten minutes later the trawler was buzzed by a twin-engined German seaplane, which appeared 'as if by magic' and fired off a sequence of red and green recognition flares. Risking a low pass above the dark waves, the enemy aircraft then flashed a call sign in Morse.

Doctor Rantzau had arrived.

Roused in a hurry by the first mate, McCarthy kept his wits

about him and ordered Walker to extinguish all lights on board. 'We managed to keep Owens below until Jerry flew away. After careful consideration I advised the skipper to pull back the net and make for home. This we did. Owens, when he heard the net gear working, asked what was the matter. The skipper told him the net had fouled and they had to pull it back to shoot.'

Mac acted properly in aborting the mission. Rantzau had arrived way ahead of schedule, a move apparently anticipated by Owens, and further evidence that he was deceiving MI5. Responding in kind, Biscuit continued to hoodwink Snow. 'After a couple of hours the ship was well on the way back to Grimsby. Owens enquired again where we were, and why no fishing. He was told we were proceeding to a place near the rendezvous.'

Owens swallowed the lie but remained nervy and restless, and as dawn drew closer McCarthy sensed new danger. 'It was obvious Owens expected something to happen. I was afraid he might go on deck, and signal if he saw anyone.' If Snow read the magnetic compass, moreover, he might deduce that the trawler was heading in the wrong direction. Therefore, at five o'clock on Tuesday morning, Mac settled on decisive action. 'I went to the wheelhouse and told Captain Walker my plan to tie Snow up and search him. It was necessary for the skipper to take the first mate into his confidence. They both gave me all the assistance I wanted, which was much appreciated.'

While the mate fetched a suitable length of rope, McCarthy ordered Owens to his feet and frogmarched him into Walker's cabin. Outnumbered, with nowhere to run, the Little Man offered no resistance as his wrists and ankles were tightly bound. A thorough search of his pockets failed to produce the note scrawled at Peterborough station, but did turn up the highly incriminating IP menu card.

'Can we talk?' Owens tried to bargain, his tone imploring.

'Shut up.'

'Are you a real German agent?'

'Heil Hitler, you bastard.'

Owens nodded, deaf to the sarcasm in McCarthy's voice. 'I thought so. My man in London tried to warn me about you.'

Rolph? Gagen? God only knew.

'Look, it's not me you want – it's the other fellow, at Sackville Street. Absolute gospel. I'm spying on him!'

Mac hesitated, torn between conflicting roles. Should he admit that he had been working for Robertson all along, or maintain the charade that he was a traitor, willing to spy for the other side?

'Play fair and I'll help you,' he said quietly, rounding on Snow, his posture menacing. 'If Rolph is the one double-crossing, just come through with it. Don't try to mug me.'

'Some line, that is. You must think *I'm* the bloody mug!'

Each man was walking a different tightrope – both of which threatened to snap. Unaware of Snow's detailed history, and unable to phone Robertson for further instructions, McCarthy had no choice but to leave Hitler's chief spy in England hogtied.

As morning turned into afternoon, the last leg of the ill-starred voyage was completed beneath a cloud of fear, confusion and paranoia. With an ocean of bad blood between them, Owens still failed to grasp that Mac was an MI5 asset. 'About an hour afterwards, Snow called for me and asked to have the rope around his wrists loosened. I asked the mate to loosen it, and while he was doing so Owens even asked him if he was a German agent.'

After thirty-six hours spent – quite literally – at sea, the *Barbados* reached Grimsby on Tuesday evening. Guards stood waiting on the fish dock, permitting no one to disembark until Owens had been placed under close arrest and removed to a cell on a nearby naval vessel, HMS *Corunia*. The silence of the trawlermen was bought off with cash payments of £5 each; Captain Walker received £25. None of the crew showed the slightest enthusiasm for returning to sea with any more 'government observers'.

Robertson was sanguine, and discounted suggestions that those on board the *Barbados* had lost their nerve. 'Mac was of the opinion that they had been tailed all the way from Grimsby. This, to my mind, is not very likely, but it is quite possible that the Germans sent a machine out to see whether the trawler was anywhere near the rendezvous. The crew were not expecting to meet anyone that night, and would naturally be rather scared at seeing a strange plane signalling to them.'

Be that as it may, the premature return of the trawler at least served to expedite Robertson's ambitious Venlo reversal. Now known as Operation Lamp, the revised plan called for the *Barbados* to return to sea with a regular navy crew, along with a protective shadow from HMS *Salmon*, an S-class submarine based at Harwich. Hopeful of rustling up air support, Tar had also visited Adastral House on Kingsway, where he spoke to Air Commodore Archie Boyle, the genial Director of Air Intelligence. Boyle listened politely, but declined to play ball.

Crucially, would rogue Agent Snow?

On Monday morning, as the *Barbados* put out from Grimsby, Robertson travelled by car to Harwich. There he met with Commander Edward Bickford, the skipper of HMS *Salmon*, matelot and sub wreathed in Phoney War glory after sinking U-36 on a North Sea patrol. Following interim orders from Robertson, Bickford instructed an officer from the 7th Destroyer Flotilla to pick seventeen reliable ratings to man the *Barbados* on its second voyage. Lieutenant Lionel Argles, a torpedo officer, had served under Bickford before and was considered a 'suitable type', as was his second in command, a fellow lieutenant named Paterson. Their scratch crew would be armed with rifles, pistols and hand grenades, augmented by an Oerlikon cannon manned by a team from the gunnery training school at Portsmouth. A powerful anti-aircraft autocannon of Swiss origin, the Oerlikon was capable of firing several hundred 20 mm shells a minute, and was likely to make short work of Rantzau's transport if he chose to return by seaplane or trawler.

If the Doctor surfaced in a U-boat, HMS *Salmon* would intervene and add to her tally. With Owens and McCarthy at sea, however, Robertson was still unsure how his German counterpart would make his way to the rendezvous point on Thursday evening.

While Argles set to work up-gunning the *Barbados*, Robertson confronted Owens in the brig on board HMS *Corunia*. Now, for the first time, Colonel Johnny learned that his sidekick McCarthy had been working for British intelligence all along. 'I took McCarthy with me but kept him outside,' Tar recorded. 'I asked Owens a few questions relating to his recent voyage and to the various remarks he had made to Mac. I told him quite straight that I considered he was double-crossing me, which he flatly denied. Owens said that he was never going to allow the meeting to take place, and that he thought that Mac was a German agent and leading him into a trap.'

Rightly sceptical, Robertson called in McCarthy and again quizzed Snow about the IP card, as well as the so-called blueprints. With nowhere to run, Owens freely betrayed his source: William Rolph. 'He was extremely hard up for money,' Tar learned, 'and very anxious to go over to Germany as an agent. He gave Owens the IP Club list and told him that he was, at all costs, to get £2,000 from the German organisation, which Owens was to hand over to him. Rolph told Owens that he regarded Colonel Hinchley-Cooke and I as scoundrels.'

All this because MI5 had apparently welched on a paltry payment of ten pounds. The only positive to emerge from the entire fiasco was that Biscuit was plainly incorruptible. So far as McCarthy was concerned, Owens' antics during the train journey from King's Cross to Cleethorpes, and his Nazi saluting at the Dolphin Hotel, were evidence of genuine treason. Robertson was inclined to agree. The early arrival of Doctor Rantzau on Monday also raised the possibility of some secret means of communication between Owens and the Abwehr, as yet undiscovered by MI5. The visiting Lascar seamen? Perhaps Rolph had queered these inquiries too. Whatever the truth, had Snow not retired below decks mere minutes before the seaplane arrived, matters might have ended very differently, with Mac behind bars beside Stevens and Best in Berlin.

Alone with Owens once more, Tar delivered Colonel Johnny a chilling ultimatum. Rather than £2,000 for a menu card, or £50,000 for a Spitfire, the numbers now under discussion were Regulation 18B, and Section 1 of the Treachery Act 1940. Though not yet in force, this draconian emergency Bill was due before Parliament in two days' time and sought to impose a mandatory death penalty on any person convicted at trial of acts likely to assist the enemy or impede operations by His Majesty's forces. Though MI5 begged to differ, Churchill had declared himself particularly keen to execute Nazi spies, with maximum publicity *pour encourager les autres*. Indeed, his office took steps to force the Bill through in just two short weeks.

Quite deliberately, the new legislation bypassed ancient rules that required two witnesses to prove an act of treason. Thus McCarthy alone held his hand on the lever of the gallows trapdoor beneath Owens' cold feet.

'I told Snow that he was going back to sea in the trawler and would be accompanied by a crew of armed naval ratings,' Tar continued, appalled that Owens had been willing to sacrifice McCarthy. 'If there was any sign that he was double-crossing us when the rendezvous took place he would probably never come back to this country.' Owens could atone for his sins only by luring Ritter on board the *Barbados*. 'If he was instrumental in inveigling Rantzau onto the ship, and enabling us to capture him, I might consider his case again. But in the meantime I was perfectly convinced that he was double-crossing me, and that he had given my name already to the Germans.'

Closing the cell door behind him, Tar savoured the agreeably terminal clang of cold steel and deadlocks.

Back on the fish quay, Robertson furnished Lieutenant Argles with final orders that were nasty, brutish and short. Snow would accompany his crew to the treff with Rantzau, with Argles authorised to take 'any suitable action' if his charge attempted to sabotage Operation Lamp. One option was a length of rope and more tight nautical knots. Another was a bullet to the head.

These distasteful chores concluded, Robertson returned to London with Sam McCarthy, still uncertain as regards Snow's long-term prospects. 'I find it exceedingly difficult to make up my mind one way or another. Snow's mind is a very odd affair and it does not work on logical lines. The arguments he put up for the things he said to McCarthy were not exactly convincing, but at the same time held a certain amount of water.'

But not much. After conferring with Guy Liddell and Jasper Harker, Robertson put in for a new Detention Order under 18B, to be served on Owens should he refuse to return to sea to abduct Rantzau. Truly the Little Man now found himself thrust onto the very tip of the spear.

Resolving to sweep clean the Augean stable, Robertson also ordered the belated detention of the coconut widow Mathilde Krafft, who was duly escorted from Bournemouth to Holloway gaol. B1A officers were also instructed to interrogate other Snow associates whose loyalties were in doubt, including Lily Bade, her maid Anna Johnson and the dubious shipping broker Samuel Stewart. To this list of ignominious names Tar also added that of William Rolph, whom MI5 and the Branch found suddenly elusive.

While Owens sweated bullets in his cell, Argles and his crew worked at a feverish pace to ready the *Barbados* for action.

Besides sourcing suitable wireless equipment, the most time-consuming task was the installation of the deadly Oerlikon quick-firing cannon, whose powerful recoil required a robust yet discreet steel mounting, something like that of a Great War Q-ship. Richman Stopford took care of other more mundane details, arranging with the Ministry of Shipping to charter the trawler for a further week and taking steps to ensure that her name and registration number would be changed after she returned to Grimsby. 'This is to be done in order to save the lives of the crew on their future fishing expeditions in the North Sea,' Tar minuted. 'It is quite plain that GY71 will be a marked ship after this trip.'

Late on the evening of Wednesday, 22 May the *Barbados* cast off once again and steamed out into the North Sea. HMS *Salmon* was already in position, submerged at periscope depth five miles from the rendezvous point and briefed to intercept enemy hostiles. With the ageing trawler capable of no more than ten knots, the outward journey lasted eight tense, uncomfortable hours, during which weather conditions steadily deteriorated. As the iron-grey sky and sea merged into one, and the *Barbados* began to pitch heavily, so too did Snow's stomach.

Racked by nausea, and haunted by visions of draconian laws and dangling nooses, Owens poured out his heart in an emotional letter, addressed jointly to Lily and his loyal son Bob, Snow Junior. This lachrymose note was entrusted to Lieutenant Argles, who in due course passed it to Robertson. 'The letter was written under a great strain,' remarked Tar. 'Argles considered he was quite genuine, as it had been made quite clear to Snow that if he made a false step he would never see land again. From what they told me, Owens had a pretty rough passage, but at the same time appeared to be most anxious to get hold of Rantzau either alive or dead, and was willing to play the game as far as he possibly could.'

Some line.

Three hundred miles east, on the picturesque North Sea island of Sylt, Major Nikolaus Ritter relied once more on the Luftwaffe to convey him to his watershed treff with Colonel Johnny.

On Thursday afternoon the Doctor again journeyed from Hamburg to List, where a maritime reconnaissance unit designated *Kustenfliegergruppe* 506 operated Heinkel 115 floatplanes from the sheltered harbour. While these planes were sturdy enough, the North Sea treff required a larger aircraft type with greater range, prompting Ritter to obtain a huge twin-engined Dornier 18 flying boat with an impressive airborne endurance of twelve hours and a range of 2,000 miles. In order to reduce weight, and thus fuel consumption, the handpicked crew from KfG 506 agreed to strip out their protective armour plating. This gambit was a brave one, since the lumbering Dornier 18 boasted the dubious distinction of having been the very first Luftwaffe aircraft type shot down by the RAF.

To reduce the risk of interception a circuitous flight plan was adopted, taking full advantage of low-level cloud. 'I wore a flying suit over my civilian clothes in case we fell into enemy hands,' Ritter recalled in his postwar memoir. 'Not that I was worried. Johnny's code was unbreakable, and varied from day to day. The weather was clear and visibility good. However, when we reached the agreed position there was no boat to be seen. I told the pilot to begin flying in a search pattern – but still we found nothing.'

Long hours passed. As darkness fell over the grey-green surface of the Dogger Bank, Lieutenant Argles and his crew kept their eyes peeled for the faint silhouette of a distant seaplane, or the menacing shadow of a submarine conning tower. Meanwhile the changeable North Sea weather continued to close in and before long the navy men found their efforts thwarted by dense fog. No aircraft circled to fire off starlight flares, no gunboat crept close on muffled engines, no U-boat broke surface to flash signals in Morse. The appointed time came and went with no sign of Doctor Rantzau. After waiting for several more blind, silent hours Argles reluctantly decided to extinguish Operation Lamp.

Shivering fearfully in the wheelhouse, his protesting stomach knotted tighter than a drum, Arthur Owens counted his blessings.

Ritter had given up long before. 'There was no trawler, and fortunately no enemy aircraft to shoot down our Dornier. Eventually, with fuel running low, we headed for home. The operation had been a failure. I was disappointed, and in my mind turned over every stage of the plan.'

For all concerned, the intricate trawler treff was destined to remain a riddle wrapped up in an enigma. The following year, under close interrogation, Owens stubbornly insisted that Rantzau flew out to meet the *Barbados* not once but twice, firing green signal flares on the first occasion but thwarted by fog on the second. Fully thirty years later, Ritter's own unreliable account contradicted the version accepted by MI5, contending there had been no fog, and no initial reconnaissance flight on Monday. According to the Doctor, Captain Walker had developed cold feet, his fear then infecting the crew and McCarthy.

Zeppelin shells.

In reality, Owens and Ritter prevaricated in order to conceal some secret means of communication to which neither was prepared to admit, even decades later. It seems unlikely that Owens could have contacted the Doctor after boarding the *Barbados* at Grimsby, which tends to suggest that Rolph was complicit. These tantalising intrigues aside, Ritter could count himself fortunate that his hand-picked Luftwaffe aircrew failed to locate the trawler second time around, since the quick-firing Oerlikon cannon would have made short work of the cumbersome Dornier 18.

The *Barbados* arrived back in Grimsby shortly after six

o'clock on Friday evening. Shattered by the rough sea voyage, and in the certain knowledge that his dual careers as Snow and Johnny were both sunk in the groggy shallows of the Dogger Bank, charcoal-eyed Owens was immediately returned to his cell on HMS *Corunia.* Meanwhile Robertson and Richman Stopford took a verbal report from Argles and Paterson, and after satisfying themselves that Owens had behaved himself correctly paid the Little Man a visit.

'To put it mildly, he was in the most frightful mess,' claimed Robertson. 'Snow complained of a duodenal ulcer and really looked desperately ill. He was taxed by us for over two hours. Had he been a normal human being he would have broken down, but we could get very little satisfaction from him. Although he continued to deny emphatically that he was double-crossing us, it was quite clear that he was fully expecting to be put into prison.'

Already Owens had rehearsed his defence with considerable care. Harking back to his successful reconnaissance of Kiel harbour in 1936, Snow now claimed that copies of the photographs had somehow reached Rantzau, who then confronted him in Germany and extracted a confession 'on pain of death'. By way of unpleasant consequence, Owens had been 'living in a reign of terror from the Gestapo' for several years.

This convenient alibi was nothing more than artful bluff, conjured up on board the *Barbados* as Owens contemplated a date with the hangman under the Treachery Act, in force now for twenty-four hours. A defence of duress would allow him to claim that his acts had been involuntary, committed against a backdrop of clandestine events on foreign soil that defied investigation and which might well sway an ordinary jury. Like Peal and Hinchley-Cooke four years earlier, Robertson and Stopford considered the merits of a criminal case long and hard. Since the IP menu card had not found its way into enemy hands, however, and Owens was indisputably a British agent, B1A were forced to conclude that there was 'no possible chance' of securing a conviction.

Besides which, the new Treachery Act meant that espionage trials had suddenly become counter-productive. A live spy, even if he could not transmit messages, was always of some use as a reference source to MI5. Whereas a dead spy was no use at all.

Robertson returned to London with Stopford on Saturday morning. Among several competing priorities in the disappointing aftermath of Operation Lamp was a searching interrogation of William Rolph. Unfortunately Snow's errant business partner was found to be absent from the basement office on Sackville Street and from his service flat nearby. Only a determined effort by Stopford succeeded in running Rolph down by telephone, and secured his reluctant consent to a meeting next day.

Owens travelled back on Saturday afternoon under armed escort. Although the new 18B Order drawn up five days earlier had not yet been served, he was placed under house arrest at Marlborough Road and instructed to contact Wohldorf that night. Following his customary weather report, together with a brazen request for additional funds to pay off the skipper of the *Barbados*, Owens demanded to know why Rantzau had failed to appear at the rendezvous.

The operator acknowledged his signal but gave no useful reply. Once again Stelle X appeared to have lost confidence in Colonel Johnny.

For his part, Robertson paid close attention to the new hidden microphone in the dining room and disconnected the private telephone line. Both as Snow and Johnny, the Little Man's future – and freedom – were dangling by the slenderest of threads.

On the far side of the Channel the Allied position grew equally precarious. A British counter-attack at Arras stalled with the loss of 40 precious tanks, the small Belgian army was close to collapse and too many French military formations were reluctant to fight with sufficient vigour. With the strategic ports of Calais and Boulogne about to fall into German hands, almost half a million Allied troops became trapped in a shrinking pocket around Dunkirk. Curiously, Hitler chose this moment to endorse a command which would spark much controversy and on Friday morning approved the so-called 'halt order' proposed by his senior commander, General Gerd von Rundstedt, who sought to preserve his armoured divisions in order to defeat the main French force in the south. Rotund Luftwaffe chief Hermann Göring lent his weight to the argument, bragging fatuously that his bombers were more than capable of dealing with the Tommies and *poilus* bottled up in the north.

For two days the Luftwaffe bombed and strafed without mercy, prompting Berlin to announce that the fate of the Allies in Flanders was sealed. King George VI responded by declaring Sunday a day of national prayer, and left Buckingham Palace to attend a packed service at Westminster Abbey, joined by Winston Churchill and the Archbishop of Canterbury. 'The last three days have been the worst I ever spent for some considerable time,' Guy Liddell confided to his diary. 'The news has been so bad that it made me feel physically sick.'

At ten o'clock on Sunday morning Robertson and Stopford descended the short flight of steps at Sackville Street. Plainly agitated even as he answered the door, Rolph tried to distract his visitors with items of trivia gleaned from his wife, a busy socialite. Robertson allowed this clumsy charade to run its course, then informed Rolph bluntly that Agent Snow had attempted to sell out MI5 with a dinner list.

'Rolph expressed astonishment. When questioned, he said that he could not understand how the IP card had got into Owens' possession. We then asked him if he was prepared to turn out his drawers and his safe, where Owens said blueprints of MI5 were kept. This he did.'

From inside the safe Rolph produced a brown paper package secured with a rubber band. Inside it Robertson found a medal presented to Rolph by the King of Belgium, as well as several older IP Club menu cards and two slim folders. On examining the latter, Tar found details of PMS2, a shady counter-intelligence unit set up during the First World War to monitor the British socialist movement. Rolph had occupied a senior position, though his section had been shut down in 1917 after the controversial trial of Alice Wheeldon, a pacifist suffragette framed for plotting to assassinate David Lloyd George with a poison dart. Wheeldon had died after going on hunger strike in prison. Then, as now, Rolph's conduct had evidenced a worrying lack of scruple.

Robertson's patience was fast wearing thin. 'After looking through these papers, and the papers in the drawers of his desk, we were unable to trace his copy of the May 1939 dinner list. By this time Rolph was becoming a little bothered and never gave us a straight answer to any of our questions.'

A desk jockey rather than a field agent, Rolph was no match for Owens where quick-witted fibbing was called for. At first he denied that Snow and Lily had visited the office on Saturday evening, and instead blathered tangentially about soldering irons and coffee pot repairs, followed by supper in a cosy little restaurant where the maitre d' was a close personal friend.

After ten dissembling minutes Robertson decided to reveal his hand. 'Look, we know for a fact that you were here at seven, because you answered the telephone when McCarthy called. Then Mac spoke to Snowy.'

'All right. I admit that I saw them here on Saturday at seven.'

'Did you give Owens the list?'

'Certainly not – though I may have shown it to him to prove my credentials. Then ... then he must have slipped it in his pocket.'

This might have stood as a credible alibi had Rolph not

blown it almost immediately, changing his story yet again. 'Rolph said that Snow asked Lily to leave the room as he had some business to discuss. Afterwards Rolph went out to call Lily, and when he came back he saw the 1939 list lying on his table, and put in back in the drawer. He was immediately tripped up on this point, and then said that Snow must have come back to the office after it had been locked up and broken open the door.' Robertson might as well have been describing his own exploits in snaring the communist mole John King, but for one inconvenient fact. 'The break-in would have been an almost impossible feat, for Snow would have had to climb over the railings to access the basement, and did not have a key to the outside door.'

By now the two MI5 men were 'morally certain' that Rolph had given the list to Owens, and made arrangements for the Little Man to be driven over from Richmond. While they waited Rolph entered a fugue state, becoming 'rather fussed' and confused, pacing endlessly from room to room. Stopford followed as best he could, observing as Rolph retrieved a small object from a drawer in his desk, then quickly tore it apart. Retrieving the fragments from a waste bin shortly afterwards, Stopford found an alphabet mounted on cork and cardboard, clearly intended as some sort of coding device.

'He could give no satisfactory explanation,' confirmed Tar, 'except to say that in learning the buzzer he thought it better to learn with a code rather than straightforward lettering. The explanation is obviously fatuous.'

Owens arrived half an hour later. Rolph, he insisted, had produced the IP list from his safe and quoted a price of £2,000, payable in dollar bills. He swore also that the two of them had devised the alphabet code together, and that Rolph had known all along about the trawler treff with Rantzau. Careful to avoid self-incrimination, Owens failed to mention that his business partner had already been numbered agent A.3554 by Stelle X.

'Ultimately Rolph admitted he knew Snow was going in a boat. Stopford and I were both very badly impressed by the way he delivered his information. He told lies continuously, repeatedly changed his story, and only with the utmost difficulty was it possible to extract from him anything at all. We are both perfectly convinced that he gave the list to Snow. It is also quite clear that Rolph is exceedingly hard up and is being pressed for money by his various creditors.'

The MI5 party finally left Sackville Street towards the end of the afternoon, taking with them four automatic pistols, a firearms certificate and a desk diary. Grudgingly, Robertson agreed with Stopford that the troublesome Snow case should now be shut down and the Little Man removed somewhere safe – perhaps even as far away as Canada. Meanwhile Owens was driven back to Marlborough Road, and dutifully buzzed his weather report at two minutes to midnight: *'Visibility 4,000 yards. Cloud ceiling 3,000 yards. Wind velocity 1. Direction south-east. Temperature 62 Fahrenheit.'*

No mention at all of the gathering storm.

Alone with his thoughts, and deprived of his firearms, Rolph had pause to reflect on the vicissitudes of fate, the new Treachery Act and the lethal toxicity of coal gas. Some while later he walked back to his flat in Dover Street, opened the tap on the gas oven and waited to die. Thanks to the high carbon monoxide content of unburned town gas, and the smallness of the room, his blood became saturated quickly, with asphyxia complete in no more than fifteen minutes, lending his corpse a curious pinkish hue.

Dark indeed was the hour. Less than a mile away in Whitehall, Vice Admiral Bertram Ramsay received orders from the Admiralty to implement Operation Dynamo, the hastily prepared plan for the evacuation of the BEF from the shrinking perimeter around Dunkirk. During the course of Sunday afternoon the German halt order had been lifted, and the key port of Calais captured. 'Dynamo was to be implemented with the greatest vigour,' recalled Ramsay, 'with a view to lifting up to 45,000 of the BEF within two days, at the end of which it was probable that evacuation would be terminated by enemy action.'

The last-ditch operation was scheduled to commence at 19.00 hours. Already, a curious flotilla of ships ranging from destroyers to passenger ferries and pleasure craft had been warned to assemble at backwater ports such as Sheerness and Ramsgate. Now this improvised armada weighed anchor and shaped course across the Channel, negotiating lengthy detours to avoid minefields and long-range artillery fire. Many of the little ships were still manned by their selfless civilian owners and crews. Like the king's congregation at Westminster Abbey, everyone hoped for a miracle.

At Dover Street the cold body of William Rolph lay undiscovered for several days. Even in death the Swiss double agent presented something of a quandary for MI5, since any whisper of suicide might lead the Abwehr to conclude that A.3554 had been compromised, and perhaps even murdered. After conducting a mandatory post-mortem, coroner William Bentley Purchase was prevailed upon to doctor the paperwork, certifying the cause of death as 'rupture of aorta atheromatous and ulceration of aorta' – a heart attack, in so many words, and therefore attributable to natural causes.

Bentley Purchase was a firm friend of the intelligence services and three years later would again bend the rules for a far more significant corpse caper, when a dead Welsh tramp was recycled as 'Major William Martin' of the Royal Marines and planted on the Abwehr during Operation Mincemeat. The *Barbados* too now switched her identity. On 30 May, as the little ships of Operation Dynamo helped bring about the miraculous deliverance of 338,000 men from Dunkirk, the registration of the scruffy Grimsby steam trawler was quietly closed. Without further explanation GY71 became GY323 and returned to sea as *Alsatian*, surviving an otherwise uneventful war before being retired and scrapped in 1955.

Donning kid gloves to interview expectant Lily Bade, Robertson quizzed her on the precise sequence of events at Sackville Street on 18 May. 'As I expected, before I had finished the question she had practically answered it. It was quite clear that she had rehearsed this answer very carefully with Snow, and in all probability telling a lie.'

Thanks to the bug at Marlborough Road, Tar knew perfectly well that Owens had taken Lily aside the previous evening and warned her that MI5 would be paying a house call.

'You know what you've got to say?'

'Yes,' replied Lily, far calmer than Owens. 'Do you want me to repeat it?'

'No – I think you know it all right.'

Lily was nervous around Robertson, and not without reason. In a matter of weeks she would be giving birth to a daughter in comfortable surroundings underwritten by MI5 and the Abwehr. Without Owens, the former seamstress was merely an unmarried mother with no visible means of support. 'I said that it would be in her interests to see that Snow played the game by me,' Tar observed coldly. 'As if he did not I would take steps to have him removed.'

This was no idle threat. On confronting the Little Man face to face Robertson made no attempt to hide his displeasure, nor his sense of personal betrayal. 'Snow was in bed at midday. I told him I was not at all satisfied with his conduct, but that much against my wishes I had been persuaded by McCarthy to carry on with the show. I said I would have nothing further to do with Snow personally, and if he wished to communicate with me he was to do so through Mac. Owens insisted that Rolph had double-crossed him, and asked if he could have some protection as he was afraid of the Gestapo.'

Robertson responded with his own double bluff. 'Just as I left the room I informed him that Rolph was dead. I left before he had any chance to question me or show any surprise.'

For Owens, the travails of the past ten days had been profoundly disturbing. Robertson had threatened to have him killed if he refused to assist in the capture of Doctor Rantzau. Now Rolph had expired in circumstances that seemed highly suspicious. With France and the Low Countries under German occupation, further meetings with Ritter on neutral ground seemed nigh on impossible, as did the prospect of escape to the safety of the Reich. Canada, too, was out of the question. Aggrieved Captain Robbie would surely see to that.

The best Hitler's chief spy in England could hope for now was unconditional surrender to the Nazi regime, or a successful German invasion of the British Isles.

8

Nazi Frightfulness in Surrey

The month of June 1940 saw the Allies lurch from one disaster to another, like punch-drunk victims of a violent mugging. Italy declared war on Britain and France in opportunistic fashion, spurring Stalin to trump Mussolini by ordering the Red Army into the Baltic states. Beaten on the field of battle, the French armed forces surrendered, only to suffer a double humiliation when Hitler insisted on staging the armistice ceremony in the forest at Compiègne where Germany had signed her own surrender in 1918.

Of the 123,000 French troops rescued from Dunkirk just 7,000 stayed in Britain to fight on with General de Gaulle. Britain now stood alone, and was seemingly ripe for invasion. Already Churchill had vowed to fight the enemy on the beaches, in the fields, and in the streets and hills; now he sanctioned the use of mustard gas in the last resort, and dum-dum bullets rather sooner. Visiting a rifle range near Checkers, the defiant Prime Minister blazed away at targets with a favourite Mannlicher rifle. 'He also fired his revolver with commendable accuracy,' recalled his young private secretary, John Colville. 'Despite his age, size and lack of practice, Winston acquitted himself well. The whole time he talked of the best method of killing Huns. Soft-nose bullets were the thing to use, and he must get some.'

On 11 June Churchill also fired Sir Vernon Kell, the veteran Director-General of MI5, after thirty years in post. Kell was replaced by Brigadier Jasper Harker, a former Indian Police man described as 'good-looking but not clever', and who was highly rank-conscious. 'The blow has fallen,' mused an ambiguous Guy Liddell, who stepped into his shoes as head of B Division. Harker's first act as new broom was to plaster the Scrubs with copies of a fatuous pamphlet, *Go To It!* This ill-judged opening gambit prompted two dozen overworked typists to tender their resignations and one staffer to remark that Harker was 'a sort of highly polished barrel which, if tapped, would sound hollow. Because it was.'

In the wake of the trawler fiasco Tar Robertson felt much the same way about Agent Snow. On the last day of May he instructed Owens to press Rantzau on the subject of future German intentions, and float the idea of a treff with McCarthy in Lisbon. *'Getting worried,'* buzzed Colonel Johnny. *'When is South African coming to help? Believe safer if my man meet you Portugal and bring papers. He will replace me when in Canada.'*

In fact Owens' messages were now being keyed by Maurice Burton, with Snow little more than a brand name for MI5 disinformation. Unperturbed, Ritter replied straight away, keen to obtain certain secret documents promised at sea a week earlier and demanding to know if Johnny's latest sidekick was reliable. *'McCarthy hundred per cent friend,'* promised Owens, through gritted teeth. *'Shall I try Portugal bringing all dope?'*

Previously a backwater for MI6, the fall of France transformed the port city of Lisbon into the espionage capital of Europe virtually overnight, with everything and everyone apparently for sale. Filled to overflowing with displaced persons and dubious characters, the single MI6 officer attached to passport control was swiftly overwhelmed, and soon reinforced by none other than Richman Stopford, who relinquished his role as Robertson's assistant at B1A. Despite this improvement, Tar could hardly risk sending rogue Agent Snow abroad and so instructed McCarthy to travel alone. With seats on commercial flights to Lisbon unobtainable at short notice, Mac booked a ticket on a passenger ship due to sail from Southampton.

'Friend representative wines,' Johnny buzzed at the beginning of June, confirming Mac's cover as a commercial traveller. *'Stay one week.'* Yet precisely what happened next is unclear. On 17 June Wohldorf learned that McCarthy had sailed two days earlier. Accordingly Ritter set out for Lisbon, travelling via Berlin, Lyon and Madrid under diplomatic cover and freighted with a parcel of baby clothes for Lily, a gift from his wife Irmgard. However, a week later Owens revealed that Mac had been taken off the boat due to some unspecified illness. *'Can you wait till McCarthy better? Cannot recommend anyone else. Secret documents safe. Visa for self week to ten days, probably more.'*

Had Biscuit crumbled, or had MI5? It might have been that picky Richman Stopford felt security was lacking in Iberia. Or perhaps hard-drinking McCarthy had dropped his guard and gone on a bender. Whatever the truth, for the second time in a month the Doctor found himself stood up by his chief spy in England, previously so reliable and punctual to a fault. Disenchanted, Ritter returned to Hamburg with the large cash payment intended for the London stelle. The baby clothes remained in Lisbon.

The good Doctor's anger would soon be displaced. Within a week of the collapse of France, with no pre-existing plan or armada, Hitler set his sights on a cross-Channel invasion of the British Isles. On 22 June all Abwehr stellen across Germany and Occupied Europe were warned that the gathering of intelligence on England was now priority number one. Since Owens was feeding back little in the way of useful information (*'Enquiries pending on coastal defences'*), Stelle X was instructed to dispatch new reporting agents with minimum delay. 'Johnny was unable to gather all the intelligence required on landing grounds,' said Ritter by way of excuse, 'and some of it was stale by the time it filtered through. So we sought out volunteers who were prepared to jump into England by parachute, or land from fishing boats. The training and insertion of these parachute agents was entrusted to me. There was no handbook to follow, and no time to lose.'

Ritter christened this hasty scheme Operation Lena, while the broad-front invasion between Ramsgate and the Isle of Wight became Operation Sealion. Given that later Allied planning for the Normandy landings in 1944 took fully two years, the glorified river-crossing envisaged by the German high command stood less chance of success than a snowball in hell, just as the Abwehr's so-called 'espionage offensive' faced equally long odds. Indeed, Germany had just three suitable spies in training, one of whom was the Afrikaaner already promised to Snow. This first party arrived off County Cork on the night of 7 July, with the two South African Germans named Tributh and Gärtner joined by Obed Hussein, the disaffected Indian who had bribed Lascar seamen to drop wireless valves at Sackville Street. Now Hussein hoped to blow up targets in London with nitrocellulose and thermite, cunningly concealed in tins of peas.

After rowing ashore in Baltimore Bay the trio were arrested as they boarded a bus to Dublin. All three would spend the next seven years in Mountjoy Prison, the Abwehr war diary speaking of lessons hard learned: 'Message received that agents landed in Operation Lobster have been detained. Equipment provided incriminating evidence. By director's decision further sabotage acts are to be made direct against England.'

At the same time Hitler issued Directive 16, describing as 'hopeless' Britain's military situation. 'England still shows no willingness to come to terms,' carped the Führer, confused and aggrieved by such impudence. 'I have therefore decided to prepare – and *if necessary* to carry out – a landing operation to eliminate the English motherland as a base from which the war against Germany can be continued.'

Though Operation Sealion was largely an exercise in brinkmanship, verisimilitude demanded that preparations be completed by the middle of August, after which all or part of the British Isles would be placed under occupation in much the same way as France. But before the invasion fleet sailed it was imperative that the Luftwaffe should wrest air superiority from the Royal Air Force. So began the Battle of Britain, in which radar – the so-called 'wireless cloud' – held the key to victory. With MI5 controlling his radio, however, Colonel Johnny was no longer able to deliver any fresh intelligence coups. *'Difficult due to new military areas and regulations,'* buzzed the impostor Burton from Marlborough Road. *'Southern England all travellers questioned by sentries. Details you require scattered over country. All roads heavily guarded and mined.'*

Stelle X was already prepared, so that instructions flashed from Wohldorf during the second week of July seemed calculated to deceive British military leaders. 'Snow has been in communication with the other side,' observed Liddell. 'Some time ago we heard that the points for invasion were Anglesey, Scotland and the south-east coast. The latest message to Snow may mean that the Germans will go for Ireland first, and subsequently Wales. This may indicate a change of plan.'

Or did it? Liddell was typically indecisive. 'On the other hand it seems to be an indication that an attack here is not likely, or impending.' In reality, the apparently incompetent Abwehr was playing the double-cross game rather more effectively than MI5.

Matters became confused further still when MI6 reported that Spain, Portugal and Gibraltar were under threat. Worse still, code-breaking work at Bletchley Park remained painfully slow and haphazard, with Enigma ciphers used by the German army and navy all notably secure. In June intercepts of Abwehr traffic were suspended to allow valuable personnel to concentrate on

Luftwaffe signals. These were at least readable, yet none of them indicated where Operation Sealion would actually beach.

This was truly a looking-glass war. While the Abwehr fed Johnny contradictory hints about Scotland, Ireland and Wales, the disinformation played back on Snow's transmitter by MI5 was correspondingly vague. *'New super landmine adapted for marine use against barges with shallow draft. Tests show three barges destroyed at once . . . Orders given no evacuation in invaded areas. Orders to bomb English civilians if necessary. Tommy guns now issued to all British troops.'*

There would be no surrender. To emphasise the point, Churchill posed for a photograph cradling a Thompson sub-machine gun, the weapon of choice for Al Capone and John Dillinger, while also sporting a chalk-stripe suit and a fat cigar. In a rare instance of German wit, this ambiguous image soon appeared on a fake 'Wanted' poster dropped by the Luftwaffe, on which Britain's 'gangster' PM was charged with 'incitement to murder'.

'The whole German machine seems to be concentrated on defeating us through propaganda,' mused Liddell. 'Practically nothing has happened in the way of sabotage. Neither Snow nor the incident of the two Afrikaaners and the Indian arriving in Ireland with two suitcases full of bombs suggests anything very thorough in the way of organisation.'

Meanwhile Britain kept calm and carried on. During the third quarter of 1940 almost half a million adult males joined the armed forces, although most new recruits found themselves drilling with broomsticks, the army having lost much of its weaponry in France. Concrete 'pillbox' bunkers sprang up, signposts were torn down, sandy beaches sprinkled with mines, and open spaces scarred by tank traps and improvised obstacles. Restyled as the Home Guard by the end of July, a ramshackle citizens' militia took delivery of uniforms consisting of little more than an armband, backed up by a million rounds of solid shotgun ammunition, said to be capable of 'killing a leopard at 200 yards'.

Preparations for Operation Sealion along the Channel coast continued apace, in a highly visible show of strength intended to force Britain to the negotiating table. Delivering a long speech to the Reichstag on 19 July, Hitler issued a so-called 'last appeal to reason', urging Britain to step back from the abyss. The gist of this interminable rant, whose length robbed it of impact, was that Germany wished only for peace with honour, and for Britain to acknowledge her rightful position in Europe. 'I can see no reason why this war should go on,' Hitler concluded, an unlikely pacifist. 'Possibly Mr Churchill will again brush aside this statement of mine. In that case, I shall have relieved my conscience with regard to the things to come.'

This blunt invitation to capitulate was widely reported, and distributed by the Luftwaffe as a propaganda leaflet, gifting needy Britons a supply of free lavatory paper. Perpetually defiant, Churchill maintained a forbidding silence, informing trusted aides that 'I do not propose to say anything in reply to Herr Hitler's speech, not being on speaking terms with him.'

Throughout this tense interregnum Arthur Owens marked time in a gilded cage at Marlborough Road, a double agent in name only, his significance diminishing as Lily grew larger. The closure of the Sackville Street office had shut down direct communication with Ritter, leaving the Snow show in the horny hands of his sidekick-nemesis Sam McCarthy. Indeed, Biscuit's eclipse of Agent Snow threatened to become total, so much so that some within MI5 were under the impression that the belligerent Canadian had already disposed of the Little Man in the middle of the North Sea.

But if Snow was anxious, Robertson was desperate. Finally, at the end of July, McCarthy was given a second chance to travel to Lisbon to treff with Doctor Rantzau. He departed on the 24th, flying out from Britain's last operational civilian airport at

Whitchurch, a grass field outside Bristol, and again masquerading as a wine wholesaler. On arrival in Lisbon he booked into the Grande Hotel Duas Nacoes, where it quickly became apparent that everyone was a spy, or a racketeer – or both. 'The hotel proprietor Wissman is a double-crosser,' Mac reported afterwards, plainly in his element. 'He proposed I should help two Jews to get to the USA. The price was 30,000 escudos, to be divided equally. The head porter is a Portuguese and in German pay. He could not be bought.'

Preoccupied with Operation Lena, Ritter was delayed for fully twelve days, leaving Mac in the care of a local liaison named Henri Döbler. A former German army officer who had amassed a fortune in the Argentine, Döbler raced yachts and kept a glamorous Portuguese mistress, said to be close to Salazar, the country's authoritarian leader. 'He frequents the bars and hotels in Lisbon where English and American people go,' Biscuit noted with approval. 'Part of his work is sending explosives to the United States. He seems to be quite fond of drink, and on one occasion I was able to drink him under the table.'

By the time Ritter reached Lisbon, the fake wine merchant's face was well known in every expatriate bar from Estoril to Marvila. An alcoholic, more or less, McCarthy's foibles were confirmed by Joan Miller, another of Max Knight's counter-subversion agents, who had recently brought down a spy ring centred on a cipher clerk named Tyler Kent at the American Embassy. 'The life of an ordinary agent in wartime is hazardous enough,' she explained. 'With a double agent, though, the psychological pressures are almost unimaginable. The need for constant alertness, unremitting duplicity – none of these is conducive to ease of mind. There's a danger of falling into a mental state akin to a kind of self-imposed schizophrenia. At the very least, the characteristics required are a steady nerve, a high degree of self-control and a relish for excitement.'

McCarthy, dismissed as an 'unedifying Canadian' by Miller,

found juggling all three qualities somewhat problematic. Nor was Ritter much impressed when he arrived on 5 August, discerning bug-eyes ('like Basedow's syndrome') and the sweaty demeanour of a petty criminal. Biscuit, in turn, was disconcerted by the Doctor, judged to be an 'exceedingly common Bavarian type' with a penchant for swearing and filthy stories, quite unlike the urbane playboy described by Snow. 'He speaks with a broad New York accent,' Mac noted, sizing up the stocky, broad-shouldered lout with a critical eye. 'But despite the discrepancies there is little doubt that the two doctors are identical.'

Having taken twelve days to reach Lisbon, Ritter remained in the port for just twelve hours. 'The Doctor said that he thought Owens' work was falling off,' McCarthy related with undisguised glee. 'He had done some very good work in the past, but was getting a little slack.' Sticking to the script dictated by Robertson, Mac excused the lack of Sealion intelligence by fibbing that Colonel Johnny was worried about Lily, whose pregnancy had developed complications, and was unable to get around much 'owing to the fact that he had to be on the radio every night'. Yet again, Ritter promised that at least one new agent would soon arrive by parachute in England and asked McCarthy to locate a suitable drop zone.

The crux of the treff remained the 'secret documents' promised by Snow two months earlier. There were no MI5 blueprints, and no menu cards listing senior Intelligence People. Instead, after surrendering his passport to a photographer, who copied it front to back, Mac handed over a National Registration Identity Card along with an ordinary ration book. Counterfeit copies were desperately needed for the new Abwehr agents assigned to Operation Lena, whose misfortune it was that the documents delivered by Johnny's 'hundred per cent friend' McCarthy had been carefully doctored by MI5 to include a number of telltale mistakes. The ID card, for example, was machine-folded, whereas genuine examples were folded by hand. The ration book, too, was non-standard, being of a type issued only to travellers, and pink instead of buff yellow.

With luck, the next Nazi agent sent to Britain would land at a spot chosen by McCarthy, carrying incriminating papers guaranteed to secure a conviction under the Treachery Act. That, or a rapid conversion to the double-cross cause, thus expanding the XX network. For the first time since the outbreak of war, the vexed case of Agent Snow looked set to deliver a positive result for MI5.

Absolute jake.

Mindful of the threatened invasion, McCarthy put across an 'extremely exaggerated and totally inaccurate' picture of British ground defences. Rantzau was dismissive and told Mac to concentrate instead on gathering information about RAF fighters and forward airfields, urging also that Owens' son Bob take a job in an aircraft factory. Inevitably, the conversation turned to the North Sea debacle. 'Rantzau said he was there on the Thursday night, and that it was their plane which had circled over the trawler on Monday. From what I could gather, it seemed that Snow knew it was the Doctor and that he was coming on Monday.'

Ritter's parting shot took the form of a warning, opaque and ominous in equal measure. Göring's Luftwaffe, he said, planned to 'open the birdcage' on 14 August. 'But the big show will not begin then, and will start later.'

Having nibbled cautiously at Biscuit, the 'exceedingly common Bavarian type' Doctor hastened home with the vital identity documents, leaving McCarthy to await further instructions and drink Döbler under many more tables. 'Biscuit got so drunk in Lisbon,' sneered Owens some time later, consumed by hatred of the rival agent who had tied him in knots on board the *Barbados*. 'Made himself ridiculous and threw away money.'

Be that as it may, several days later the thirsty double agent took delivery of a brand new Afu short-wave transmitter and several thousand dollars in cash. With his mission accomplished, Biscuit returned home on a Japanese merchant ship, the *Suwa Maru*, eventually disembarking at Liverpool on 19 August after a full week at sea. 'Biscuit has returned with an up-to-date wireless set in a suitcase and £950,' Liddell reported with evident pleasure. 'His whole visit seems to have been a thorough success.'

The Abwehr's newfound confidence in the London stelle was confirmed when Wohldorf buzzed Owens on the new Afu transmitter to request twenty sets of specimen names and serials for forged ID cards. After consulting with the Registrar-General, the incomparably named Sir Sylvanus Percival Vivian, the Wireless Committee obliged with a dozen candidate identities. The first eight were genuine, and included Owens, Lily, Maurice Burton and Gwilym Williams. The remainder were wholly fictitious.

Meanwhile, Hitler issued a fresh Directive calling for the complete destruction of the Royal Air Force. As the air battle above the Channel intensified, the Luftwaffe also paid tentative visits to industrial targets around Birmingham, Liverpool and Southampton. This ongoing strategy of tension meant that London was spared for the time being, although at the end of July a searchlight battery in Richmond Park was sprayed with machine-gun fire, prompting the local golf club to draw up a set of emergency rules. Players were politely requested to collect bomb and shell splinters to avoid damage to mowers; balls moved by enemy action could be replaced as near as possible to their original position. Best of all: 'A player whose stroke is affected by the simultaneous explosion of a bomb or shell or by machine-gun fire may play another ball from the same place.'

Penalty one stroke.

While not a club member himself, highly strung Arthur Owens was abnormally terrified of air raids and begged Tar to allow the dispatch of a lie intended to discourage the return of war to his doorstep. *'New anti-dive bomber machine gun. Special sight. Very accurate. Mass produced.'*

Snow buzzed in vain, and Biscuit docked at Liverpool too late to warn British intelligence of the Luftwaffe's plans to 'open the bird cage' on 14 August. Codenamed *Adlertag* (Eagle Day), the command issued by Göring to his air fleets was typically grandiloquent: *'Operation Adler. Within a short period you will wipe the Royal Air Force from the sky. Heil Hitler.'* The fat Reichsmarschall envisaged a campaign lasting no more than two or three weeks, by which massed waves of bombers would attack targets within 100 miles of central London, creeping gradually closer day by day, thereby forcing Britain to capitulate. Enigma decrypts betrayed a modicum of detail to Bletchley Park before bad weather forced a change of the German plan. As a result the RAF were largely unprepared when, on Monday, 12 August, two days early, the Luftwaffe attempted to blind the British fighter-control system by pinching out radar stations at Dunkirk, Dover, Rye, Pevensey and Ventnor, the latter perched on the edge of the Isle of Wight.

Eleven months earlier, Colonel Johnny had identified Chain Home as a priority target for Germany. *'I repeat – do everything you can to jam these signals, or knock out the power source.'* A determined, accurate Luftwaffe strike threatened to punch open the vulnerable 'channel' revealed by Snow to MI5 at the time of the Munich Crisis in 1938. Now, with most of Continental Europe vanquished or supine, such a gap might even lose Britain the war.

'If I'm successful,' Owens had told Walter Dicketts on the eve of this landmark betrayal, 'I'll be able to do anything I like.'

Son of a bitch.

The attempt to blind Britain was tasked to an elite precision-bombing unit, *Erprobungsgruppe* 210, which operated Messerschmitt-110 heavy fighters from a forward airfield at

Calais-Marck, and whose businesslike unit insignia framed the British Isles in the cross hairs of a gunsight. Early on Monday morning a force of sixteen aircraft sped across the Channel towards the Kent coast, splitting into four groups of four above the garden of England. Erpro's unit commander, Hauptmann Walter Rubensdörffer, took the first section inland towards the Chain Home station at Dunkirk near Canterbury, where observers on the ground watched with dread fascination as the lead aircraft circled the target and released a ring of coloured smoke, through which one fighter after another dived to plaster the site with eight 500-kilogram bombs.

The same deadly pattern was repeated at Dover, Rye and Pevensey, wrecking buildings, cutting off electricity and shaking the foundations of the tall steel towers. All except Dunkirk went off-air, tearing a gap in the radar screen that stretched for almost one hundred miles. Through it swarmed several squadrons of gull-winged Stuka dive bombers, striking airfields at Hawkinge and Lympne without loss. Shortly before noon close on a hundred Junkers-88 bombers followed through with a fierce attack on Portsmouth docks, during which fifteen of the raiders peeled off to attack Ventnor from the blind landward side. A dozen direct hits put the radar off-air, setting fire to most of the buildings and obliging the RAF to rush mobile equipment to nearby Bembridge.

While the four mainland stations were back on air within twelve hours, a second visit by Stukas left Ventnor out of action for eleven whole days. Erpro 210 lost no aircraft on the Monday morning and returned to Kent in the afternoon, hitting the airfield at Manston particularly hard and triggering a collapse of morale there later described by some as a mutiny.

Humdinger.

Disappointingly, the humdrum message keyed on Snow's transmitter that night failed to capture the drama of the moment. *'Food situation normal.'*

Despite inclement weather, the doors of the birdcage were again flung open on *Adlertag* proper the next day. Commencing at dawn, wave upon wave of German fighters and bombers pounded airfields, factories and dockyards across southern England, inflicting a good deal of damage on the ground but paying only cursory attention to radar installations. As a result the Luftwaffe failed to significantly impair the ability of Fighter Command to defend British air space, while the persistence of the 'wireless cloud' above southern England caused Göring to make a decisive error. 'It is doubtful whether there is any point in continuing attacks on radar sites,' he told senior commanders gathered at Carinhall, his luxurious hunting estate near Berlin, far removed from the field of the battle. 'None of those attacked so far has been put out of action.'

At a stroke, the inept Reichsmarschall entirely negated the value of Arthur Owens' biggest single contribution to the Nazi war effort. Further muddled thinking was evident as Eagle Day turned into night. In an effort to spread alarm and despondency among the general public, the Luftwaffe dropped bundles of espionage paraphernalia over the Midlands, including maps, rucksacks and rubber rafts. More arrived next day, suspended below parachute canopies stencilled with oversized Nazi eagles, and backed by claims on German radio that paratroops in British uniforms and civilian clothes had linked up with a homegrown Fifth Column. The scare triggered a round of exhaustive searches by police, troops and the Home Guard, though none of the 'phantom parachutists' were found, allowing the Ministry of Information to dismiss the entire exercise as a clumsy propaganda stunt.

So far as Ritter and Operation Lena were concerned, this ill-judged experiment in psychological warfare proved a disastrous own goal for it served to place the British public on a state of high alert about spies. Likewise, both for MI5 and the Wireless Committee, the Battle of Britain was no sort of Finest Hour.

According to an unsubtle report keyed by Burton as Johnny on 14 August: *'Home Defence staff anxious for invasion. Defence measures terrific. Large forces ready to attack you if invaded here.'* Buzzings such as this carried the pungent whiff of propaganda, while a run of aviation dope was similarly crude: *'Air Ministry friend informs plane production above expectation. Making new Super Spitfires. Increase in rate of fire very formidable. Supply dumps full of spares. British and American confidence in RAF greatly increased. New machines give good results.'*

Unlike the junk passed for wireless transmission by British intelligence, which served only to confirm to the Abwehr that A.3504 was transmitting under control. Perhaps Ritter imagined that the Afu set handed to McCarthy in Lisbon was free of hostile interference. Desperate for evidence that the RAF was being ground down in a war of attrition, Ritter now instructed Owens to monitor key fighter stations such as Hornchurch, Croydon and North Weald and report back on bomb damage and numbers of serviceable aircraft. *'Let McCarthy do nothing else.'*

Robertson interpreted this signal to mean that Biscuit should concentrate exclusively on airfields. Predictably, Owens insisted that Rantzau in fact trusted McCarthy to do nothing at all.

Ein glas bier! for the Abwehr.

Kein glas bier for MI5.

Fortunately Operation Adler already showed signs of faltering after three days of ferocious aerial combat. The heroism of Fighter Command aside, Göring's tactical decision to cease blitzing British radar stations was compounded by operational setbacks, including a disastrous raid on Croydon airport by Erpro 210, which cost the elite unit seven out of 23 aircraft dispatched, including that of its commander, Walter Rubensdörffer. On 15 August just 30 RAF fighters were lost in combat, set against punishing Luftwaffe losses of 75. Less happily, the raid on Croydon left 62 civilians dead, with residential streets in Kingston wrecked by bombs soon after and a crowded cinema hit in Wimbledon. Though Richmond remained untouched by aerial bombardment, alarmist rumours spread that a group of German parachutists was at large in the Old Deer Park. Popular reaction to this mounting savagery found expression in a single outraged newspaper headline: *NAZI FRIGHTFULNESS IN SURREY.*

Amidst the shock and awe of Operation Eagle a stork descended on Marlborough Road. On 15 August, as Croydon bled, Lily almost died giving birth to a daughter, Jean Louise Owens, during a lengthy and complex delivery. If, as seems likely, Agent Snow was ambivalent about fathering a third child on the wrong side of forty, in the midst of the Second World War, the difficult arrival of Jean Louise at least promised to plug the emotional hole left by the loss of Patricia, his daughter with Irene, still hopelessly estranged from her father. The birth suited MI5 too, excusing as it did the lack of hard intelligence relayed to Wohldorf by Colonel Johnny.

Seeing as Nikolaus Ritter had taken the trouble to carry baby clothes from Hamburg to Lisbon, Owens might have been expected to put his good news on air, using CONGRATULATIONS code. However, A.3504 was no longer drafting his own reports, and therefore the message keyed by Burton that evening was strictly business. *'Croydon raid hit one oil tank, one components factory and landing ground. Getting more dope.'*

Or rather, Biscuit got dope. True, Agent Snow was virtually a prisoner in Richmond, yet his rival McCarthy now harboured a planet-sized grudge against idle Arthur Owens, deeply resenting the fact that the Little Man lived in the lap of luxury while still receiving a monthly salary of £250 from Germany. Meanwhile, Mac did the work of both men and crawled home to a drab room in Paddington. On one visit to Marlborough Road the bullish Canadian went out of his way to needle Burton and Price, the resident minders, by leaving a generous £30 tip in the hallway 'for the staff'. McCarthy then travelled up to Manchester to meet Charles Eschborn, who Tar hoped might take on Snow's old klamotten. There, too, Mac caused grave offence, wheedling the photographer for inside information, then rubbishing much of his latest material.

'Biscuit is succeeding in upsetting everyone,' wrote a dissatisfied Robertson. 'This is not adding to the smooth running of the case.'

Worse still, McCarthy was found to be hopeless in the field. Dispatched to Somerset at the end of August, McCarthy teamed up with the local Regional Security Liason Officer (RSLO), Captain Theakston, to scout suitable drop zones for incoming parachute agents. The pair eventually settled on Little Quantock Farm, nestling in the hills near Crowcombe, then notified the local Chief Constable and rounded off a long day with a session in the local pub. 'I am certain that it would be unwise to let this man work in any country area alone,' Theakston concluded in a bemused report. 'He is completely lost, has no sense of direction, and is obviously out of place among country people.'

It hardly helped that Agent Biscuit was a belligerent drunk. Due to travel back to London by train the day after, Mac set out for the station but was back within the hour, having left his revolver under a pillow. Imbibing heavily on the long journey home, McCarthy became mired in a slough of despond. Of the £950 handed over by Henri Döbler in Lisbon, he had been permitted to retain just £100, from which penny-pinchers at MI5 had deducted the cost of his slow voyage home. Owens, meanwhile, was earning more than a cabinet minister, yet seldom even keyed his own wireless transmissions and often stayed in bed beyond noon.

What happened next was faithfully recorded in the duty log at Marlborough Road. 'McCarthy turned up very drunk and threatened to murder Snow, Lily and the baby and all their connections unless he had some more money. He ultimately extracted a cheque for £200.'

Reporting to B1A the following morning, Burton confirmed that McCarthy appeared to be suffering from delirium tremens but was deadly serious about bumping Owens off. While his threats to kill Lily and two-week-old Jean Louise carried rather less weight, Burton also disclosed that Mac had become far too well known at The Marlborough, where 'he gets very tight on double whiskies and shows off in a most disgusting manner.'

The Security Service was not amused, a duty officer noting peevishly that 'Mac is due for a right royal raspberry.'

The timing of this latest double-cross crisis was exquisitely poor, since Wohldorf had warned Snow that an Abwehr agent would shortly arrive in Britain by parachute. 'A suitable spot is being found,' wrote Liddell. 'The great difficulty is to get the man down alive and prevent the Home Guard from getting at him.' After all, spies captured in public sight could not be turned and would have to stand trial. Dead spies were no use at all. Nor were dead-drunk Canadian receivers on the ground.

Ritter also faced something of a quandary. In just ten weeks he had managed to recruit and hastily train a half-dozen parachute agents for Operation Lena, at least three of whom looked promising on paper. One of these V-men was a close personal friend named Wulf Schmidt, a Dane from Jutland who had tramped the globe as a cattle hand and banana farmer. Another was Gösta Caroli, a stocky Swede of German origin, with the benefit of two years spent living in Birmingham pre-war, masquerading as a travel journalist but in fact reporting to Stelle X. Still more intriguing was Karl Goose, a special-forces officer educated in North America, and drafted in from the Abwehr's very own Brandenburg commando unit.

'With Lena the selection criteria were far more stringent than for ordinary agents,' Ritter claimed later. 'Aside from the fact that they had to be prepared to jump out of an aircraft, they had to be physically fit, no younger than 20 and no older than 30, and intelligent enough to view their tasks in a wider context. On landing, their chief priority would be to get the wireless transmitter working as quickly as possible.'

Ritter also created a clandestine Luftwaffe drop unit. Led by Hauptmann Karl Gartenfeld, a specialist in long-range reconnaissance and navigation, the small flight operated a twin-engined Heinkel-111 bomber, painted funereal matt black, its bomb bay adapted to drop agents rather than high explosives. The exacting insertion technique devised by Gartenfeld required a degree of bravery and skill on a par with that of Erpro 210. Flying low over the English Channel to avoid radar, the unwieldy Heinkel would climb steeply to 20,000 feet over hostile territory, press onward inland, then throttle back its twin Daimler-Benz engines for a quiet diving glide as the drop zone approached.

Disappointingly, the first Lena mission washed out. On the night of 1 September Ritter drove to an airfield near Rennes with his most experienced V-man, the Swede Gösta Caroli, who had left Britain only in December and would now return under the codename Nilberg. The two men shook hands on the tarmac, after which A.3719 hauled his transmitter and baggage into the belly of the sinister black Heinkel while Ritter retired to a hotel to await Gartenfeld's return. Over the course of the next hour Caroli endured freezing temperatures in the cramped bomb bay, scarcely able to move, and green with fright at the prospect of a low-altitude jump over blacked-out enemy territory. But the drop was scrubbed. On crossing the English coastline Gartenfeld encountered searchlights and deteriorating weather, and elected to return to base with his human payload still on board.

At daybreak, McCarthy and the various reception parties positioned on the ground by MI5 left the Quantocks disappointed.

More Zeppelin shells, or so it seemed.

For the Abwehr, Caroli's failure to leap into the clutches of MI5 masked a lucky escape. Regardless, the hastily planned espionage offensive would suffer another serious blow the following evening when Hilmar Dierks, the spymaster who had first recruited Owens back in 1936, was killed in a car accident after a night on the tiles with a trio of agents bound for Scotland. 'He drank too much and had to be persuaded not to drive,' lamented Ritter. 'In spite of blackout regulations they were dazzled by the headlights of an oncoming car and hit a tree. Everyone else walked away with minor cuts and scratches. But Dierks was dead.'

To add insult to injury, Ritter then found himself beaten to the punch by a colleague, Kurt Mirow of Abwehr II in Cologne. During the early hours of Tuesday, 3 September, a party of four ill-prepared spies crept ashore at Romney Marsh in Kent. Trained to work in pairs, José Waldberg and Carl Meier made landfall at Dungeness, their companions Charles van den Kieboom and Sjoerd Pons arriving a few miles further along the coast at Dymchurch. After enjoying a liquid lunch and celebratory meal at Le Touquet the previous day the group had set out from Boulogne, crossing the Channel in a fishing smack under cover of darkness before transferring to dinghies and rowing ashore in the early hours. All were short-term reporting agents, with rations sufficient for no more than a week. The beaches on which they landed were among those targeted by Operation Sealion, the invasion front having been narrowed to a 40-mile strip between Eastbourne and Hythe.

Unlike the aborted mission of Gösta Caroli, who was controlled from Stelle X, MI5 received no advance warning of the four Cologne agents via Snow's transmitter. Even blessed with this advantage, however, each would be captured within hours, their comic misadventures soon passing into the invasion folklore of 1940.

Waldberg and Meier were particularly inept, dropping their

maps and codes overboard even before reaching dry land, then dozing off beneath an abandoned lifeboat. As dawn broke the two spies moved inland onto Romney Marsh, where they holed up beneath a large holly bush and pondered how best to proceed. Both were severely hungover, so that thirst became a major distraction. After several parched hours Meier decided to walk into Lydd in search of a drink, and immediately aroused suspicion by asking for a bottle of 'champagne cider' in the Rising Sun pub at nine-thirty in the morning, well outside normal licensing hours. On being challenged by alert locals, Meier pretended to be a Dutch refugee and foolishly let slip that he was not alone.

Meanwhile Waldberg rigged their transmitter in a tree and managed to send off two messages, one reporting *'no mines, few soldiers, unfinished blockhouse'*, the other vowing to *'resist thirst until Saturday – long live Germany'*. A third signal, scribbled later and probably not transmitted, disclosed that Meier had already been captured. That night Waldberg was also detained, following a thorough sweep by police and troops.

Kieboom and Pons failed to match even this modest achievement. After landing on the shore beneath the Napoleonic fort at Dymchurch Redoubt the two slept for an hour in an empty bungalow, then unpacked their transmitter and set about ferrying their kit across the narrow coast road. Towards dawn a patrolling sentry from the Somerset Light Infantry glimpsed a flicker of movement in the long grass opposite the beach. Upon further investigation, Private Tollervey found himself confronted by a Eurasian-looking man with 'slit eyes' and 'smooth, coloured skin'. Kieboom (whose mother was Japanese) was soaking wet and wore binoculars draped around his neck, along with a pair of white shoes. Tollervey marched the bedraggled ex-clerk to a nearby seaside villa which served as battalion headquarters, where Kieboom demonstrated a tighter grasp of fieldcraft by flushing his linen codes and secret ink down the lavatory.

Pons was arrested a half-hour later, after approaching a group of bystanders to ask where he was. 'They were given no contacts in this country,' noted Guy Liddell with grim satisfaction. 'In fact, they were singularly badly directed. To anybody with any knowledge of conditions here it should have been apparent that none of them could hope to succeed.'

Questioned at Seabrook police station, the Romney Marsh Four confessed to being Nazi espionage agents. They were next transported to Latchmere House, the forbidding interrogation centre established by MI5 on Ham Common, just two miles south across Richmond Park from Snow's London stelle on Marlborough Road. During the Great War the large Victorian mansion had been used as an asylum for shell-shocked infantry officers and still boasted a functional padded cell. Now known simply as Camp 020, and liberally seeded with listening devices, this uncompromising home for hostiles was run by a fearsome monocled commandant, Colonel Robin 'Tin-Eye' Stephens, whose interrogation team included Edward Hinchley-Cooke, Owens' former nemesis at MI5.

'The initial onslaught was against Waldberg,' remarked Stephens, 'described by his companions as the enthusiast of the party.' A classified document until 1999, Tin-Eye's eccentric official history of Camp 020 omits to mention that prisoners were sometimes obliged to strip naked and stand to attention for several hours, while an openly unimpressed female secretary took shorthand notes. 'Meier and Pons spoke readily enough in their spleen against the shabby preparation of their adventure by the German secret service. Kieboom required less gentle persuasion. All four had been given a short-term operational mission: to report on troops, airfields, anti-aircraft defences, ships and civilian morale. They had been assured that their precarious life in England would be short, and that the German armies would soon rescue them.'

Since Waldberg had used his transmitter unsupervised, none

of the four could safely be used as double-cross agents. According to Stephens – though no one else – Kieboom agreed to contact his German controllers and fib that the party had gone into hiding after Pons caught a bullet. With bitter irony, Pons alone would escape execution after the hapless quartet were sent for trial at the Old Bailey under the unforgiving Treachery Act.

With battalions of spies descending on Kent, Tar Robertson had no option but to try to mend fences with Agent Snow. On the evening of 3 September, as the spy sweep concluded on Romney Marsh, Robertson paid the Little Man a visit at Marlborough Road. 'I asked if he would be prepared to continue working with McCarthy. Snow consented to do this, but said that Mac behaved extremely badly and was most abusive. Not only to him, but to people in the local pub, and this created a very bad impression with all concerned. I said that in future Mac was going to take all his instructions directly from me, and I would instruct him when I wanted him to go down to Richmond.'

Arthur Owens was tickled to death. After three months in double-cross purgatory, living under virtual house arrest, Hitler's chief spy in England was set to stage a comeback to shame Lazarus.

Unlike the Swede codenamed Nilberg. Late on Wednesday evening Gösta Caroli clambered back on board Hauptmann Gartenfeld's matt black Heinkel-111 and steeled himself for another nauseous, sub-zero white-knuckle ride. By a curious coincidence, Adolf Hitler chose precisely the same moment to address a mass rally of nurses and female workers at the vast Sportpalast in Berlin, seeking to ramp up the war of nerves and sending his audience into transports of delight. 'In England the people are filled with curiosity,' teased the Führer playfully. 'They keep asking – why doesn't he come? Be calm. He's coming! He's coming!'

In truth only one man was coming. Shortly after midnight Caroli finally hit the silk over Northamptonshire, landing hard and fast on farmland near the remote village of Denton. Gartenfeld had warned A.3719 to deploy a secondary parachute for his heavy transmitter equipment, but the Swede chose to ignore this advice and jumped from 5,000 feet with the Afu set strapped to his chest. His descent was correspondingly rapid, the wireless connecting with his chin on impact and knocking him senseless. Several hours later, at 6.30 a.m., Caroli regained consciousness, cut himself free from his harness and dragged his gear into a ditch. Still concussed and decidedly groggy, Agent Nilberg then fell asleep.

Towards the end of the afternoon a labourer working in Twenty-Acre Meadow noticed a pair of feet protruding from a hedge. The mysterious sleeper was duly reported to Cliff Beechener, a tenant farmer and local Home Guard volunteer. After fetching a shotgun, Beechener set off to investigate and quickly deduced that Caroli was a foreigner by virtue of an unusually large knot in his necktie and his curious orange leather shoes.

'It occurred to me that I would not think much of a chap with shoes like that,' Beechener joked forty years later. 'On closer inspection I saw he was lying on a parachute. I took him to the house and made a call to the police, and I remember the sweat pouring off him. I had the BBC news on the wireless. Stuart Hibberd was reading about the RAF bombing Hamburg, and the poor chap put his head in his hands. He said he had a wife and family there.'

By nightfall Caroli was in police custody in Northampton. Having arrived by parachute with a wireless transmitter, incriminating maps, £200 in cash and a Mauser automatic pistol, the Swede could hardly deny that he was a German spy. Due to intransigence and petty rivalries, however, fully forty-eight hours would pass before Ritter's first parachute agent was handed over to MI5, thereby confirming Guy Liddell's worst fears about losing track of incoming agents as they fell to earth. As a result, Caroli was transferred to Camp 020 only on Saturday, 7 September.

'For all his Swedish identity he was a fanatical Nazi,' vouched Tin-Eye Stephens. 'The first interrogation elicited the names of several Abwehr officers in Hamburg, his controlling stelle, and elsewhere. He claimed to have been recruited for his mission only some two months earlier, but admitted that he had been in England, working as a journalist for a Swedish press agency, in 1938 and 1939.'

There was also the small matter of his forged identity papers. These were made out in Caroli's own name, but carried telltale serial numbers buzzed by Snow three weeks earlier. 'Pressure on Caroli reached its most acute stage when he was asked to disclose details of other agents who might follow in his footsteps,' boasted Stephens. 'He prevaricated, then gave slightly. There was another agent, due to arrive by the same means in a matter of days.'

The V-man waiting in the wings was the Dane Wulf Schmidt, codenamed Leonhardt by Ritter. Caroli was deeply reluctant to betray his colleague, for the pair had struck up a close friendship during training for Operation Lena, besides which the Swede was genuinely loyal to the Hitler regime. Under intense psychological pressure, however, not least the threat of trial and execution, Agent Nilberg revealed all in exchange for a shrewd promise by MI5 to spare the lives of both men.

For all involved in the double-cross system the breaking of Gösta Caroli at Camp 020 was a eureka moment. Within two short days Robertson, Liddell and MI5 had found themselves gifted with a new XX agent, codenamed SUMMER by B1A, along with a head start on a second Nazi spy whose name, background and physical description were now a matter of record.

For Tar in particular, it was the first piece of truly good news since Sunday, 3 September 1939.

Cliff Beechener found less to celebrate. Having relieved Caroli of £200 in cash, a windfall he dutifully handed over to the police, the enterprising farmer later tried to claim back the money, citing an obscure ruling from 1768 which held that a British subject was entitled to keep any property confiscated from an enemy of the king.

The police referred the matter to MI5, from whence there came no reply.

9

Summer and Snow

On the morning of 7 September, Black Saturday, code-breakers at Bletchley Park ascertained that the Luftwaffe were again preparing for action on a grand scale. By the middle of the afternoon Chain Home radar plots confirmed that approximately 350 bombers and 600 fighters were poised to cross the Channel, a vast formation one and a half miles high and occupying 800 square miles of sky. Having travelled from Carinhall to assume personal command of the renewed aerial assault, Göring watched from a collapsible chair perched on the cliffs at Cap Blanc Nez, the sense of imperious valedictory picnic underscored by a nearby table groaning under the weight of sandwiches and champagne.

The target, finally, was London. 'The moment is a historic one,' the chubby Reichsmarschall crowed above the hum of a thousand aero engines. 'The Führer has decided to deliver a mighty blow!'

As the huge aerial armada formed up in the skies above Northern France, intelligence gleaned from the growing menagerie of spies at Camp 020 seemed to confirm that the British Isles were about to be invaded. Waldberg, the leader of the Romney Marsh Four, had hoped to hold out until Saturday, thirst permitting. Caroli, too, anticipated liberation within a fortnight. Furthermore, two miles to the north across

Richmond Park, Snow's new Afu transmitter hummed with a series of urgent requests from Stelle X: *'Where are troops, tanks etc stationed for counter-attack? What kind, how many? Fortifications near coast between Isle of Wight and Margate – guns – anti-aircraft – barbed wire – mines – are they flooded at high tide? Are they stronger where coast is steep, or where it is flat?'*

On any view, the disparate fragments gathered by the Joint Intelligence Committee during the course of Saturday afternoon promised Armageddon by air and sea.

Finally Hitler was coming.

At five-twenty that afternoon, as the first German bombs began to fall on the East End, Churchill assembled his Chiefs of Staff in Whitehall. Weighing the evidence provided by Ultra, radar, MI6 and Agent Snow, as well as additional data on moonlight and tides, and the rising number of landing barges in the Channel ports, it was decided to bring Britain's defences to the highest possible state of alert. At 20.07 GHQ Home Forces flashed the ominous codeword 'Cromwell' to Eastern and Southern Commands, signifying that invasion was imminent and probable within twelve hours. Regular troops stood to as instructed, while in several areas eager Home Guards set church bells tolling in the mistaken belief that landings were already in progress. Bugles sounded on the cliffs at Dover, and in Lincoln a party of Royal Engineers attempted to blow up the railway station. Countless sticks of German paratroops were reckoned to have been shot on the wing, Mass Observation recording one wild rumour that 500 had landed near Newport, all but one of them dispatched in three seconds flat.

Meanwhile London endured its first night of aerial Blitz. Fresh from his own interrogation of the Romney Marsh spies at Camp 020, Maxwell Knight watched the conflagration from the roof of Dolphin Square. 'By the evening the East End was ablaze,' wrote his faithful assistant Joan Miller. 'With M by my side I watched the docks burning. The heat and smoke were appalling, and the sky was lit with an unearthly glow. Before morning, a thousand Londoners would have died in this unspeakable attack.'

To this grim tally the Luftwaffe almost added Double Agent Snow. Having failed to buzz weather or damage reports for two days, Owens resumed contact with Wohldorf on the evening of 11 September in a state of high dudgeon. *'Richmond – what hell? Windows gone, time bomb in garden.'*

On Monday, Owens' safehouse at 14 Marlborough Road had almost been destroyed by a brace of German air raids, the first in the wee small hours, the second at six in the evening. 'It became very noisy during the early morning and bombs began to drop all round,' wrote Marie Lawrence, a youthful diarist and near neighbour. 'Then suddenly a plane came right overhead and there was the noise of the big gun in the park, then a whistling sound as the bomb came down. It was the most awful thing I have ever known. I laughed and cried as we sat in the bogey hole.'

A stick of bombs straddled Marlborough Road, some of them fitted with delayed-action fuses. If anything, the evening raid was even more severe after the RAF split up a large daylight attack, causing rattled Luftwaffe crews to jettison bombs across several London suburbs. 'The noise was terrific and bombs were flying everywhere,' Marie Lawrence continued, once again seeking shelter below stairs. 'Whistle upon whistle, bang after bang. As we sat in the cupboard the floors and windows shook and seemed to go in and out. Every second we thought was our last.'

The arrival of an unexploded bomb in Snow's garden forced the evacuation of the London stelle for two whole days. 'As there had been a great number of bombs dropped round him,' noted Robertson drily, 'Owens expressed a wish to move to a quieter place. I said I would have a look round.'

Erpro 210, the radar specialists, were also busy, visiting the

Vickers aircraft factory at Brooklands just as the afternoon shift clocked on, killing 83 and wounding more than 400. Production was brought to a standstill, though this devastating strike cost the unit its second commanding officer in as many weeks. Other Luftwaffe raiders hit the Hawker Hurricane works at Kingston, and Shorts near Rochester – both targets to which Owens had paid close attention, and had discussed at length during treffs with Ritter.

Had MI5 known the true extent of Snow's treachery, Hitler's chief spy in England might have been left to defuse his own UXB. Instead, his Afu transmitter was now employed to deflect attention away from London, with details of fictive targets buzzed over to Wohldorf, beginning with a dummy munitions plant erected near Stafford.

Although the Blitz would continue for 57 consecutive nights, the fierce air battle above southern England finally began to peter out. On 15 September, a Sunday, the RAF claimed 186 German aircraft destroyed in a single day, set against the loss of just 13 British pilots. In truth, only 56 enemy raiders had been shot down, yet the figures hardly mattered. The defeat of the last mass raid put up by the Luftwaffe in daylight marked another critical turning point. The unfastened 'birdcage' of Operation Eagle had failed to force Britain to capitulate. Electing to postpone Operation Sealion, Hitler turned his attention instead to the Soviet Union.

On the very same Sunday that Fighter Command won the Battle of Britain, MI5 turned another corner in the double-cross war. After reluctantly agreeing to act as an XX agent, the sour Swede Gösta Caroli was escorted from Camp 020 to Aylesbury, where an attempt was made to establish wireless contact from a pigsty behind the home of the Chief Constable of Buckinghamshire. 'We could not take any chances on the Germans "fixing" a location,' wrote Caroli's controller Ronnie Reed, a former BBC engineer. 'If an agent told them he was transmitting from Aylesbury, he would actually have to be located at or close to Aylesbury.'

Since the pigsty was too low, and the aerial too short, Caroli and Reed tried again from a cell at Aylesbury police station. With contact finally established, Agent Nilberg informed Hamburg that he had sustained injuries on landing and was now living rough in the countryside between Oxford and Buckingham. With bad weather closing in, the message continued, he proposed to seek shelter by posing as a refugee.

At 11.15 on the morning of 15 September, Snow received an anxious signal from Wohldorf. *'Swedish friend in fields near Oxford. How can he contact you at once please? Standing by for your answer.'*

Robertson immediately conferred with his superiors in B Division. It was, he insisted, impossible to overestimate the significance of this latest development. 'There is a strong possibility that this single spy Caroli may be the forerunner of a whole battalion. Upon the action now taken really depends all the months of work spent on Snow.'

Verisimilitude demanded that the rescue mission should actually take place. With his plan approved by noon, Robertson instructed Burton to send the following reply: *'Can meet booking office High Wycombe railway station. Will wear white buttonhole. Password: Have you* seen *the stationmaster. What time?'*

Still unwilling to trust Agent Snow, Tar called in Mac for a last-minute briefing. The following morning the volatile Canadian would make his own way to the busy market town, wait at the station at the appointed time, then walk Caroli along the main road towards London. Wary of lurking Nazi agents, or some sort of triple-cross, Tar warned McCarthy to keep his wits about him and not to let the recalcitrant Swede escape. Once watchers from B6 were certain that the pair had not been followed Caroli would be spirited away by car, leaving McCarthy to return to London alone.

The elaborate plan also took account of McCarthy's perennial

Achilles heel: booze. 'Biscuit was not slow to appreciate that High Wycombe is a very large town, and that he had a fairish walk in front of him. In anticipation of his probable reaction to this unaccustomed exercise he was instructed not to visit any public houses en route.'

Biscuit could ill afford another right royal raspberry. On Monday morning, sporting a smart white buttonhole, Mac followed his instructions to the letter. The tall, bespectacled stranger appeared at eleven o'clock, and confirmed that he had seen the stationmaster. After a lengthy stroll along the A40 Caroli was driven back to Camp 020, leaving Mac to relay his report to Tar. Naturally enough, the version of events played back to the Abwehr was entirely different. Transmitting as Snow that evening, Burton informed Wohldorf that the 'Swedish friend' was being sheltered by McCarthy, having fallen ill after a week spent living in the open.

So far as Owens was aware this was perfectly true. 'We don't want to tie Summer to Snow,' Tar explained, lighting on a pleasing seasonal metaphor. 'For then they stand or fall together. Snowy readily assented to this and is willing not to meet Summer. As the "master mind" he is quite agreeable to being kept in the background.'

For services rendered McCarthy was handed a ten shilling note. Unaware that Stelle X was now being spoofed by British intelligence, Ritter expressed delight at the prompt rescue of Caroli. *'Thanks for help to friend. Won't forget. Expecting reports of his trip. Please try to give daily reports, no matter how little. Paramount importance constant observation of airports, planes etc. Friend knows.'*

This opaque parting shot referred to Wulf Schmidt, the Dane who had bonded with Caroli during training for Operation Lena, and even entered into a rash wager to meet him again at the Black Boy Hotel in Nottingham on 20 September. Then a prominent landmark in the city, the building was an apt rendezvous for visiting German spies, boasting a Gothic façade and a Bavarian balcony, and enough gables, turrets and spires to shame mad King Ludwig. However, as Agent Leonhardt prepared to climb aboard Hauptmann Gartenfeld's black Heinkel-111 and bale out over the Midlands, he had no inkling whatsoever that his friend Nilberg had already betrayed him to MI5.

This sudden expansion of the double-cross system spurred Guy Liddell to form a small steering group, comprising six senior officers from MI5, MI6 and the Wireless Committee. Soon this cabal became the Twenty Committee, so-called because in Roman numerals the figure twenty is represented by a double cross (XX). 'We did much more than practise a large-scale deception,' averred its chairman John Masterman, in peacetime an Oxford history don. 'By means of the double agent system we actively ran and controlled the German espionage system in this country. This is at first blush a staggering claim, and in the first place we could not bring ourselves to believe that we did so. Nevertheless it is true, and was true for the greater part of the war.'

Constantly undermined by Agent Snow during the first year of war, MI5 had finally begun winning the double-cross game with the arrival of McCarthy's Afu transmitter from Lisbon, and the fraudulent rescue of Gösta Caroli at High Wycombe on 16 September. Now, three days later, their confidence was further buoyed by the arrival of Wulf Schmidt, dropped by Gartenfeld over the Fens a half-dozen miles north of Cambridge. 'It was only yards from a searchlight battery defending RAF Oakington,' Schmidt recalled cheerfully many years later. 'The crew were asleep when I landed.'

Codenamed Leonhardt by Ritter, Wulf Schmidt was a Danish national born in South Jutland in 1911, who had acquired a solid command of English following spells as a cattle hand in Argentina and a banana grower in the Cameroons. Like his colleague Caroli, Schmidt jumped attached to his suitcase transmitter and landed heavily after his canopy snagged in telegraph wires. Irked that his wristwatch was shattered, but confident of passing unnoticed in England, the next morning Schmidt hobbled into the nearby village of Willingham where he bought a new timepiece and a daily paper, ate breakfast in a café and bathed his swollen ankle under the village pump. Predictably enough, his foreign accent and smart blue suit soon raised eyebrows.

'Someone must have been suspicious and reported me to the police,' Schmidt confirmed, 'because I was arrested as I slept in a field close to my parachute.' By midday the V-man designated A.3725 had been transferred into the custody of the local Home Guard. Following a preliminary interrogation by Major Richard Dixon, the RSLO based in Cambridge, the dubious refugee with forged identity papers in the name of Harry Williamson was driven to Camp 020.

His chauffeur was Jock Horsfall, a former racing driver attached to MI5's transport section who excelled at covering miles fast. On the way to Ham Common Horsfall took his powerful Citroën on a detour past Trafalgar Square, followed by the Houses of Parliament. 'I had been told England was on the brink of collapse,' noted Schmidt with dismay. 'That there was no food in the shops, and that London was in ruins. None of it was true.'

Despite this dispiriting excursion Schmidt showed no sign of cracking at 020, displaying a haughty arrogance, adamant that he had arrived by boat three months earlier as a Danish refugee. As a result MI5 brought in several external officers to question the new arrival, one of whom was Colonel Alexander Scotland, an intelligence veteran charged with the interrogation of enemy prisoners of war at the so-called 'London Cage' in Kensington Palace Gardens. As recorded by Guy Liddell, what followed was decidedly un-British. 'Malcolm Frost found Scotland in the prisoner's cell. He was hitting Schmidt in the jaw and I think got one back for himself. We cannot have this sort of thing going on in our establishment. Apart from the moral aspect, I am quite convinced that these Gestapo methods do not pay in the long run.'

Liddell took the matter up with the Director of Military Intelligence, Paddy Beaumont-Nesbitt, and demanded that Scotland be barred from 020. Undeterred, a day later the slap-happy colonel returned to Latchmere House armed with a hypodermic syringe full of truth serum. Lying judiciously, Tin-Eye Stephens told Scotland that Schmidt was in no fit state to be interrogated further. A formal complaint about Scotland's techniques was later made by Maxwell Knight to the Secretary of State for War.

Eschewing brutality, MI5 simply informed Schmidt that he had already been betrayed by his colleague Caroli, who would not be available to meet him in Nottingham. There was also the small matter of the Treachery Act and mandatory capital punishment. By way of a final trump card, Schmidt had landed with forged papers bearing telltale defects put across by McCarthy, and incriminating serials supplied by Owens.

'His reaction was immediate and dramatic,' wrote Stephens. 'Schmidt lost all his previous composure, cursed "the swine Caroli" and blurted out that he would tell the whole truth.' The Dane held back little, telling of his recruitment in Hamburg, his training under Doctor Rantzau, of meeting other Lena agents in Brussels, and revealing his intended mission. 'He was persuaded that his betrayal had not begun with the capture of Caroli, but had been implicit in the cynical carelessness of his preparation and dispatch. In his new standpoint Schmidt seemed to be a sound XX prospect, and agreed to work as a double agent.'

'No one ever asked me why I changed my mind,' Schmidt told intelligence historian Nigel West four decades later. 'But the reason was very straightforward. It was simply a matter of survival. Self-preservation must be the strongest instinct in man.'

Thus late in the evening of 21 September the erstwhile banana farmer became Agent TATE, so called on account of his close resemblance to Harry Tate, the popular music-hall comic, lately deceased. Under Schmidt's direction, MI5 returned to Willingham and recovered his transmitter from a field near Half-Moon Bridge. The device was then installed on the top floor of Latchmere House. Despite the dubious ministrations of Colonel Scotland, just two days after arriving at 020 the former National Socialist zealot buzzed Wohldorf to report that he had landed safely and was making his way to London. *'Roads blocked with refugees. Most of them look Jewish.'*

Absolute jake.

Still there was no invasion. Reporting on a meeting of the Twenty Committee, Guy Liddell alluded to a bold proposal by the then Director of Military Intelligence. 'Paddy Beaumont-Nesbitt was rather in favour of encouraging them to come over. But on referring the matter to the Chiefs of Staff it was decided not to let them have the truth about the strength of our defences.'

Snow, Summer and Tate duly obliged, reporting on a coastline bristling with troops, anti-tank guns and machine-gun nests, backed up by mobile reserves and over a million Home Guards. The tallest of these tales, such as the supposed importation from Australia of 200 man-eating sharks for release into the Channel, were unlikely to perturb the planners of Operation Sealion. Nevertheless, the art of strategic deception now came of age. Established under the auspices of MI6, the Underground Propaganda Committee set about devising rumours known as 'sibs', including stories of crateloads of Tommy-guns and barge-busting super-mines – both fictions already transmitted to Wohldorf by Snow. In the wake of the Cromwell invasion alarm, stories also began to circulate that a landing had actually been attempted on the night of 7 September, leaving the Channel white with German dead.

North American papers such as the *New York Times* proved particularly receptive, happily reporting that drifting Nazi corpses were disrupting fishing in Sweden, with a miserly reward of 75 cents offered for each body recovered with its uniform intact.

Rumours of up to 80,000 dead stormtroopers undoubtedly boosted morale in Britain, and at the same time helped to maintain vigilance in the face of a grave and ongoing threat. As with the material transmitted by MI5 double-cross agents, however, the fiction of the bodies on the beach also required some limited foundation in fact. The arrival of a dead *Wehrmacht* anti-tank gunner at Littlestone-on-Sea was reported in *The Times*, while in late September British troops were detailed to collect ripe German corpses between Hythe and St Mary's Bay. One of those tasked with this macabre detail was Gunner William Robinson of 333 Coastal Artillery Battery, who helped retrieve a dozen bodies over a two-day period, then carted the remains to a field near New Romney.

'They had been in the water a considerable time,' Robinson recalled of this unpleasant fatigue. 'We were given twenty Woodbines, which we collected each day, and additional pay of two shillings – which we collected some time later.'

For Germans, so it seemed, Romney Marsh was a must to avoid. Besides the two Scandinavian V-men, Caroli and Schmidt, the roll-call of detainees at Camp 020 still included the hapless quartet of spies who had arrived on the Marsh by boat. None of the four could be used as XX assets, and all faced trial under the 1940 Act. As a general rule the Twenty Committee opposed execution, arguing that 'intelligence should have precedence over bloodletting', and that the 'human library' of captive spies at Latchmere House was always useful as a reference source. Nevertheless, it seems probable that the trial and inevitable execution of the Romney Marsh Four was sanctioned in full by MI5, *pour encourager les autres*. The loss of Waldberg and his team also increased the chances of the Abwehr directing future agents towards Snow and the London stelle.

The night Blitz was far less convenient. While the B1A office in St James's escaped largely unscathed, on 28 September the Luftwaffe attempted to spark a second Great Fire of London with tens of thousands of incendiaries, several of which landed on Wormwood Scrubs. The only human casualty was Jock Horsfall, MI5's virtuoso of the wheel, who fell through the glass roof of C Wing, almost breaking his neck. Serious though this was, Horsfall's injuries were as nothing compared to the damage inflicted on the precious Registry after the night-duty officer failed to locate the correct keys. 'Hosepipes had to be worked through the barred windows and doors and the mess was simply awful,' observed a clerk next day. 'The half-burnt files were soaking wet and there was a disgusting smell of burnt wetness.'

The result was an unmitigated disaster for the Security Service. Fire and water badly damaged the central card index as well as hundreds of files, not all of which had yet been copied to microfilm. This entirely avoidable calamity prompted a hasty move from prison to palace. Standing in two thousand acres of landscaped parklands near Woodstock, Blenheim Palace was the monumental ancestral seat of the dukes of Marlborough – and the birthplace of Winston Churchill. Privileged evacuees from Repton School were hurriedly evicted and the tenth duke confined to a single wing, leaving MI5 staff incongruously split between grand staterooms and draughty Nissen huts. For shell-shocked survivors of the Scrubs, however, the enforced relocation to rural Oxfordshire was a godsend. Bombing, ack-ack barrages and sleep deprivation soon became torments of the past, with staff even treated to edifying tours of the Palace by Anthony Blunt, an art historian recruited into MI5 by Guy Liddell – and a Soviet spy to boot.

For Agent Snow, too, the Blitz paid dividends. Following the arrival of a UXB in his garden at Marlborough Road, the devastating fire at the Scrubs served only to underline the need to move Owens – and his transmitter – to a safer haven. This turned out to be Homefields, a detached house on Spinney Hill in Addlestone, owned by a Major Whyte of Section B23, who was among those transferred to Blenheim. 'In view of the great difficulty in obtaining a suitable house it is submitted that the terms are favourable,' advised Tar on receipt of the bill. In addition to rent of four and a half guineas a week there was also the cost of the housekeeper's wages, and those of a gardener. 'This will amount to an additional two guineas a week, in return for which all the vegetables in the garden will be available for the occupants.'

No pigsties or prison cells for Hitler's chief spy in England. Yet again, the resilient Little Man had fallen firmly on his feet.

The evacuation of the London stelle into the leafy Surrey countryside also involved Lily Bade, baby Jean Louise, Maurice Burton and the pool of watchers from B6. Since Homefields was some distance from the nearest railway station, permission was obtained to spend £70 on a second car. With the war costing seven million pounds a day, and Abwehr cash running short, Robertson paused to undertake a searching review of Snow's finances. As B1A understood matters, Owens earned a basic salary of £250 a month from Hamburg, plus generous expenses. These excluded food, drink and clothing, but did include rent. In picking up the tab for Homefields, therefore, MI5 were subsidising not only absent Major Whyte but also Hitler's war of aggression against the British Isles.

'I explained to Snow that the other side ought to pay for all the expenses incurred on their account. These include McCarthy's salary, and all the mythical expenses they thought were being incurred. For example, journeys which are not taken because we already know the answer.'

After protracted negotiations, Owens agreed to hand over all monies received from Germany and request additional funds from Rantzau whenever B1A deemed it necessary. In return, the Abwehr master spy was permitted to keep his extravagant monthly salary, whereas MI5 would meet out-of-pocket expenses such as travel and Mac's trifling wage. 'This arrangement will suit us very well,' reasoned B1A. 'It relieves Snow of the money actually spent on running his organisation, and out of the sums notionally spent we ought to be able to build up a fund out of which we can pay all those expenses chargeable to the other side.'

For Nikolaus Ritter, Operation Lena had yet to turn a profit. At the end of the month three more Lena agents reached Britain by sea, landing by dinghy on a remote stretch of the Banffshire coast after flying from Norway by seaplane. Ritter had inherited the team following the sudden death of Hilmar Dierks, killed in a car smash four weeks earlier. Incredibly, this accident left one of the spies a widow, since glamorous Russian émigré Vera Erikson had married Dierks a short while before, despite being younger than him by twenty years.

Unperturbed, Erikson promptly embarked on an affair with her co-agent Karl Drücke, after rejecting the advances of a rival V-man who tried to impress her by chewing on a wine glass.

The lovers' mission to England was equally futile. Having lost their bicycles as they rowed ashore, Erikson and Drücke were detained within hours of landing. At Portgordon an alert stationmaster grew suspicious of their wet clothes and alerted the police after the pair purchased third-class rail tickets from a wallet stuffed with banknotes. A search of Drücke's luggage revealed a familiar inventory of incriminating equipment, including an Afu transmitter and codes, a Mauser pistol, a torch stamped 'Made in Bohemia' and a half-eaten German sausage. Both spies carried forged ID cards bearing serials transmitted by Snow (along with telltale number 7s crossed in the Continental style) and pink ration books based on the example supplied by

McCarthy. The third member of the party, Werner Walti, was arrested later that day at Waverley station in Edinburgh, reaching for his weapon as the police closed in but being quickly overpowered.

Unlike the Romney Marsh spies, Drücke and Walti were experienced espionage agents; both withstood harsh interrogation at Camp 020, and could not be turned. Declining to offer up full confessions, the two men claimed to be couriers, a fiction maintained even after Vera Erikson betrayed both of them. On trial for their lives at the Old Bailey nine months later, Drücke remained silent, while Walti swore that his mission involved nothing more significant than the delivery of a suitcase transmitter to Victoria station. Cross-examined by the Solicitor-General, Sir William Jowitt, Walti described his contact in London as a man in a grey pinstriped suit, with a scar on his forehead and a pidgin-English password: 'I am coming from Glasgow.'

Nikolaus Ritter can hardly have imagined that Sam Stewart or Alexander Myner were still viable V-men. Could it be that the 'friend' Walti expected to meet was in fact a short Welshman with brown boots, shifty eyes and nicotine-stained fingers, coming from Pontardawe?

10

The Executioners

Newly promoted to the rank of major, Nikolaus Ritter dispatched his third parachute agent to England on the night of 3 October 1940. On paper at least, Kurt Karl Goose was eminently qualified for Operation Lena: after three years spent in the United States as a geology student, his English-language skills had earned him a place in the Abwehr's highly secretive Brandenburg commando unit, who specialised in false flag operations behind enemy lines. Less impressively, as Goose dropped through the bomb doors of Gartenfeld's Heinkel-111 he lost control of his bowels, and therefore landed in Northamptonshire in a state of some disarray.

Seeking shelter from a downpour in an agricultural shed, the elite special-forces commando was accused of stealing eggs by a market gardener and marched off at the point of a pitchfork. By nightfall Goose was doing bird in a cell at Wellingborough police station and admitted to being a parachute agent. The following day the first Brandenburg commando to fall into British hands was driven to Camp 020.

But for inclement British weather things might have turned out differently. Despite the fact that Goose was dropped in the same area as Gösta Caroli, MI5 received no advance warning, and his papers had been forged with a degree of care. True, these looked far too new, but his ID card was not based on serials provided by Snow and was clean of telltale Continental figures. In the debit column, Goose had retained his German army pay book and a Luftwaffe uniform in the belief that, if captured, he could expect to be treated as an ordinary prisoner of war. This hope was forlorn, since trial by court martial only entitled him to be shot instead of hanged.

The new arrival readily agreed to work as a double-cross agent, using the droll codename GANDER. 'Goose is a poor fish who never wanted to be a spy,' observed Liddell, bemused. 'He joined his regiment, and when a sergeant asked who spoke English he rather foolishly put up his hand.'

Unaccountably, Gander had been issued with a one-way transmitter and was therefore unable to receive any incoming messages. Whether or not this was some inscrutable Abwehr ploy, Kurt Goose was allowed to fulfil his original mission under the supervision of Ronnie Reed, (mis)reporting on weather and morale in the Midlands for a period of several weeks. The case was closed down in November, Goose having 'blotted his untidy copybook' by attempting to bribe one of the guards at Latchmere House into posting a letter to the German embassy in Dublin.

A case for his prosecution under the Treachery Act was drawn up but not pursued. Gander escaped death by the skin of his teeth, yet just three days after his arrival at Camp 020 Robertson and B Division once again found themselves battling to prevent the conspicuous execution of captive Nazi agents. 'Lord Swinton came down today and cross-examined us about the spy cases,' complained Liddell. 'The Prime Minister has evidently been asking why we had not shot some of them.'

A personal appointee of Churchill, Ernest Swinton headed the Security Executive and was hell-bent on reforming MI5. Imperious and intolerant, he had even recruited a business-efficiency expert, all of which smacked of Mussolini and trains running on time. 'I am still in ignorance of what Swinton's position is,' carped Liddell, polishing his gloves and preparing for battle. 'All we know is that he appears to think he is head of MI5, and to some extent even of SIS. He quoted some minute and said that in future nobody was to be offered his life without his authority. I told him that information was really by far the most important matter to be considered.'

Ironically, as MI5 argued to save lives, Gösta Caroli attempted to take his own. Like the troublesome Snow menage, the Swede codenamed Summer had also been evacuated from Blitz-torn London, taking up residence at The Old Parsonage in Hinxton, an isolated village a dozen miles south of Cambridge. Supremely secluded, the safehouse offered plenty of space for aerials and minders, to whom Caroli began speaking too freely about his pre-war espionage career. 'Inevitably Summer found his way back to Camp 020,' wrote Tin-Eye Stephens, who set about fresh interrogation. 'He remained at heart a Nazi, and made an attempt at suicide by cutting the arteries in his wrists with a razor blade. He was found in his cell in a pool of blood, but prompt action saved his life.'

On recovering, Caroli admitted that he had spied in the Midlands from October 1938 onwards, living in Handsworth while posing as a journalist and sending back regular reports on utilities, harbours and factories. He had left England only in December 1939; an attempt to return at the beginning of 1940 came to grief when his transport was torpedoed in the North Sea. That Caroli had not been entirely frank during his initial questioning was a cause for concern, but after several sessions with the in-house psychiatrist at 020, Dr Harold Dearden, he was allowed to return to the 'Home for Incurables' at Hinxton.

John Masterman wrote of a lesson hard learned. 'A double-agent is a tricky customer and needs the most careful supervision. His every mood has to be watched, and his every reaction studied. Only unremitting care and some psychological finesse could coax a converted parachutist along safe lines and into a better way of thinking.'

Since Caroli was plainly unstable, Robertson decided to employ a stand-in to compile Summer's field reports. His choice was none other than Walter Dicketts, the veteran confidence trickster who had attempted to sell Snow a phoney patent for squeezable mustard six months earlier, only to stumble headlong into a nest of counterfeit Nazi spies.

During the intervening period Dicketts had tried and failed to rejoin the air intelligence branch, lurching always from one financial crisis to another. 'So long as he is not given large sums of money to play about with he should be perfectly satisfactory,' Robertson had assured MI6, to no avail. The hapless crook then suffered a serious accident in the blackout, collecting three broken ribs and a dislocated thumb. By the beginning of October, however, Dicketts was sufficiently recovered to begin XX work for B1A. 'The news you gave me yesterday is the best I have had for a very long time,' he wrote to Tar from a seedy bedsit in Maida Vale. 'I am anxious to start work and very pleased to hear that you may be able to arrange an advance of £50. The money is a godsend as I am again really at desperation point. I have fourteen pawn tickets and nothing left to pawn.'

Awarded the curious cryptonym CELERY, on a salary of £10 per week, Dick moved into the Home for Incurables at Hinxton, stepping gladly into Caroli's mustard-coloured shoes. His first spoof espionage tour, in November, visited Nottingham and Grantham, where he infiltrated the British Manufacturing & Research Company ('I could very easily have destroyed part of the factory if I had had two Mills bombs in my pocket') and surveilled various aerodromes. A week later he was in Birmingham, poking around the Webley small-arms factory, followed by a trip to Bristol, where he found morale dangerously low after heavy bombing.

'There is more raid panic in Bristol than in any other of the large manufacturing towns I have visited,' Dicketts concluded. 'I made a comprehensive tour of the aircraft factory, and as I had a badge on and was walking briskly without hat or coat, I was not questioned.' For the unreformed confidence trickster, adept in the dark art of false identities, the Celery role was a cakewalk.

At the Addlestone Home for Incurables, Agent Snow was also observed to be 'feeling his oats' once more after a long period of quiescence, anxious to return to active double-cross duty. The increasing importance of Tate (Schmidt) and Summer (Caroli) further threatened his tenure as Hitler's chief spy in England, and might yet exhaust his usefulness to Robertson and MI5. This in turn raised further alarming possibilities, for meddlesome Lord Swinton was now insistent that even redundant spies should be considered for prosecution, regardless of any past services rendered.

Fortunately for Owens, Ritter kept Colonel Johnny in play by pressing for a treff in Lisbon or Canada. For MI5 this latest proposal raised a multitude of ticklish concerns. 'Snow must be watched very carefully,' advised Liddell. 'The question of putting a microphone into his new house is being considered.'

Concerns were also raised that Owens' wireless operator, Maurice Burton, was in danger of going native in the wilds of Surrey. 'Snow and Burton are always going out to the local pub drinking,' noted one visitor to Homefields. 'Burton is running round with a girl, who he says comes from Winchester, and who he has known for a very long time. The reason for this is apparently to create a good impression locally and not arouse suspicion.'

Unlike boozy ex-dope smuggler Sam McCarthy. While engaged in a spoof spy tour of the Midlands the volatile Canadian aroused the suspicions of the owner of a Grantham hotel, who reported his guest to the police. Displaying commendable initiative, an inspector named Curry listened in on his telephone calls, then posed as a Fifth Column agent to entrap the mysterious stranger. After responding favourably to Curry's overtures, McCarthy found himself lifted as a German spy, a victim of verisimilitude run wild.

This latest manifestation of 'excessive zeal' saw Agent Biscuit ordered to lie low by MI5. 'This message was sent to the other side,' scoffed Liddell. 'They replied asking where Lielow was.'

Surprisingly, the previously dormant Welsh Ring now stirred to pull off a spectacular coup. In September Agent G.W., the former police inspector Gwilym Williams, received a letter from a Spanish journalist named Piernavieja del Pozo, who requested a meeting in London. Owens buzzed Wohldorf to check his credentials and learned that del Pozo was an emissary from Witzke, the hard-drinking 'Commander' with whom Snow and G.W. had mixed bathtub explosives in Antwerp a year earlier. A rendezvous was duly arranged for 10 October near the Spanish Embassy in Belgrave Square.

Less a treff, more an *encuentro*.

Del Pozo, it transpired, was a fascist Falangist with film-star good looks, installed in a plush suite at the Athenaeum on Piccadilly and writing up 'unbiased' reports on an island under siege for the Spanish press. Astonishingly, what was in effect an Abwehr stunt had been sponsored by the British ambassador in Madrid, Sir Samuel Hoare, with the ludicrous result that an enemy sympathiser was invited to visit airfields, dockyards and the headquarters of 7 Corps. At his meeting with Williams, the dilettante spy nicknamed POGO by MI5 handed over a fresh questionnaire together with a tin of talcum powder containing £3,900. This enormous sum, the equivalent of £175,000 today, was intended for A.3504, Colonel Johnny.

Humdinger.

G.W, however, had other ideas. 'Williams is very incensed at having the money taken away from him and threatened to resign,' noted Liddell. 'Marriott managed to calm him down. He is a rather unpleasant type who is obviously on the make.'

As the case developed Williams was encouraged to dispatch doctored reports via the Spanish diplomatic bag, though del Pozo soon shot his own fox by giving an indiscreet interview to the *Daily Express*. 'I am pro-German and think Hitler will win this war,' Pogo told their reporter, wearing pyjamas at noon and somewhat refreshed. 'You may be fighting against dictatorship, but you will have to adopt dictator's methods if you want to win.'

Disastrously, the *Express* article confirmed that del Pozo was sending back secret reports through official channels. After the talkative Señor asked to visit 'troops in the trenches at Dover' and take part in a Bomber Command raid on Berlin, Guy Liddell devised a cunning plan. 'Pogo's bomber would return to some Home for Incurables, where he would be kept for the remainder of the war. A notice would appear in the papers to the effect that three of our bombers did not return. In this way we should not endanger the position of Snow or G.W.'

The ambitious plan fell through after del Pozo was prevailed upon to moderate his tone. 'I have seen Britain stage a come-back which we in Spain did not expect,' he explained in a subsequent – doctored – piece for the *Express*, having experienced a Damascene moment (or been flipped) in his rooms at the Athenaeum. 'She has the means and the determination to wage a long war and to fight to the end for victory.'

Pogo had bounced, Rolph had vanished and McCarthy sent into exile in Lielow. A controlled request from Agent Snow to treff in Northern Ireland was politely rejected by Ritter, who no doubt recognised another bold attempt by MI5 to engineer a reverse Venlo and add the elusive Doctor Rantzau to the living library at Camp 020. The conspicuous failure of Operation Lena was equally disconcerting and served to aggravate doubts sown first by the abortive trawler treff in May, then by Owens' subsequent no-show in Lisbon in July. Moreover, much of the wireless dope feeding back was blatant propaganda.

What on earth was going on in Perfidious Albion?

In an effort to discover the truth, on the night of 2 November Gartenfeld dropped another parachute agent into England. Masquerading as a Dutchman named Jan Willem Ter Braak, the latest V-man touched down near Haversham in Buckinghamshire, just a few miles north of the top-secret code-breaking station at Bletchley Park. While his real name, Engelbertus Fukken, suggested a predisposition to misfortune, there were no sprained ankles, no prowling Home Guards and no imprudent forays into public houses. Ter Braak simply abandoned his parachute in a field and made his way unobtrusively to Cambridge. There he obtained lodgings at 58 St Barnabas Road, conveniently close to the railway station, and explained to his landlords, a couple named Sennitt, that he was a scientist who had fled to Britain after the German invasion of Holland.

This story was entirely plausible, and his false identity papers passed unremarked. These, too, were based on serials transmitted by Snow in August, marking Ter Braak as a Lena agent dispatched from Stelle X. Why then did Nikolaus Ritter decide to send another V-man to Cambridge when Gösta Caroli was already in position, seven miles south of the city in sleepy Hinxton? In all likelihood, Ter Braak's mission included checking up on the 'Swedish friend' with an injured ankle, just as the tall, bespectacled stranger had called on Snow at Norbiton Avenue in October 1939.

Certainly Ter Braak was of a higher calibre than previous Lena agents. Despite flawed papers the fake Dutch scientist was able to rent an office on Rose Crescent, plumb in the centre of the city, where he installed his suitcase transmitter. Stranger still, Ter Braak was living within fifty yards of MI5's RSLO in Cambridge, Major Richard Dixon.

Wulf Schmidt's situation was even more intimate. During his

first few weeks as a XX agent Tate remained under lock and key at Camp 020, with his Afu set housed in a nearby equestrian centre. Now Wohldorf learned that Leonhardt had found lodgings in Barnet, and established contact with Caroli. Both statements were true – up to a point. The meeting with Caroli took the form of an anguished confrontation at 020, while his digs were an MI5 safehouse called Round Bush House near Radlett. Indeed, so pleasant were his new surroundings in Hertfordshire, and free from German bombs, that Schmidt soon found himself joined by Tar Robertson and his wife Joan, together with their young daughter Belinda and a nanny. Soon Schmidt was helping with household chores, and honed his skills as a photographer by taking family snaps. The only catch was his colourful language, which favoured expletives such as *scheisse*, and *Götz von Berlichingen*, an oath derived from Goethe meaning 'kiss my arse'.

For the Romney Marsh Four life was rather less comfortable. At the end of November Waldberg, Meier, Pons and Kieboom filed into the dock at the Old Bailey, each charged with assisting the enemy under the Treachery Act. Although the four spies faced trial by jury the hearing was held in camera, with Court Number One securely locked and guarded, its windows covered over with sheets of brown paper. So keen were the Security Executive to obtain convictions that the case was presented in person by the Solicitor General, Sir William Jowitt. 'They were not difficult cases to prosecute,' Jowitt wrote. 'The only possible defence the accused could put forward was that they had been forced by the Germans to undertake espionage, and were resolved to give themselves up directly they landed. This was the line of defence in fact adopted.'

Waldberg, their leader, did not trouble to give evidence on his own behalf, having sealed his fate by using his transmitter. Indeed none of the four were truly innocent. Rather than surrender on arriving in Lydd, Meier had dithered in shops and pubs, and Kieboom had flushed his code down a lavatory. Pons laid claim to having deliberately dropped his transmitter in a waterlogged ditch, but a corporal from the Somerset Light Infantry testified that the set had been found in the corner of a field, hidden by long grass, in perfect working order.

The trial lasted a week, after which the jury returned guilty verdicts on Kieboom, Waldberg and Meier. Surprisingly, Pons was acquitted. 'It was a merciful if not entirely logical view,' admitted Jowitt. 'I do not think that the complete truth was ever revealed to us.'

MI5 also found the verdict contrary. If Kieboom had in fact assisted B1A by sending a controlled message from Camp 020, the jury heard nothing of it. The Eurasian spy subsequently complained of being tricked, and alone among the four lodged an appeal. Meanwhile Pierrepoint, the public hangman, was warned to expect trade the following month.

It was indeed a murky business. As if in retaliation, at the end of the month the Luftwaffe deposited a parachute mine on the roof of Latchmere House, causing extensive damage and killing an internee. 'Evacuation was advised,' wrote Tin-Eye Stephens, 'but we carried on just the same. Interrogations took place in the mortuary, and precedence in the bath was granted only to prisoners due for trial at the Bailey.'

Charles van den Kieboom's hopes of reprieve were forlorn. Under close interrogation at 020, Karl Drücke fingered the distinctive Eurasian as a former cashier at the Hotel Victoria, known to be a centre of Abwehr activity in Amsterdam. This contradicted claims by Kieboom to have been unemployed in July, after losing his job at the YMCA. In the light of this damning disclosure the spy who had landed below Dymchurch Redoubt with binoculars and tennis shoes draped around his neck could do little but hope for a miracle.

Fifteen miles west of Ham Common, at Homefields, Agent Snow's transmitter once again began delivering results. Though the arrival of Jan Willem Ter Braak had passed unnoticed, at the end of November Wohldorf warned Owens to expect another batch of spies and asked for three extra ID serials, including one suitable for an unmarried woman. These were followed by yet another urgent demand, this time requesting details for a male living in London at an unverifiable address. After due consideration, Snow (or rather B1A) obliged Wohldorf with James Rymer, identity number ARAJ 301-29, residing at 33 Abbotsford Gardens.

The dope was plausibly specific. However, James Rymer was the long-dead author of countless Victorian penny dreadfuls, including *The First False Step*, and the house he called home, an unremarkable semi in Woodford Green, had already suffered damage in an air raid. Any V-man using this telltale name and address would find his own cover blown sky high.

Inconveniently, Ritter continued to press to meet Owens in Lisbon, where fierce rivalries had flared up between MI5 and its overseas counterpart, MI6. The rapid expansion of the double-cross system required an unprecedented degree of cooperation between the two warring agencies, yet at the same time the potential for territorial friction was also increased, not least because MI6 set about recruiting their own double agents in Spain, Portugal and Turkey. The first of these was a libidinous Yugoslav playboy named Duško Popov, codenamed TRICYCLE on account of his penchant for three-in-a-bed sex. Popov was soon followed by Juan Pujol Garcia, who as GARBO would go on to become the most successful XX agent run by B1A. Unhelpfully, SIS Section V fought long and hard to keep these exotic assets for themselves, even going so far as to withhold vital intelligence from the all-powerful Twenty Committee.

For Tar Robertson there was also competition from within MI5, after a new Wireless (W) Branch threatened to poach work – and even agents – from B1A. After one especially savage spat with its director, an incomer from the BBC named Malcolm Frost, Tar found himself threatened with exile to Jan Mayen Island, a barren volcanic outcrop off the coast of Greenland. Liddell lodged a complaint with their shared nemesis, Lord Swinton. 'I said that I did not see how there could be any peace while Frost remained. He was obviously an intriguer first and foremost. This cannot continue, and Robertson and the double-cross business must come back where they belong.'

Against this background, the complexities of sending rogue Agent Snow on a mission to Lisbon were a headache that B1A would not suffer gladly. With McCarthy still exiled to Lielow, and Rolph still dead, Tar was obliged once again to cast around for a suitable sidekick – one with sufficient experience to undertake such a delicate assignment, yet also robust enough to resist being corrupted by Owens. Ironically, the only viable candidate was Walter Dicketts, the amiable fraudster whose work with Gösta Caroli at Hinxton had been put on hold following the Swede's messy suicide attempt at 020.

In a clumsy stab at serendipity Owens ran into Dicketts at his local pub in Addlestone, a chance reunion carefully choreographed by B1A. 'Dick knew a hell of a lot more than I thought he knew,' the Little Man rued later. 'In the first place he was very much against Major Robertson and leaning towards the German organisation. He came down to The Otter and showed me letters from Robbie and said he'd had a rotten deal right from the beginning. Registered letters with a pound here, two pounds there. He said, "How can I and my wife live on this dirty deal?"'

In truth both men were playing one other, just as they had over drinks in The Marlborough eight months earlier. 'Dicketts says that Snow is very artful,' wrote Robertson, 'and keeps laying traps to try and find out why Dick has been put in touch with him.'

By December relations had improved sufficiently for Dicketts to relocate from Hinxton to Homefields, joined soon after by glamorous chorus girl Kay. Her presence provided company for Lily, and welcome help with the baby, Jean Louise. 'Celery is back in the bosom of the family,' Tar remarked wryly. 'He is to take his lead from Snow. If Snow becomes pro-German he is also to become pro-German. And if by any chance the opportunity presents itself for Dicketts to go into Germany then it should be taken.'

For all concerned, the prospect of sending Agent Celery to Hamburg or Berlin stirred a strange sensation of déjà vu. Sam McCarthy had accepted the same hazardous assignment in May, only to be deterred by Snow's antics on the train journey to Grimsby and the early arrival of Ritter's seaplane off the Dogger Bank. So far as Robertson was concerned, Owens was no more trustworthy now than when he had connived with Rolph to sell a list of Intelligence People to the other side, and thrown Nazi salutes in a Cleethorpes hotel. Then again, Doctor Rantzau had recently paid over £3,900 to the London stelle via Pogo, the dilettante Spaniard. If Snow failed to show in Iberia, his threadbare network seemed likely to fall apart entirely.

Upping the ante still further, it was decided that Dicketts would pose as Jack Brown, a disgraced Royal Air Force officer cashiered for dishonesty, with financial worries and an axe to grind. On Monday, 9 December, Robertson summoned Dick to London for a meeting at White's, the private members' club used as an unofficial office by MI5. Neither man's journey was easy, for the previous night the capital had suffered its worst raid for several weeks, during which German bombers dropped 100,000 incendiaries and 400 tons of high explosive over twelve hours, igniting ten large fire areas. Two hundred and fifty civilians died, with more than 600 seriously injured. For war-weary Londoners, the fact that British and Commonwealth forces were drubbing the Italians in North Africa came as small consolation.

At White's Dicketts ordered his customary gin fizz. No less predictably, Agent Celery claimed to be in low water and required a sub of £20, along with a docket for six gallons of petrol. The atmosphere at Addlestone was much improved, so he said, although Dick expressed concern that Snow seemed to know 'a tremendous lot' about his colourful past.

'That's probably Gagen,' guessed Tar. 'The Special Branch inspector. They keep in touch, apparently.'

'What about Burton?'

'He's perfectly all right, so far as I know.'

'Because it's odd. Burton says he doesn't like Owens, but they're thick as thieves – always sloping off to the pub together and having private conversations. Kay doesn't like him much, either. She says he's fast.'

'What about Lily?'

'Oh, Lil can look after herself well enough. The Little Man's drinking worries her though. I tell you, the bottles disappear like magic. Yesterday I saw him fill a tumbler of Scotch at half past seven in the morning. When he's not tight, he's bone idle.'

'And pro-German?'

'He's still playing both ends against the middle. And I swear he's in contact with the other side.'

'How so?'

Dicketts leaned forward in his chair. 'Yesterday afternoon he warned me about the big raid on London. He was desperate to get hold of his son.'

Tar nodded. Snow Junior had recently been conscripted into the Auxiliary Fire Service and was based at Chertsey. The Blitz had already cost the lives of more than a hundred London fire-fighters. His father, meanwhile, remained preternaturally terrified of air raids.

'What time was this?'

'Oh, several hours before the sirens went. I'm telling you, Snowy has a line of communication we know nothing about.'

Robertson considered this for a moment. Rolph was dead, the Sackville Street office closed and Owens had been rusticated to the Surrey countryside. If Agent Snow had managed to suborn Burton, or still had access to a secret transmitter, it meant that much of the double-cross system was insecure, and perhaps even blown. The implications were horrendous beyond words.

'This trip to Portugal,' ventured Dicketts. 'Just how important is it?'

'Very,' confessed Tar.

'If I do get into Germany, and I don't come back, I need to know that my boy will be properly looked after. Kay as well.'

'Agreed.'

'Because we're not married . . . '

'I know.'

Dick cleared his throat. 'I had in mind three pounds, ten shillings a week for life. That, or a lump sum.'

'How big a lump?'

'Say, six thousand pounds?'

A single cruiser tank cost far more. Robertson already knew that Jasper Harker, the Director-General of MI5, was unlikely to authorise even half this amount. 'I'll see what I can do,' he hedged. 'You'll be working overseas, so it may be that MI6 can contribute.'

'I must be in the wrong game,' snorted Dicketts. 'Snow reckons to buy Lily a fur coat for Christmas. Says it'll cost £1,500.'

Half a tin of talcum powder, in fact.

Just dandy.

For three of the Romney Marsh Four life seemed rather more cheap. At Pentonville prison the following morning José Waldberg and Carl Meier were each pinioned in the condemned cell, then bustled into the green-painted execution chamber and dropped by an inexperienced hangman named Stanley Cross. It is not known whether the two V-men died side by side, the preferred procedure for double executions, although an official report would call into question Cross's fitness for the job. Drop lengths, it seemed, were the problem: too short, and the prisoner strangled slowly; too long, and the neck was likely to be severed. Charles van den Kieboom followed his colleagues to the scaffold a week later, having withdrawn his appeal. Once again the job did not run smoothly, and despite having practised on three worthless spies Stanley Cross was never again employed as a principal executioner.

'Some had to perish,' offered Masterman coolly. 'Both to satisfy the public that the security of the country was being maintained, and also to convince the Germans that the others were working properly and were not under control. It would have taxed even German credulity if all their agents had apparently overcome the hazards of landing.'

Following Churchillian diktat the executions were afforded maximum publicity. Black-bordered death notices were prominently displayed on the prison gate, and photographs of the suitcase transmitting sets distributed to national newspapers as an aid to recognition. Wrote *The Times*: 'In official quarters it is suggested that their capture emphasises still more the need for the public to exercise the greatest care when talking among strangers.'

Not everyone took note. In Cambridge, the missing parachute agent Jan Willem Ter Braak failed to register with the police as an alien and, despite being reported to the authorities by his landlady, the lead was not followed up. Not long afterwards an alert official at the local Food Office identified Ter Braak's pink ration book as a forgery, and discovered that the serials on his identity card belonged to a man named Burton, who lived a hundred miles away at Homefields, Addlestone, Surrey. Asked to provide further information, Ter Braak hurriedly quit his lodgings in St Barnabas Road and moved across town.

Complacent local police reassured Mrs Sennitt that her missing tenant would register in his own good time. Meanwhile the marshalling yards in Cambridge suffered several timely raids, causing locals to remark that the Luftwaffe seemed oddly well informed.

In Addlestone, too, paranoia ran riot. Concerned about the reception he might receive from the Abwehr in Lisbon, Owens alleged that half the village knew Homefields was chock-full of Nazis. 'The rumour went round we were all German spies. One of the code papers got picked up and taken to the police.' His reputation was even less savoury in war-torn Stratford, where Lily's mother Louisa Virgiels, as well as several members of the Ferrett family, still lived. 'Dicketts accompanied Snow on a visit to his mother-in-law,' noted Tar, 'and was not allowed out of his sight. Snow also gave Dick the impression that he is afraid of being seen out in that locality.'

Owens was right to be afraid of a lynch mob. By now MI5 had finalised plans for the evacuation of less reliable XX agents to North Wales in the event of a German invasion, still regarded as a clear and present danger. Under Plan Hegira, Arthur Owens, Wulf Schmidt and a half-dozen others would be dispersed to various hotels around Llandudno, a complex operation jokingly referred to as Mr Mills' Circus. The local RSLO even took to using appropriate animal metaphors in correspondence with B1A: 'I have now completed arrangements for the accommodation of the animals, the young and their keepers,' Captain Finney wrote gaily. 'It has been impossible to arrange cheaper accommodation in boarding houses, as naturally the proprietors of these want definite dates.'

Some double-cross agents, like Sam McCarthy and Gwilym Williams, were considered sufficiently trustworthy to make their own way to safety. Those who were not – chiefly Owens and Schmidt, but also Lily Bade and Snow Junior – would be arrested and driven to Wales under armed escort. Twelve sets of handcuffs were borrowed from Scotland Yard, together with half a dozen Webley .455 revolvers and 54 rounds of soft-nosed ammunition – for in the last resort the circus animals would be shot.

'If there is danger of any of the more dangerous cases falling into enemy hands they will be liquidated forcibly,' Robertson told Tin-Eye Stephens. 'As Snow is a great believer in German efficiency it is highly probable that he would attempt to join the Germans immediately, and could blow our whole show.'

Although necessary, this brutal approach was tempered with mercy. On Christmas Eve, Wulf Schmidt was driven from Round Bush House to the Old Parsonage at Hinxton, where he and Gösta Caroli were permitted to enjoy the festive holiday together, albeit under heavy armed guard. Despite having slashed his wrists ten weeks earlier, the Swede seemed to have shaken off the 'black mood of despair' diagnosed at Camp 020 and been coaxed into 'a better way of thinking' by the 'unremitting care and psychological finesse' applied in the light of his suicide attempt.

Then, with the season of goodwill over and gone, Caroli attempted to throttle his guard and took to his heels.

11

Double Trouble

Shortly after lunch on 13 January 1941, Gösta Caroli was surprised but pleased to find himself under the supervision of a single military guard. 'I was sitting playing a card game when Summer suddenly attacked me,' Sergeant Paulton explained afterwards. 'He sprang from behind with a piece of rope about 20 inches long and tried to garrotte me. I naturally struggled, and succeeded in throwing myself sideways.' The two men fell on the floor in front of the fireplace. 'Still holding the rope like a pair of reins, Caroli got his knee into the small of my back and told me not to struggle.'

Exhausted by the struggle, Paulton blacked out momentarily, enabling the desperate Swede to tie his hands. 'He expressed regret for his treatment of me, and said that I would only have to wait to six o'clock. He said that he had to do it. He knew it was a hanging job, but he could not go on. I told him I could not lie tied on the floor all that time, and asked him to put me on the Chesterfield. Then I asked him to put a pillow under my head – this he did.'

It was fortunate indeed that Tar Robertson had chosen Round Bush House over The Old Parsonage as his family home. Running through Paulton's pockets, Caroli located the keys to the safe in the study, from which he removed his ID papers, two quartz transmitter crystals and £5 in petty cash. A wider sweep of the house netted maps, matches, a torch and a child's magnetic compass, as well as a chunk of cold beef from the larder, along with tins of sardines, pilchards and pears. By now twenty minutes had elapsed. Packing his escape kit into a suitcase, Caroli left the house through the kitchen, taking care to close the shutters and doors behind him.

Paulton lay still, then wriggled off the sofa and stood upright. 'In the half-light I spotted my penknife on the table, and groping behind my back I succeeded in picking it up and set to work.' After cutting himself free, Paulton crept into the study and called Major Dixon, the RSLO in Cambridge.

Dixon told Paulton to alert the London office. Even as they spoke the still-shaken minder was alarmed to see Caroli pass by the window, pushing a Douglas motorcycle and struggling to carry a collapsible canvas canoe. The machine belonged to another guard (whose unauthorised absence had triggered Summer's bid for freedom) and was stored in an outbuilding. Paulton made a note of the registration number, then watched as Caroli coaxed the engine into life, wobbled slowly down the drive and disappeared in the direction of Newmarket.

It was hardly the Great Escape. Nonetheless, if V-man Nilberg managed to reach the coast, and paddle back to Holland, the entire double-cross system would sink like a stone. Luckily Caroli was no T. E. Lawrence, and after repeatedly toppling off the unfamiliar machine he decided to surrender to a cordon of police at Newmarket station. By nightfall the recidivist Swede was back behind bars at Camp 020. 'Clearly Summer can never be allowed to use his transmitter again,' Liddell noted with genuine regret. 'We have all come to the conclusion that somehow or other he must be eliminated. This is not, however, an easy matter.'

Via Snow's transmitter, Ritter learned only that their mutual 'Swedish friend' had sent a letter to McCarthy, warning that he was being watched by the police and meant to hide by enlisting on a merchant vessel. In the interests of verisimilitude Caroli's wireless set was left in the cloakroom at Cambridge station, then offered to Sam Stewart. After Wohldorf confirmed to Snow that the shady shipping agent was still 'believed to be all right', Stewart found himself interned for the duration under Regulation 18B.

Gösta Caroli spent the rest of the war at 020R, a secure internment camp near Huntercombe, finding a measure of peace by tending the kitchen garden. 'Summer remained at heart a Nazi,' reflected Tin-Eye Stephens. 'Although now disciplined and not otherwise troublesome, his escape mania was a constant menace. He was the only prisoner at either camp who ever attempted to cut his way out through the formidable apron of wire surrounding buildings and compounds.'

Despite Summer's sudden end, the double-cross system burst suddenly into bloom. That same month a British-born agent named George Kilburg (aka DRAGONFLY) returned from Lisbon with a sophisticated wireless hidden in a gramophone player, while in New York the fun-loving Yugoslav playboy Tricycle set about bilking the Abwehr for £20,000, a scam dubbed Plan Midas. The Twenty Committee also approved Plan 1, a scheme to fool the Germans into bombing a dummy munitions dump. Wulf Schmidt buzzed map coordinates to Wohldorf, after which Ritter recommended his loyal friend for an Iron Cross. The undeserved medal was eventually delivered to his family in Germany, though the Luftwaffe never troubled to bomb the imaginary target.

Indeed, Doctor Rantzau's own career now assumed a downward trajectory. The deaths and disappearances of so many Lena agents raised concerns at Stelle X, causing rival officers to call loudly for his scalp. At the same time attention shifted from Europe to North Africa, where British and Commonwealth troops had routed the Italians and swept up 130,000 prisoners in just eight exhilarating weeks. Gravely humiliated, Mussolini begged help from Hitler. The result was the Afrika Korps, a new army for a new theatre of war, capably commanded by Erwin Rommel, soon to pass into legend as the Desert Fox.

On 20 January Ritter received orders to proceed to Tripoli, tasked with forming a special *Sonderkommando* to insert agents behind Allied lines in Libya and Egypt. Climate aside, the job looked a lot like a punishment posting, opposite yet equivalent to Robertson's threatened exile to the sub-Arctic scrub of Jan Mayen Island. Before leaving Hamburg, however, the departing master spy found himself locked in a puzzling double-cross duel with Tar Robertson over airborne interception technology.

On the morning of 23 January Wohldorf alerted Owens that a 'friend' in England had acquired valuable intelligence on infrared. This experimental technology promised to help night fighters find their quarry in the dark, albeit dimly, since research on both sides tended to suggest that airborne interception (AI) radar would do the job far more effectively. In Blitz-torn Britain, operational trials with AI were concealed behind fibs and sibs that RAF pilots ate nothing but carrots, thereby ingesting large quantities of vitamin A and cultivating acute night vision. Soon gullible civilians seized on the idea, hoping to avoid bumps and bruises in the blackout.

This disquieting signal appeared to confirm earlier claims by Owens that Doctor Rantzau had a mole inside the Air Ministry. 'Snow is rather inclined to put the thing on a high plane and meet this man himself,' mused Guy Liddell. 'My inclination is to bump him off. Eventually we decided to suggest that within the next twenty-four hours at a given time the unknown informant should drop his information through a letterbox.'

The letter box chosen was at 14 Craven Hill, a property in Bayswater leased by MI5 and occupied by Sam McCarthy. On the same afternoon that the message was received, Tar Robertson passed several hours with Owens and Dicketts at White's. 'I went to great pains to impress on Snow that information about the infrared process was of vital importance to this country, and must on no account be disclosed to the enemy.'

For once Owens did as he was told. *'Informed infrared stunt of vital importance and great hope here,'* he buzzed Wohldorf next evening. *'If you trust your friend and he is safe, suggest he put material through letterbox at specified time when I can arrange to receive it. Reply in time for material to be taken to Manchester, 10.15 train.'*

A team of B6 watchers descended on Bayswater to stake out Mac's letter box, and at the appointed time a cine-camera operator trained a telephoto lens on the door of Number 14. A floorwalker from Whiteley's department store on Queensway aroused suspicion, but ultimately there was no delivery of dope, no secret documents and no hurried trip north to microdot photographer Charles Eschborn.

Nothing but Zeppelin shells, in fact. Without the benefit of an all-seeing infrared beam it was impossible to make out who was spoofing who.

Besides, there were bigger stunts to consider. During the closing phase of the Battle of Britain an eminent German geopolitical theorist named Albrecht Haushofer had posted a letter from Lisbon to Scotland's premier peer, the Duke of Hamilton, a firm friend since the Berlin Olympics in 1936. An enthusiastic supporter of the pre-war Anglo-German Fellowship, Hamilton was now a Wing Commander in Fighter Command, and as a sitting member of the House of Lords was thought by Haushofer to wield considerable political influence. His letter dealt chiefly with family matters, but concluded with a guarded invitation to meet 'somewhere on the outskirts of Europe' for a one-to-one talk.

'Archie Boyle is prepared to send Hamilton on some mission to Lisbon,' confided Liddell to his diary on 11 January. 'The whole case looks rather like a peace offer of some sort.'

Another Last Appeal to Reason, in fact. British intelligence did not yet know it, but Haushofer was acting on behalf of Hitler's deputy, Rudolf Hess, who had also met Hamilton at the Berlin games and shared his passion for aviation. After sitting on the note for several months MI6 summoned the blue-blooded flyer to London for a meeting, which Tar Robertson also attended. Without consulting Lord Swinton, let alone the Prime Minister, the Twenty Committee subsequently invited Hamilton to treff with his old friend Haushofer in Lisbon. Preferring Spitfire sorties to cloak-and-dagger work, the Duke replied that he would do so only if ordered.

For the moment, Robertson and MI5 would have to remain content with sending a fake RAF officer to Portugal: disgraced desk pilot Jack Brown, aka Walter Dicketts, aka Agent Celery.

In stark contrast to Hamilton, Double Agent Dick was keen as mustard to begin his Iberian mission, having negotiated a handsome fee of £200, payable up front. On receiving the money from Robertson, the personable fraudster promised to place it on deposit until his mission was successfully concluded. 'This,' Tar noted drily, 'seems too good to believe.'

As Dicketts prepared to leave the country, Agent Snow added a measure of XXX intrigue to an already complicated double-cross scenario. Besides Owens and Lily, and Dick and Kay, the Snow ménage at Homefields now included Ronnie Reed, the former BBC engineer now being groomed as a B1A case officer but left temporarily idle by the sudden end of Summer. Owens, resentful at yet another intrusion by MI5, muttered darkly in turn that Reed was grooming Kay for 'mucky business' while Dick was away.

'Dicketts is convinced that Owens is mad,' Tar sighed wearily. 'He also confirmed the impression that Snow is double-crossing us, and has people everywhere. Possibly even in this department.'

Certainly Owens was insistent that all dope and samples should be 'especially good' in advance of the Lisbon treff, and not merely ersatz chicken feed. Frustratingly, however, there was still no sign of the infrared man, nor any encouraging updates on Summer or Biscuit. Indeed, the best intelligence continued to flow in the opposite direction. For on 3 February Colonel Johnny received yet another startling transmission from Rantzau: *'Dropped man 31st thirty miles south of Peterborough. Was badly hurt leaving plane. Perhaps dead. If you hear anything please let me know.'*

Ironically, the latest Lena parachute agent was already receiving medical treatment at Brixton prison. Defiantly alive, but nursing a broken ankle, 'James Rymer' of 33 Abbotsford Gardens, Woodford Green, was in fact Josef Jakobs, a dentist by training, who risked a low-altitude jump over fens on the last night of January and came to grief in a potato field near Ramsey. Surrounded by his equipment, Jakobs endured a long night of agony and at daybreak announced his presence by squeezing off shots from his Mauser pistol. Two smallholders responded and summoned the police, who transported Jakobs into captivity on a horse-drawn cart, together with his transmitter, codes, maps and currency – and obligatory chunk of German sausage.

Plainly a spy, Jakobs was taken to Camp 020. After a short preliminary interrogation, conducted on a wheeled gurney, the truculent German was transferred to the hospital wing at Brixton. Questioned further, he claimed to have been imprisoned in the concentration camp at Oranienberg and had volunteered to jump over England with the object of making his way to America, where an aunt resided in Illinois. The story closely resembled that offered up by Kurt Goose, the Brandenburg commando captured in October, and briefly turned as Agent Gander.

'It is difficult not to be sceptical about these people,' wrote Liddell. 'Firstly, it seems almost incredible that, if his story is true, the Germans could imagine he was going to be of any real value. Secondly, why did they give him an identity card with no letter prefix? We know that the Germans are extremely crude and sketchy in their methods, but a clerical error is difficult to believe. Did they intend that Jakobs would be captured, or send him over to test Snow in some way? The Germans must now be wise to the game of collaring an agent and forcing him to use his wireless set in our interests.'

Liddell was closer to the truth than others in B Division dared to admit, Robertson included. But what the Twenty Committee had no way of knowing was just how many unknown German agents might be at large in Britain, and which of the agents already turned were still considered reliable by the Abwehr. 'We could not bring ourselves to believe that we did in fact control the German system,' Masterman recalled of this baffling period. 'Innumerable precautions had to be taken on the assumption that they had several and perhaps many independent agents of whom we had no knowledge, and that these could be used to check the reports of our own controlled agents.'

Like Jan Willem Ter Braak, still at large in Cambridge with a working Afu transmitter, and living just fifty yards from the local RSLO.

Owens' credibility was partially restored a week later when he was asked to assist yet another agent in distress, this time Wulf Schmidt. After faithfully transmitting from England for sixteen weeks, and in the process winning an Iron Cross, verisimilitude dictated that the V-man codenamed Leonhardt should run short of money. Since Josef Jakobs was missing in action, along with £497 meant for Schmidt, Wohldorf again asked Johnny to help a friend in distress. *'Please send hundred pounds to Mr Williamson, Radlett General Delivery, with fictitious addressor. Mail letter in London on Feb 11th.'*

Schmidt was still residing with the Robertson family at Round Bush House, and received the money safely. For Jakobs, however, the breaks remained bad. 'He was manifestly unemployable as a double agent,' recalled Tin-Eye Stephens, 'and blank as a tome of reference in the living counter-espionage library at 020. There was no good reason why he should continue to live.'

Lord Swinton, at least, would be pleased.

As these various strands unravelled Walter Dicketts set out for Lisbon, sailing from Liverpool on 4 February on board the SS *Cressado*, a cargo steamer bound for Gibraltar as part of convoy OG.52. As a commercial traveller in 'sardines, corks, fruit and wolfram', verisimilitude dictated that Dick should travel steerage; the Little Man would follow on Valentine's Day, by air. If the *Cressado* was hardly the *Queen Mary*, the long sea voyage at least allowed Dicketts time to rehearse his mission as disgraced air force officer Jack Brown – and set up a profitable card school. 'He is a first-class cribbage player,' an observer told B1A, 'and spent most of his time playing with the chief steward.'

No doubt giddy on gin fizz, Dick also dropped hints that he was an important government agent, whose business in Lisbon was strictly hush-hush. 'As a matter of fact he got the captain to give him £10, for which he gave him a cheque from Barclays Bank.'

Back in London, Owens continued to clamour for high-grade intelligence and was rewarded with a counterfeit contact inside the War Office. The lucky officer concerned was an urbane lieutenant named Richardson, then acting as a personal assistant to General Sir Robert Haining, Vice-Chief of the Imperial General Staff. Richardson carried off his role with no little aplomb, joining Owens, Lily and Kay for a meal at the Anchor Hotel in Shepperton, then reporting back in bemused fashion to Gilbert Lennox, a deception specialist.

'Owens seemed very keen to get my address and telephone number but I managed to avoid this. He appeared to be well-known at The Anchor, and at dinner there appeared to be no secret about the fact that he was an agent, or the fact that Mrs Celery's husband was also an agent. Several toasts were drunk to Owens, wishing him luck on his forthcoming travels abroad. Apparently the hotel people at The Anchor had been instrumental in obtaining a maid for Lily, and, in turn, they were trying to get a nursemaid through him.'

Richardson found Owens' table manners sorely lacking. 'Owens has one peculiar habit. He only wears his false teeth when he is eating, and has a sort of sleight-of-hand trick of slipping the dentures into his mouth under cover of a handkerchief before a meal.'

True to form, Owens attempted to suborn Richardson, inviting him for cocktails the following Tuesday. The young lieutenant politely demurred. 'I excused myself, as I thought I had probably done enough.'

Passing on his report to Robertson, Lennox observed that young Richardson seemed wasted in a Whitehall posting.

As Dicketts steamed onwards to Lisbon, Owens put the frighteners on Kay. 'He told her that she could expect me to be away for six months or longer,' Dick groused later, 'and that I should be in a situation of great danger the whole time. He painted a very vivid picture of what I might be going through, and how only he could look after me. The poor girl was worried to distraction.'

With good reason. According to the scheme hatched by Robertson and Dicketts, renegade flyboy 'Jack Brown' would reach Lisbon ahead of Owens, meet Rantzau, usurp Snow, and proceed on to Germany if all seemed well. Regrettably, in war even the best-laid plans seldom survive first contact with the enemy – an aphorism doubly true of U-boats. Convoy OG.52 consisted of thirty merchant vessels, one of which, the SS *Canford Chine*, was torpedoed off the west coast of Ireland six days out, with the loss of all hands. Moreover, the need to avoid German bombers operating from the coast of Brittany necessitated a long, circuitous Atlantic passage, added to which the convoy encountered bad weather. The result was that the *Cressado* was delayed by a week, triggering panic in Addlestone and Hamburg.

Beside herself with worry, Kay demanded a meeting with Robertson at the Grosvenor Hotel. 'She was of course very worried because she had not heard from her husband, and asked me a great many questions with regard to the possibility of him going into Germany. I said that this rested entirely with Snow and Rantzau, but that I was sure he would not take any unnecessary risks. This did not altogether convince Mrs Celery.'

When Robertson met Snow for a final briefing they were joined by Felix Cowgill of MI6, whose support was required in Lisbon. 'I reminded Owens that he must be ready to discuss his North Sea trip with Rantzau, and gave him very brief outlines of Summer and Pogo. He is going to complain of the inadvisability of sending agents over here without previously warning him.' For the rest, Tar spoke more in hope than expectation. 'If it was at all possible he was to get information from Rantzau about any impending invasion since this would be of real assistance, as well as anything relating to secret weapons.'

Ten remarkable months after his last treff with Ritter, Agent Snow finally flew out from Whitchurch on 14 February, posing as a sales agent for a large manufacturing concern. After a long, anxious flight over a thousand miles of grey Atlantic waves Colonel Johnny touched down at Sintra airport and was faintly astonished to see the field ringed with Axis aeroplanes – Italian machines decked out in dazzling white, and Lufthansa trimotors adorned with crooked swastikas. Security was tight, with armed Portuguese guards beside each and every aircraft. No doubt Owens wished he had a pistol of his own. Lisbon was, as Mac had warned, full of rats.

Agent Snow took an antiquated taxi into Lisbon and checked in to the Metropole Hotel, an opulent deco establishment facing onto the smart Pedro IV Square. Still there was no sign of Dicketts. Following procedures rehearsed during earlier treffs on neutral ground, Owens left a cryptic note at the Grande Hotel Duas Nacoes, then returned to the Metropole to wait. In due course instructions came back to stand outside the main entrance at nine o'clock. His nerves winding tighter as the minutes ticked past, Colonel Johnny sought refuge in the hotel bar.

At nine-fifteen Henri Döbler drew up in a grey Opel saloon. Sprawled across the back seat was Major Nikolaus Ritter, gold tooth flashing behind the widest of smiles. As Döbler drove the two men through the glittering port city, worlds away from the inky blackout of London and Hamburg, Johnny and the Doctor swapped notes on events since their last treff in Antwerp in April 1940. 'He asked me if I had sent £100 to this Williamson man as arranged,' recalled Owens. 'I said that as far as I knew it had been sent. "Well," he said, "he is one of my best friends and I don't want anything to happen to him." The conversation then turned to more general matters, such as conditions in England, and Lily and the baby. I showed him some photographs, and he said his wife wanted to be remembered to me.'

This, at least, was how Snow reported their happy reunion to MI5. In reality, with the London stelle blown wide open and everything to lose, Owens delivered Dicketts to Ritter on a plate. In a comfortable apartment on the Rua dos Sapateiros, a bottle of Scotch loosened the Little Man's tongue with remarkable speed. 'I built Dicketts up,' confessed Owens. 'Told Rantzau all about his past history.'

Initially Ritter was not best pleased. 'Owens immediately told me that his sub-agent was working for British intelligence. I asked why, if that were the case, he had taken the risk of bringing Dicketts to Lisbon. Owens replied that he dared not break off the relationship, as to do so would be regarded as a sign of guilt.' Ritter noted that Johnny was 'abnormally difficult' to interrogate, and told his story in a confused, disjointed and reluctant manner. 'Owens added that he had first met Dicketts approximately ten weeks before in a public house.'

Kein glas bier.

Interrogated by Allied intelligence officers five years later, Ritter weaved a narrative which carefully avoided any hint of triple-cross. 'If, as Owens said, a British agent had been in touch with him for ten weeks, it was practically certain that the authorities already knew enough to arrest him. Moreover, his sub-agents might already be implicated, and perhaps under arrest, including Schmidt. I told Owens plainly that I would have to consider if it would be safe to allow his return to England, seeing how much he knows, and that I should have no difficulty in liquidating his case promptly in Lisbon. Owens was clearly very much frightened by this threat.'

No Iron Cross for Colonel Johnny. Nevertheless, with Operation Lena long abandoned, and a brand new mission in mind, Ritter tempered his ire with mercy. 'In view of our long acquaintance I was satisfied that Owens was telling the truth so far as he knew it. He said that despite Dicketts' connection with British intelligence, he could, if properly handled, be recruited by us. For Dicketts was an extremely greedy man.'

A bemused Abwehr subordinate later summarised the situation rather more succinctly. 'It was all a big tangle.'

Jack Brown, so it seemed, was already dead. Word now reached Lisbon that the *Cressado* had been sunk by a U-boat, with only a handful of survivors landed on the island of Madeira. Ritter made discreet enquiries, and after satisfying himself that the steamer was still afloat handed Owens a generous bounty of £5,000. Taxed by Robertson on this payment some time later, Owens spoke of a reward for his ongoing loyalty. In truth the vast pile of dollars and sterling was meant as bait for Walter Dicketts, the 'extremely greedy' British secret service agent due in port any day.

Ritter, however, was a man in a hurry. Desperate for news of the *Cressado*, Owens checked in with the British Embassy, where Richman Stopford was now head of station for MI6. The result was a flurry of anxious telegrams, one of which Owens sent directly to Lily at Homefields. *'Dick not arrived. Worried. Can you help? See that Kay doesn't break down. I will cable as soon as he arrives.'*

Effectively a hostage in Lisbon, Owens joined Ritter for a refresher course on sabotage at a hillside villa in fashionable Estoril. There, in a well-kept garden, a technician named Rudolf demonstrated how to use a wristwatch as a timing device, as well as a range of novel explosive devices disguised as batteries, flashlights and fountain pens. Ritter rejected an example of the latter, patiently explaining that while Pelikan might be a fine German brand, V-men operating in England might be best advised to carry Montblanc or Parker.

'I hadn't spotted that!' said Johnny approvingly, nodding.

Impressive though this was, Ritter's belated grasp of elementary fieldcraft came too late for the unlucky Lena agents dispatched to England bearing chunks of German sausage, torches stamped 'Made in Bohemia' and poorly forged ID papers bearing 7s crossed in the Continental style.

There was more. As well as a brand new code book, based on *Warning From the West Indies* by William Macmillan, Ritter dropped dark hints of arcane new developments in chemical warfare, against which British respirators would offer no protection. Poison gas and Pelikans aside, Owens undertook little if any useful work for MI5 while in Portugal, being laid low, so he said, by Lisbon Fever. 'I was ill at that time and in bed,' he swore later, complaining also of duodenal ulcers. 'My temperature was 104. I was in such a state that I couldn't carry on. If I thought I could go out I saw people outside. At other times they came to my room. I could only just manage to crawl around.'

In reality, the Little Man's wretched state owed far more to nervous exhaustion brought on by the threat of prompt liquidation by the Abwehr, a grim situation made worse by his excessive consumption of alcohol and Veronal. A barbiturate commonly used as a sleeping aid, Veronal was freely available in certain less scrupulous Lisbon drugstores, with no prescription required.

It was especially good dope.

After seventeen interminable days at sea the *Cressado* finally reached Lisbon late on the evening of Friday, 21 February. The tortuous voyage had reduced Dicketts to a state almost as miserable as Owens, in desperate need of a hot bath and a change of clothes, and racked by fears that Agent Snow and Doctor Rantzau had lost hope and moved on without him. Finding the immigration sheds closed on their quay, Dick managed to persuade the chief steward to smuggle him ashore, then made his way to the Hotel Metropole. Disconcertingly, there were no messages at the desk, leaving worried Agent Celery no option but to sneak back to the *Cressado*.

As 'Jack Brown' waited impatiently to clear passport control, Ritter prepared to return to Germany. 'He'd put off several important appointments in Hamburg and Berlin,' explained Owens. 'So that night I shook hands with the Doctor and he went back, so far as I knew.'

Landing legally the following morning, Dicketts returned to the Metropole at noon. There were still no messages, but as he filled out a registration form at the desk Owens suddenly emerged from the dining room, apparently having dressed with a shovel and considerably refreshed by rather more than *ein glas bier*.

'Good old Dick!' Colonel Johnny exclaimed, turning heads.

Dicketts' heart sank into his boots. 'The Little Man was so pleased to see me that he very nearly fainted. He had drunk a great deal of liquor. I'm quite convinced his alcoholic state was his relief at seeing me. The Germans had given me up all round.'

Owens hastened to his room to phone Döbler, leaving Dicketts to wire an urgent cable to Kay: *'Just arrived darling. Very bad trip. All my love sweetheart. Things are NOT going well.'*

Matters quickly improved upstairs, where Dick sank a gin fizz or three, then watched as Snow threw open his wardrobe and lifted up a pile of dirty laundry. Beneath it sat a small mountain of banknotes.

'That's £5,000,' Owens crowed. 'Look at the way the Doctor gives money away. See how these people treat me. The German organisation doesn't quibble about expenses at all.'

Already Celery was beginning to wilt. £5,000 easily trumped the miserly £200 fee paid by MI5 for the Lisbon mission, and his penny-pinching salary of £10 a week. Owens softened Dick further with several punches thrown well below the belt. 'He started to talk to me about Kay, my wife, and said that at Homefields she was so afraid that she was locking her bedroom door at night because of Ronnie Reed. He told me he had done his very best to calm her fears, cheer her up and that sort of thing.'

As for progress on their mission for MI5, Snow told Celery nothing at all. 'Owens refused to give me any information,' complained Dicketts. 'Always on the feel that I was an amateur, a novice, whereas he had been in it for years. If I knew everything that was going on it would upset me, for the less I knew the better, and I should not fall into traps.'

Owens had spun the very same line to McCarthy on board the *Barbados*, only to find himself bound up in knots. Now Dicketts was about to be cast overboard, hands tied, to sink or swim.

The two slippery spies carried on drinking until Henri Döbler appeared and drove them out to the hillside villa in Estoril. Here, at last, Dicketts shook hands with the infamous Doctor Rantzau – portrayed by McCarthy as a loutish drunk with a fondness for dirty jokes, but putting Dick more in mind of a 'shrewd Midwestern American businessman', with sober tortoiseshell spectacles and perfect colloquial English. 'He was very friendly and hearty, but scarcely drank at all, and plainly commanded respect from his colleagues.'

Ritter's appraisal of Dicketts was rather less favourable. 'My first impression coincided exactly with what Owens had told me. Dicketts had all the appearance of a crook and of a man who would do anything for money. He spoke often and convincingly of being in low water financially, and of being compelled to accept work below his real capabilities.'

For the moment, no mention was made of the fact that Dicketts was working for the British secret service. Instead, under Owens' tipsy, duplicitous gaze, he carefully delivered the lines rehearsed time and again as Captain Jack Brown, talking in the broadest possible terms about Stirlings, Beaufighters, infrared and the new high-altitude Flying Fortress, twenty of which were on order from Boeing in America.

'I wanted to interview Dicketts for the first time without prejudicing any subsequent decision,' said Ritter. 'Had I revealed immediately that I knew him to be a British agent, then discovered that he was incorruptible, or a more important man than Owens supposed, it would have been impossible to allow them to return to England. On the other hand, as long as Dicketts knew nothing, I was free to act in whatever way seemed best. Clearly this could only be confirmed by careful interrogation and observation over a period of time. If it were confirmed that Dicketts could be bought, we would have to exert ourselves to the full to flatter, frighten and impress him. If not, it might be necessary to dispose of him. For either purpose Germany was the right place.'

Unaware that his cover had been blown by Snow, the former confidence man judged his own performance impressive. 'Rantzau asked me my opinions of England, the war, and my own attitude. I did not pretend any fascist leanings, but said I had a great admiration for the German system of government, and intense disagreement with my own.' Dicketts also disclosed that his mother was Irish, and that he was prepared to go to any length to stop the war. 'I told Ritter the agreed story and he apparently accepted it. It was obviously a foregone conclusion that I should go to Germany.'

Ritter, too, stayed in character, expressing interest in Dick's famous photographic memory and promising that he could be of great value to the Reich so long as he was honest and sincere. 'The Doctor wanted me to come to Berlin within forty-eight hours and see for myself how differently the people were governed, and what great satisfaction there was there.'

Whereas Dick, a practised con artist, remained calm, the highly strung Owens began to buckle under pressure, and perhaps even felt pangs of guilt. 'The Little Man stayed all through the first interview, but his hair was disarrayed and he was in a state of collapse with excitement and alcohol. He did not take part in the actual conversation, except to intersperse with remarks like, "Dear old Dick – let's have another drink. We will look after you. The Doctor is a good friend of ours."'

There were more good friends at the Arcadia, a lively cabaret club run by the Abwehr, where two hospitable dancers named Sophie and Lotti took to Dick immediately. Owens sweetened the honeytrap still further, promising Dicketts unlimited pleasures in Hamburg, the Valhalla included, and even told him to look up Fräulein Helen, his former mistress at the Café Indra.

From double-cross to XXX.

Mata Hari methods.

Things WERE going well.

12

Working For Peace

After two days of high living in Lisbon, Walter Dicketts embarked on his daring double-cross mission into the dark heart of Nazi Germany, a feat almost without precedent in wartime. The date was Tuesday, 25 February 1941. As Hitler's armies moved on the Balkans, and Allied forces deployed to defend Greece, Agent Celery kept a discreet early-morning rendezvous behind Estoril station. There he was met by Hans Ruser, a swarthy diplomatic courier, who handed him a passport in the name of Walther Anton Denker, then loaded his suitcase into the boot of a powerful Ford V8.

Lotti Schade, the youngest and prettiest of the dancing girls at the Arcadia night club, was there to bid Dick a fond farewell. So too was Colonel Johnny, temporarily sober and once more rehearsing the role of master spy.

'You're sure you want to go?' the Little Man asked Dicketts.

'So long as there's no double-crossing.'

Owens nodded vigorously. 'Captain Robbie sent you over here blindfold. If I hadn't got here first, you'd be going to your death.'

'I'm trusting you on this one, Arthur. One hundred per cent.'

The two men exchanged solemn, dissembling handshakes, followed by a theatrical embrace from lissom Lotti.

'You're a brave man, Dick,' pronounced Owens. 'Don't let me down – and don't give me away.'

Never mind gullible jewellers on Bond Street, or gramophone records and plum-coloured suits. Walter Dicketts was about to attempt his most ambitious fraud yet, with Adolf Hitler as his mark.

Ruser made for the Spanish border at Badajoz, crossing without incident and reaching Madrid after twelve hours on the road. 'At first he was very cool and informed me quite bluntly that he did not like travelling with a traitor.' Captain Jack Brown pushed back with some well-rehearsed lines about desiring peace. 'Ruser then changed his mind and agreed with me entirely. He said that he was sure Hitler was sincere in his desire for peace with England, and had no territorial ambition in Europe other than Austria, Czechoslovakia and Poland.'

In Madrid the pair stopped in at the German Embassy. Here Ruser collected diplomatic seals for Dick's luggage and paraded the prize defector before various military attachés. On Thursday Dick boarded a Junkers-52 trimotor and flew east to Barcelona, transferring there to a sleek modern Focke-Wulf Condor airliner, then sweeping gracefully across the high snow-capped Pyrenees into France, accompanied now by a doctor named Fischer. 'During the journey we became very friendly. He spoke fluent English and, while extremely pro-Hitler, was anxious to see the war over.'

Everyone, it seemed, was working for peace.

At Lyon the Condor touched down to refuel. Even though the city was situated in the unoccupied Vichy zone, Dicketts counted ten Messerschmitt 109 fighters lined up on the tarmac. There were also a hundred French fighter planes, left to rot in a corner of the airfield following the Armistice in June 1940. Few if any of the Dewoitines and Morane-Saulniers looked to have seen combat. More than any Fifth Column fairy tales of nuns in jackboots and midget assassins disguised as orphans, this sorriest of sights revealed something of why France had collapsed in just six short weeks.

On Friday the Condor flew onwards to Stuttgart and Berlin, eventually landing at Tempelhof in the late afternoon. There Dicketts was met by an athletic Abwehr officer named George Sessler, who jumped the queue at a taxi rank by waving a red Gestapo card and whisked Dicketts across the capital to the Hauptbahnhof. An express train carried them north to Hamburg. 'We had a private coupe,' recalled Dicketts, 'and over a bottle of wine became rather friendly. He had toured America and South Africa, and the whole of Europe with a Hitler Youth football team.'

By the time Dicketts checked into a plush suite at the Hotel Vier Jahreszeiten it was almost midnight. Fatigued by four days of luxury travel, Dicketts went in search of a nightcap to steady his nerves. Two watchers tracked his progress from Room 344 to the American Bar off the lobby downstairs, and stuck out like sore thumbs.

Back at the Metropole in Lisbon Owens returned to his sickbed. With £5,000 burning a hole in his wallet he could now afford the services of a nurse, who provided cold towels and Veronal in exchange for a thousand escudos a day, and the promise of some furniture. 'Nobody speaks English in Lisbon,' Owens fretted, seeking to excuse his maudlin condition. 'Eventually I got a young lady to look after me. But I still felt like hell, all the same.'

In fact the Little Man was on the up and up. 'Madame Elizabeth Fernanda stayed with Arthur in his room at the hotel,' Dicketts vouched later, 'and I believe looked after him extremely well.'

'Friend Snow is, I think, enjoying himself,' Richman Stopford confirmed, flashing an update to B1A. 'His present position has rather gone to his head, but you will no doubt bring him to his senses on his return.'

In Hamburg too there were rude awakenings. At eight-thirty on Saturday morning Dicketts was roused by Sessler, who rapped loudly on his door, then ushered in a pair of Abwehr *doktors* named Schwartz and Powell. Their interrogative style was both subtle and persuasive, and required none of the severe methods intermittently employed at Camp 020. 'Dicketts admitted his status as a British agent whose mission was to penetrate Owens' network,' Ritter recorded succinctly. 'He offered his services to Germany and these were accepted. I then made certain financial arrangements with a view to confirming his loyalty to us, and ensuring that he kept his mouth shut about Owens. Dicketts would receive a few hundred pounds as a gesture of our goodwill, but remain dependent on Owens for a much larger sum to be paid in instalments.'

Undoubtedly Celery arrived at the same conclusion as had Wulf Schmidt in his cell at Latchmere House. 'It was simply a matter of survival. Self-preservation must be the strongest instinct in man.'

Mucky business. A right dirty deal.

Things were *not* going well.

Naturally enough, Dicketts admitted none of this to MI5 and swore that all had gone swimmingly for Captain Jack Brown. 'It was a very ruthless interrogation and there is no doubt that they were suspicious. They showed extreme disbelief at my apparent ignorance on air force matters. But on the fourth evening Doctor Powell and Doctor Schwartz took me out for dinner at Schumann's, as they understood I liked lobster, and thought I was a little tired.'

Ritter appeared only on Tuesday, keen to cover his own backside before leaving for North Africa. 'I was anxious to leave something behind,' he conceded. 'Owens had been operating his transmitter since before the outbreak of war, and could not reasonably expect to last much longer. Now the case was effectively over. On the other hand, I saw that total collapse might be staved off with the assistance of Dicketts – not so much from any confidence in him, but in the hope that the case might after all be rescued from disaster.'

Not just the case, but the Fatherland itself. Codenamed Barbarossa, Hitler's colossal military assault on the Soviet Union was named in honour of a crusading emperor of the Holy Roman Empire, and provisionally scheduled for May 1941. In order to divert attention from the east, preparations for a seaborne invasion of the British Isles were to be maintained as a feint, including deception schemes known as *Haifisch* (Shark) and *Harpune* (Harpoon). Both involved bogus radio traffic, reconnaissance flights and landing exercises – and now Walter Dicketts, the corrupt double-cross agent named after a vegetable and recruited by Snow in a public bar.

For Hitler, the prospect of war on two fronts made peace with Britain an urgent necessity. Despite the fact that Churchill had ignored every 'last appeal to reason' issued from Berlin, the Nazi leadership remained firmly convinced of the existence of a large peace lobby in Britain. Dicketts, a British secret agent for twenty years, and as pliant as squeezable mustard, might conceivably make better progress than previous intermediaries such as Pope Pius XII, or Hess and Haushofer via the Duke of Hamilton. Dicketts later explained: 'The suggestion was that if I could see people in authority in Britain, and come back to Germany accredited, with the certainty that what I was doing would not be splashed all over the headlines in English papers to show a weakening of Germany, then they would welcome a peace offer.'

Agent Celery remained in Hamburg for a fortnight. After four consecutive days of 'ruthless' interrogation – or so he claimed – the fraudster was confirmed as trustworthy, advised to adopt an American accent, and given use of a car to inspect air-raid damage. 'I was extremely disappointed by the lack of damage to Hamburg docks,' MI5 learned from him afterwards. 'I then toured through the poor residential part of St Pauli and cannot understand why bombs were dropped here, as there are only low-class houses and nightclubs, and no important factory within a mile.'

Evidently Bomber Command read his mind. On the evening of 13 March clubbable George Sessler treated Dicketts to a comprehensive tour of Hamburg nightlife, including nightspots such as the Valhalla, whose tables, telephones and tarts Owens had found so seductive in peacetime. Unfortunately this expedition coincided with an RAF raid on the Blohm & Voss shipyard, the heaviest strike yet launched against Hamburg. Dicketts spent much of the night in a shelter below the main railway station, locked in awkward conversation with a group of Wehrmacht officers. 'On finding out that I was American they asked me for my opinion on the Lease-Lend Bill. They informed me that the German territorial hold on Europe was so strong that America coming into the war would only serve to prolong it, and not make any difference to the ultimate victory of Germany.'

Far more pleasurable was an invitation to supper with Ritter and his haughty wife Irmgard, herself a former secretary at Stelle X. A cosy treff at the Alster Pavilion was followed by a show at the renowned Hansa theatre, where his hosts took a box. 'She is pro-British and hates the war,' noted Dicketts, with touching naivety. 'We talked of my wife, and I was asked to bring her to Germany on my next visit. That way she would be safe from reprisals should I be found out, or should the invasion suddenly take place.'

Much to Dicketts' surprise, Doctor Rantzau confessed to being genuinely fond of Owens, *Der Kleine*. 'Arthur is a fool in many ways,' Ritter confided. 'He drinks too much and lives on his nerves. But I'm prepared to go on trusting him because I've known him for more than four years. Never, to my knowledge, has he let me down. But he's also a goddamn lazy son of a bitch who won't get going unless someone gives him a good kick in the pants.'

More violence threatened when Dicketts visited a 'Young Nazi Political Club' with George Sessler. 'We stayed there until 5.30 in the morning, drinking and singing, by which time the entire club was in a state of drunkenness and quarrels. Some of them took great exception to me and wanted to fight, as I was an American.' Dick suggested they should duke it out. Sensibly Sessler demurred, preferring to rely on his red Gestapo card. 'George called the ringleaders together, warned them of concentration camps, and told them that they were the worst kind of German. One man called him a few filthy names, so George, who was a first-class boxer, hit him twice and knocked him out. We left the club in silence, and went home.'

By his own admission, Dicketts' extended sojourn in the lively port city was blurred by long nights on the tiles and heavy drinking, added to which Abwehr staff indulged in regular drug-taking. 'At least 50 per cent of them carry Veronal and cocaine. Veronal to give them heavy sleep after a long day's work, and cocaine to help them overcome the strain. They all insist that they use the drug but that the drug does not use them.'

More especially good dope.

Back in Lisbon, despite caning Veronal rather than cocaine, Snow grew increasingly paranoid. Hoping to defect by striking a deal with Ritter's replacement, a Doctor Schneider, Owens made repeated requests to join Dicketts in Hamburg, all of which were pointedly ignored. In a last desperate throw he even cabled Lily at Homefields, suggesting that she fly out to nurse him in person, along with their infant daughter Jean Louise. 'Even if this were possible we would scarcely agree to it,' observed Liddell, smelling not just a rat but a midden.

Towards the end of his stay in Hamburg Dicketts was introduced to a senior *Reichspropaganda* official, said to be an aide to Joseph Goebbels, who worked from an office above the Alsterhaus, Hamburg's landmark department store. Here Agent Celery was issued with several pamphlets and papers, including details of supposed Polish atrocities against Germans, photos of Churchill posing with a cigar and tommy-gun, parody gramophone records and a mildly critical book by Major Philip Gribble, *The Diary of a Staff Officer.* These, it was hoped, he would circulate privately to 'people of importance' in Britain. With commendable optimism, it was even proposed that Dick should present copies in person to Winston Churchill.

'Doctor Goebbels' assistant said that he was sure people in England were getting entirely wrong information,' Dicketts told MI5, 'and that thinking people would like to end the war. My reaction to this was that I was too small a man to have any influence of that kind.'

More likely, Walter Dicketts replied in terms that would save his own skin, and secure the handsome peace dividend of £5,000 hidden beneath Snow's dirty shirts in a wardrobe in Lisbon.

On 17 March, a Monday, Sessler escorted 'Walther Denker' back to Berlin, where the prize English spy was accommodated at the plush Hotel Adlon on the Unter den Linden. Here, at the very heart of Germania, Dicketts met with a senior aide to Hjalmar Schacht, the former Reichsbank president who now served Hitler as Minister without Portfolio. By his own account, Dicketts merely gave Schacht's office fatuous tips on ways to improve Nazi radio propaganda. In fact, he took delivery of detailed peace proposals for onward transmission to people of influence in Britain – names conceivably suggested by Schacht himself, a political liberal who had been an active member of the Anglo-German Fellowship before the outbreak of war.

'They must have colonies,' the corrupt triple agent briefed MI5 back in London. 'They intend to keep Poland, Czechoslovakia and Austria, but they are not interested in the rest of Europe.' The peace plan entrusted to Dicketts also promised to preserve most of the British Empire – though with independence for India and a sharp reduction in British sea power – and would require the United Kingdom to stand back as Continental Europe was reorganised as a 'corporate state' under the iron heel of the Reich.

On Wednesday morning Dicketts and Sessler boarded a Focke-Wulf Condor at Tempelhof and commenced the long return journey to Barcelona, again stopping at Stuttgart and Lyon. 'Sessler became more and more friendly with me,' explained Dicketts, 'and said that he would like to get out of Germany and come to England. He is very pro-British and pro-American, and at loggerheads with all in his department except the Doctor.'

More credibly, the Abwehr hoped to insert Sessler into England in a new double-cross sting of their own.

Celery, so it seemed, was suddenly a magnet for spies. With no seats available on the flight from Madrid to Lisbon, Dicketts and Sessler were obliged to take a train and found themselves sharing their first-class compartment with an 'extremely good-looking' Belgian twenty-something named Marcelle Quenall. Slim, ash blonde and engagingly displaced, Dick claimed that Sessler was 'very taken' with La Quenall but was plainly smitten himself. 'She studied me intently throughout the journey. George had a large bottle of Gordon's and offered her a gin fizz. She replied that she would not drink with a German.'

Reluctantly, Dicketts and Sessler left the train on the border at Valencia de Alcántara, where they were met by Henri Döbler and his Moorish mistress Alicia, and covered the remaining miles to Lisbon by car. In order to avoid being tailed by British watchers, Dick was dropped off in the outskirts of the city and made his way back to the Metropole by taxi.

True to form, there was no sign of Snow at the hotel, nor any message at the desk. Dicketts eventually located Owens at the Arcadia club where, somewhat recovered, the Little Man was carousing with a dubious Irish couple named Nolan, as well as the lithe German dancing girls Sophie and Lotti. 'Owens was obviously very relieved to see me,' wrote Dicketts. 'I was credibly informed by several people that he had worried himself to the point of a nervous breakdown during my absence. These people, of course, did not know the reason. I said I had been to Setúbal, Badajoz and Oporto.'

But Dicketts had been to Berlin and Hamburg, and was now an instrument of Nazi foreign policy. 'It's been the most remarkable experience,' he gushed effusively, steering Owens towards a private table. 'I've got enough information to blow open the whole works.'

'Dandy. Tell me what they gave you, Dick.'

Dicketts glanced around, checking for eavesdroppers. 'I can't tell you right now, Arthur. Suffice to say that we've got to get back to London as quickly as possible. Because you and I are going to get together with Winston Churchill and settle the whole war.'

'Gospel?'

'One hundred per cent. We'll all get medals and live like kings in Germany – me, you, Kay, Lily and baby Jean. No more air raids. No more Captain Robbie or Ronnie Reed.'

Oddly downcast, the Little Man sucked on his dentures thoughtfully. 'I had no idea you were such a big nut. Where did they put you up?'

'The Vier Jahreszeiten.'

'A double room?'

'I had a suite.'

'Well – you've had a marvellous time. I never had a whole suite to myself. Damn funny, that is.'

Owens bristled visibly as Dick twisted the knife. 'By the way, I'm to call on you for as much money as I need.'

'What – they didn't give you anything?'

'Two hundred quid.' After a gap of ten years Dicketts fell back to bilking rich guests in foreign hotels with astonishing ease. 'Mind you, that's for expenses. Besides, I happen to know half that money in your room is earmarked for me.'

Having squeezed Owens for 1,000 escudos, Dick disappeared into the warm Iberian night with Lotti Schade. 'She had apparently been informed of my activities and taken a great liking to me. The two girls are German agents, and Lotti is the chief.' On the tender promise of more undercover activity Lotti gave amorous Agent Celery her address. The only catch was that the love nest was in Wilhelmsruh, a distant suburb of Berlin.

Next day, Owens and Dicketts made their way to the British Embassy, travelling in separate taxis to avoid being followed, and delivering wildly different reports. Keen to report 'certain vital information' to Churchill in person, with the hand of history on his shoulder, Dicketts instructed MI6 to put him on the first available flight back to Britain. Cables or telephones would not do, staff learned with dismay, for every phone at the Embassy was tapped by the enemy. Dicketts also insisted on diplomatic seals for the several packets of confidential documents received from Hjalmar Schacht's office in Berlin, the content of which was far too important to disclose to underlings in Lisbon.

In a separate office, Agent Snow dropped bombshells of his own. Rantzau, he told Stopford, had deduced that Hitler's chief spy in England was operating under British control some months earlier. Confronted on arriving in Lisbon, Owens told the Doctor of a raid on Homefields by 'intelligence cops' in December, who then compelled him to play a double game. The rest of Snow's remarkable story was essentially true. Rather than liquidate Colonel Johnny on the spot, Rantzau had handed him £10,000 and a brand new mission. This revolved around Walter Dicketts, who, Snow added, seemed now to be working for the Abwehr rather than for British intelligence.

This 'rather disquieting' news was immediately flashed to MI5 in London. As head of B Division, Guy Liddell took a stoical view. 'It may be that Snow has lost his nerve. There is also the curious fact that at one moment he wanted his wife and child to join him in Lisbon. The whole thing is rather unfortunate, but it was bound to come to an end sooner or later. We shall have to get other strings to our bow.'

Blissfully ignorant of Snow's latest manoeuvrings, Celery explored lively intrigues of his own devising. That evening, to his great delight, the peacemaker spotted Marcelle Quenall in the lounge of the Metropole. Making his excuses with indecent haste, Dicketts warned Owens that the beautiful blonde had glimpsed his German diplomatic passport on the train from Madrid, and must now be aware that he was a British spy.

'I'll have to spend most of my time with her from now on,' Dick blurted eagerly, already on his feet. 'Trying to square things up.'

This involved dinner, flowers and an intimate debriefing. 'I found that she was entirely without funds and living at a fourth-rate hotel,' explained Dicketts of Operation Legover. 'She was obviously ill so I got her a doctor, paid for fruit and medicine and gave her 200 escudos. She said she would like to work for the British secret service. I think she could be very valuable, as she is attractive and accomplished.'

And a Nazi spy. 'Dick gave her money because she was broke,' carped Owens, who decided to conduct his own private investigation. 'She had a very cheap room at the Hotel Franco and she was drawing money from the Repatriation Office. So what was she doing in a first-class carriage on the train? I asked him if he was clear about this woman, and not to get himself into trouble. He got in a pretty vile mood. I probably stepped on his corns somewhere.'

In London – as in Lisbon – strings were being pulled. When the RAF declined to lay on a special transport, Owens and Dicketts were found places on a scheduled KLM service from Sintra to Whitchurch due to depart on Tuesday, 25 March. Inconveniently, a storm front over the Atlantic then delayed their flight for two consecutive days. For Dicketts the wait was interminable: as well as detailed peace proposals, for urgent discussion over gin fizzes in Downing Street, his precious sealed envelopes contained hard intelligence that Operation Sealion, the long-threatened German invasion of the British Isles, was pencilled in for the Easter weekend. Would Panzers and Stukas reach Addlestone before his plane left the tarmac at Sintra? Or would Ronnie Reed remove pretty chorus girl Kay to some dubious place of safety in the wilds of North Wales?

Owens, too, was a soul in torment. In the space of a month his sidekick had usurped him as the Führer's master spy, and obtained better room service to boot. 'He went to Berlin, and he had an apartment at the Adlon – which I've never had. He went to Hamburg, had the best hotel there, and was treated like a king. What the big stunt is I don't know. By the way he talked, he'd been sleeping with Hitler – and Hitler had been talking in his sleep.'

All was confusion. On a visit to Hans Ruser, the pacifist diplomatic aide who had driven him from Lisbon to Madrid, Dicketts found his flagpole adorned with a swastika flag *and* the Union Jack.

It was all, in Ruser's own words, a big tangle.

The KLM grounding at Sintra left everyone at sea. On Tuesday morning Jock Horsfall sped down to Bristol with Tar Robertson, anxious to collect Agents Snow and Celery from Whitchurch airport and debrief each man separately in London. When the flight failed to arrive from Lisbon the MI5 party spent an impatient night in Bristol. The following morning, with no news from Portugal, Robertson ordered Horsfall back up the Great West Road.

In Lisbon, Owens killed time with his faithful nurse Elizabeth Fernanda, while Dicketts attended to Marcelle Quenall at the Hotel Franco. Poor weather did little to dampen the ardour of either man for Operation Legover.

Finally, on the morning of Thursday, 27 March, the dark skies above Lisbon cleared. In order to reduce the double jeopardy of Spanish anti-aircraft fire and interception by German long-range fighters, the stubby DC-3 headed west out into the Atlantic, then turned north to cross the Bay of Biscay. After a thousand miles and five posterior-numbing hours the British coastline drifted into view through the cabin windows. Almost immediately this welcome sight was obscured by wooden panels, hastily fitted by the steward to thwart incoming spies and saboteurs.

If Walter Dicketts had expected to be whisked directly from Whitchurch to Whitehall he was sorely disappointed. In their haste to leave Lisbon both agents had failed to obtain the correct consular endorsements on their passports, with the result that Owens was stopped short by alert immigration officials. Claiming first to be a sardine salesman, then a secret agent, his behaviour seemed calculated to arouse suspicion. An inspection of his luggage revealed two quartz wireless crystals and led to a humiliating strip search, during which Owens' loud protestations of chronic ill-health and duodenal ulcers were pointedly ignored.

'He was found to be carrying a large number of articles in his pockets including £10,000 in notes,' ran the official report from Whitchurch. 'There were also two fountain pens, which he claimed to be explosive and very dangerous.'

That these were Parker, not Pelikan, mattered not a jot. Ushered into a separate cubicle, Dicketts realised that it might have been wise to remove the maker's label from a brand new overcoat purchased in Hamburg, and also found himself stripped down to his birthday suit. Arriving too late to curtail these indignities, Jock Horsfall and Major Stratton, the local RSLO, were able to placate Agent Celery only with difficulty.

Had Dicketts known that Owens had forfeited his peace dividend of £5,000 within minutes of landing at Whitchurch, he might well have abandoned his high-stakes triple-cross mission on the spot. As it was, Agent Celery now informed Horsfall that he, too, had something to declare. At five o'clock Tar Robertson received an alarming telephone message that called for immediate action. *'Three 12,000-ton transports leaving Elbe with troops early morning of March 28th. Troops assembling on March 26th and are proceeding to the Netherlands.'*

Transports and troops on the move. Invasion, perhaps, or a large seaborne raid. While there would be no repeat of the infamous Cromwell alarm of 7 September 1940, when bridges were demolished and church bells rung, Celery and Snow were hustled into separate cars and rushed back to London. Arrangements were made to accommodate Owens at 901 Nell Gwynn House, a Chelsea apartment leased by John Bingham, one of Max Knight's assistants and later a prolific writer of thrillers. Dicketts was driven by Jock Horsfall in the speedy Citroën, which promptly broke down near Hungerford, forcing the party to stop overnight in a local hotel.

With Dick stuck in Berkshire, Robertson had no option but to pass the invasion alert to the Air Ministry and Admiralty in raw, undigested form. The following day two dozen Blenheim bombers flew coastal sweeps but spotted no enemy armada. Possibly several transports weighed anchor in the Elbe; possibly the stunt was a blind. Undeniably, the German invasion spoof known as Operation Shark was every bit as fictitious as the 200 man-eaters allegedly imported from Australia and released into the Channel in 1940.

Robertson and John Masterman set about grilling Owens first thing on Friday, arranging for a stenographer to make a verbatim transcript. The most pressing concern was his shock claim that Rantzau had known for some time that Johnny was operating under British control. If this was true, much – perhaps all – of the double-cross system was almost certainly blown. Like the IP Club menu fenced by William Rolph, it also raised concerns around the personal security of senior officers within MI5 and MI6.

'When did Rantzau tell you this?' Tar began.

'As soon as I landed in Lisbon,' lied Owens. 'He said "I've got something very important to tell you. As your friend I want a truthful answer." I said, "OK, you know me." He said, "We have information that you are in contact with British intelligence." I said, "That's perfectly true, somebody squealed on me in England. I've been trying to tell you." Then he said, "We know all about you. We've got two propositions, and if you help us we'll see you are OK."'

'So, did you help them?'

'I said I would. That's why I'm alive here today.'

'How did the Doctor respond?'

'He said they'd outlined a plan of what they wanted me to do. By the way he spoke I don't think he'd known it more than a week or ten days. He didn't try any rough stuff or anything like that.'

'No,' said Masterman coolly. 'In fact, he gave you ten thousand pounds.'

'Five thousand for services rendered to date, plus a bonus for my loyalty. Besides, I had very heavy expenses in Lisbon.'

'Did you tell Rantzau anything else?'

'I gave him practically no information – we didn't even bother with the questionnaire. I just told them Dicketts had everything, said I'd turned all the dope over to him.'

'Did he ask about the man in Radlett?'

'I said I sent £100 and took precautions. Apparently he's the Doctor's best friend so he doesn't want anything bad to happen to him.'

'What about Caroli?'

'I said he'd beaten it, so far as I knew.'

'And McCarthy?'

Owens shook his head. 'Take it from me, his name is mud. Döbler likes him well enough, but not the Doctor. Wash Mac out. By the way, they reckon the South African who never showed up came down in a canal and sank.'

Robertson cleared his throat. 'Let's be clear on this, Snowy. You admitted to the Doctor that you're operating under our control, but he's not worried any more of his agents have been compromised?'

'Not as far as I know. Charlie, Gwilym Williams – he thinks they're all one hundred per cent.'

The men from the Twenty Committee exchanged looks. Quite plainly the Little Man was lying through his acrylic false teeth. Masterman coughed loudly. 'That, to my mind, is absolutely incredible.'

'The whole thing is most mysterious,' agreed Owens. 'He knows you're in control of the whole of the wireless business, but I'm still to carry on. If a message is fake I've got to include certain words, like "on the level", "on the up and up", and so on. If those words are used then the message is fake.'

Tar cast his mind back to the confrontation with Owens aboard HMS *Corunia* after the crushing failure of Operation Lamp. There, too, the Little Man had claimed to be desperately ill. There, too, he had stubbornly refused to crack under prolonged interrogation.

'What about Dicketts?'

'Well, that's the big plan. Plus he's got instructions to buy a motorboat and pick up agents from one of the Channel Islands. Explosives and messages too. And his own transmitter.'

'It would seem he was busier than you.'

'Ah – I was that sick I could barely crawl around.' Owens lit up his umpteenth cigarette, then touched his stomach gingerly and winced as if in pain.

'You took your time telling us you were blown, Snowy,' Tar continued evenly. 'I assume you warned Dick before he left for Germany?'

'Soon as he stepped off the boat. That's why I say he isn't playing straight. He had no hesitation in going to Berlin, no hesitation in the world. If I'd come straight out the blue, like him, I shouldn't have gone. Then he comes back full of it, and he's got something important from Goebbels and Schacht.'

'You're quite certain he's working for the other side?'

'Absolute gospel. He got into places I've never been asked to go. Why should a perfect stranger be treated like that? It doesn't sound right to me.'

'A double-crosser?'

'An extremely dangerous man, take it from me. Whoever's got the most money, he'll work for. Plus he takes dope.' Owens paused for a moment. 'The thing is to find out what he's got in those sealed packages.'

'That's all taken care of.'

'Well, thank God for that. Because according to Dick, me and him have got to go round and see Mr Churchill and get the war settled.'

Robertson offered no reply. In the light of the Venlo fiasco in November 1939 the Prime Minister had refused point-blank to parlay with ambivalent Nazis who claimed to be working for peace. Though the Blitz continued to exact a horrifying toll, and Greece and the Balkans looked likely to fall, few in the know doubted the wisdom of letting Hitler invade the Soviet Union and lose the war on frozen battlefields a thousand miles to the east. Let the dictators destroy themselves.

As the hours wore on at Nell Gwynn House Owens' answers became ever more tendentious, and the detail increasingly fuzzy. 'Snow's demeanour under interrogation gives every impression of telling the truth,' concluded Masterman, weary yet bemused. 'Which, indeed, he really thinks he is doing.' But the chair of the Twenty Committee was a history don, not a clinical psychologist. And canny Agent Snow thought nothing of the kind.

Finally Robertson instructed Owens to draft a written summary of his stay in Lisbon, then drove with Masterman from Chelsea to Mayfair, where Dicketts had been installed in a flat off Berkeley Square. With his lucrative peace plan derailed by

Customs officials at Whitchurch, the hapless triple agent hastily concocted a very different version of his German odyssey, involving robust interrogation and nerves of steel, followed by lobster suppers, scuffles in nightclubs and trifling encounters with pretty young ladies and junior aides.

For B1A and MI5, of paramount concern was whether Owens had warned Dicketts that his cover was blown before entering Germany. Tar sensed that he knew the answer already. 'Snow, being the little rascal that he is, preferred the security of his own neck to that of his friend Celery.'

Adopting tactics tried and tested at Camp 020, Robertson and Masterman sought to resolve the conundrum by putting the two spies together in a room for the first time since landing at Whitchurch. With a stenographer unlikely to keep pace, the confrontation was recorded direct onto acetate discs. The date, appropriately enough, was Tuesday, 1 April 1941.

All Fools' Day.

'You must both be aware of the seriousness of the position,' began Masterman. 'For us, Arthur, the essential point is the exact nature of your warning to Dick in Lisbon.'

Owens turned towards Dicketts. 'You didn't know I was blown?'

'You never told me anything about it. When did you break it to me?'

'I believe I warned you when you came up to my room at the hotel.'

'I don't care what your beliefs are,' snapped Dicketts. 'I want to know exactly.'

'I told you in front of the Doctor, Dick. The whole shooting match – everything about me in connection with the British Secret Service.' Owens gestured vigorously with his hands, as though he were back in the room at the Metropole. 'Don't you remember sitting there, the Doctor sitting there, and me sitting on the bed with Döbler?'

Dicketts glanced at Robertson. 'I'm sorry, but I disagree with this story entirely. I encountered Rantzau for the first time at the villa in Estoril. And if I'd known anything about the Little Man getting found out I should never have gone into Germany.'

'Well, I said it all right,' the Little Man insisted.

'And I'm quite convinced that the opposite is true, because on the last night you very nearly persuaded me not to go. You were very worried and shook my hand half a dozen times, telling me what you thought of me, that you would look after me. You were wavering, in my opinion.'

'No, I wasn't. I said you were a very brave man.'

'Well, in that case you were sending me to my death. You could have done nothing about it.'

'No, I wasn't. Gospel.'

'That's my candid opinion, Arthur. If I'd known that the whole case was blown to the Doctor then I should not have left.'

'Dick, you knew perfectly well.'

'You're bluffing.'

'You know bloody well I'm not bluffing.'

Dicketts rolled his eyes. 'Bearing in mind your mentality, I'd say your memory seems awfully short.'

'Ah – so you think I'm mental, like you tell Captain Robbie?'

'Actually, I think you're a maniac, Arthur. A maniac who lives in an atmosphere of mystery.'

Over the course of several hours and two dozen acetate discs the pair failed even to reach agreement on whether gin fizz or sherry had been consumed at the Metropole, let alone whether Snow had sent Celery into Germany blindfold. 'The riddle of the Sphinx and the doctrine of the Trinity are simple and straightforward affairs compared with this double enquiry,' conceded Masterman at length. 'More than ever I am convinced that Snow is a case not for the Security Service, but for a brain specialist.'

Owens knew nothing of the doctrine of the Trinity, only artful triple-cross. With the peace plan in tatters, however, and his secret war lost, Agent Snow hardly needed a brain specialist or any other doctor to confirm that he was living on borrowed time.

13

Snow On Ice

In an effort to discover whether Agent Snow was mad, let alone even genuinely ill, Robertson arranged for Owens to visit a specialist in Harley Street. 'I remained in the consulting room while the doctor put his initial questions,' Tar remarked. 'Snow made a terrific song and dance about his various ailments, saying that he was sick and had a pain in his left side, and had been told by his local doctor he was suffering from a weak heart.'

Owens also boasted of being an alcoholic, blaming his poor memory and erratic behaviour on delirium tremens and a bottle of brandy a day. To this catalogue of woe was added the duodenal ulcer first alleged after Operation Lamp. The Harley Street specialist ordered a stomach X-ray, but after Owens and Lily left the consulting room he told Tar that there was 'really nothing wrong with Snow at all. He had the constitution of an ox if he had been drinking as much as he said.' The specialist added that in his opinion Snow was mentally sound, but very sly. 'He himself would not trust him further than he could see him. The local doctor should have a word said to him, as he had had his leg pulled.'

While Owens sank brandy, Walter Dicketts quaffed vintage champagne. During a break in the seemingly endless round of debriefs and boardings, Dicketts drove Kay to Southend-on-Sea for an extravagant lunch at the Palace Hotel, lavishing two whole pounds. No matter that he was £5,000 down, or that MI5 doubted large parts of his narrative: having merely survived three weeks inside Germany was cause enough for celebration.

In order to secure a suitable table Dicketts masqueraded as Major Richard Blake, an identity dormant since 1931 when he had bounced a cheque at a garage in Taunton. Unfortunately the head waiter at the Palace, Alfredo Carminati, knew Dicketts of old and alerted the police while the 'major' slipped out to visit his mother. 'The waiter and the manager were aware of his convictions,' noted the local CID. 'Much publicity had been given to the case in Hampshire when he was sentenced to eighteen months. In past criminal activities he frequently posed as an army officer.'

A somewhat equivocal character, Carminati was also able to produce a pair of gold cufflinks given to him by Dicketts twelve years earlier. Southend Constabulary feared the onset of a crime spree to rival Dick's desperate capers a decade earlier, but quietly dropped their investigation after the matter came to the attention of MI5.

'Celery entirely denied the accusation,' wrote Tar's new assistant, John Marriott. 'His wife tried to book a table, but was told they were full and she must wait her turn. Then the head waiter came forward and greeted him like an old friend, addressing him as Captain. Dicketts gave the name of Woods as a man of Southend who might have informed on him out of malice.'

At least Agent Celery could afford to eat. For Jan Willem Ter Braak, the parachute agent still at large in Cambridge, the future looked decidedly bleak. After operating undetected for five months, the mysterious V-man now found himself running short of cash, and unable to buy food without an up-to-date ration book. With each day that passed his situation grew ever more desperate. Finally, on 29 March, the day before fake Major

Blake dined in style in Southend, the bogus Dutch scientist quit his lodgings in Montague Road, owing rent arrears and with less than two shillings in his pocket. At the railway station Ter Braak deposited his suitcase transmitter in the left-luggage office, the method of disposal prescribed during training for Operation Lena, then solemnly retraced his steps towards the city centre.

On the morning of Tuesday, 1 April, an air-raid warden made a gruesome discovery in one of the public shelters on Christ's Pieces, a small park close by Emmanuel College, criss-crossed by pathways and planted with ornamental trees. Sprawled untidily on the earthen floor was the emaciated body of a middle-aged man, neatly dressed in an overcoat, pinstripe suit and black homburg hat, his hands sheathed in leather gloves, his horn-rimmed spectacles knocked askew by a pistol shot to the head. Police were slow to investigate, suspecting a macabre April Fool. By midday, however, a gaggle of press reporters had converged on the scene, word having spread that the body was that of a Nazi spy.

'The question of tightening up regulations will have to be gone into very seriously,' wrote Liddell, profoundly vexed on learning that Ter Braak might easily have been arrested before Christmas. 'In this case the police were entirely to blame. The joke of it is that Ter Braak has been living within 50 yards of our RSLO in Cambridge.'

The following day copies of the *Cambridge News* were hastily withdrawn after an urgent call from the Ministry of Information. For MI5, the discovery of the dead Lena agent was profoundly worrying. On the one hand, detailed technical examination of his transmitter tended to suggest that it had not been used, while his ID papers, based on serials provided by Snow, were reliably flawed. On the other, his lifeless corpse raised the dread spectre of a parallel Abwehr network, as yet undiscovered. As it was, John Masterman could only speculate on 'how much more happy and more useful' Ter Braak's career might have been within the bosom of B1A.

As if in answer to these prayers, within a week two young Norwegians named Glad and Moe paddled ashore on the Moray Firth, only to be captured immediately and turned as JEFF and MUTT. Neither carried papers based on material provided by Snow, and were straightforward sabotage agents with no connection to Lena or Ritter. Nevertheless, Arthur Owens sensed danger and called an urgent meeting with Robertson to discuss the threat of violent assassination.

'From remarks made by the barman at The Otter it appears that a number of customers have formed the impression that people living at Homefields are working for British intelligence, and that there is a secret wireless transmitter at the address. Snow was in a frightful state about this. He said that the game was up, that he and all the people working with him were blown sky high, and that his life was in jeopardy along with those of his wife and child.'

Robertson argued that the Abwehr were unlikely to bother sending over an agent just to bump Owens off. 'He was sent home still protesting, and I was very strongly of the impression that the whole of the story from Snow's point of view was in the nature of a smokescreen.'

Or Zeppelin shells. Tar's diagnosis was subsequently confirmed by the Harley Street specialist. The X-rays taken of Owens' stomach revealed no trace of duodenal ulcers, nor any other internal trouble. 'Apart from rather high blood pressure his health is good, and the doctor was unable to believe that Snow had been drinking to anything like the extent he would have us believe. He added that the local doctor in Surrey now says Snow is probably suffering from venereal disease, and has been sent up to St Thomas' Hospital for examination.'

Operation Legover, it seemed, had exacted a terrible toll. Syphilis was not schizophrenia, however, and no psychiatry would be required. 'The doctor gave it as his opinion that Snow was a consummate liar, and could not be trusted in anything he said. He had no doubt he would try to deceive us in any way which suited his purpose.'

A right royal raspberry.

Kein glas bier.

On the morning of Thursday, 10 April, as Germany steamrollered Greece and the Balkans in support of another woeful Italian effort, the Twenty Committee elected to terminate Snow. 'The facts appeared to contradict one another to an astonishing extent,' sighed its chairman, John Masterman. 'If indeed Owens had revealed all, why was Dicketts not painfully executed by the Germans, unless he had gone over to the enemy? If, again, all had been revealed, why did the Germans present Owens with £10,000? The fact that Doctor Rantzau wishes to keep the party alive is a strong argument for closing it down.'

The Little Man was a busted flush, and had entirely exhausted his usefulness to B1A. Shortly before ten o'clock Agent Snow was brought before Robertson and Masterman, with Guy Liddell's deputy, Dick White, sitting in to provide an impartial view. As Snow's long-suffering case officer, it fell to Robertson to deliver the *coup de grâce*.

'We've come to the conclusion that you're of no further use to us, Snowy. So far as you and your skin are concerned, we propose you send over a message tomorrow to say that you are exceedingly ill, that your nerve has gone, and that you are not prepared to go on with the game.'

For the first and last time in his picaresque espionage career, talkative Arthur Owens was lost for words.

'You should also ask the other side what to do with your transmitter,' Tar continued. 'Is that all right?'

'Dandy,' Owens muttered quietly.

'On your rendering of the facts, Rantzau must know exactly why you've sent such a message.'

'Quite, quite. I follow you.'

'And that will throw the ball into his court.'

'Exactly. Quite.'

'So, that's your situation Arthur. Case closed, game over.'

Owens glanced from face to face. 'Can't I do anything to help this country at all? Hell, I've got to earn a living.'

'What do you suggest?'

'I'll do anything. I'm not a fool, I've had a good education.'

'And yet you've been tremendously idle,' countered Masterman. 'You could have kept on a job with Expanded Metal.'

'I didn't want any complications in that way.'

'So you did nothing for ten months except live off an enormous salary that makes a Cabinet Minister look stupid at the present rate of taxation.'

'Quite.'

'You see our difficulty,' said Robertson. 'They know we control your transmitter. There's no more value in this particular show.'

'I shouldn't look at it that way at all,' replied Owens, rallying slightly.

'Then how *do* you look at it?'

'The Doctor seems to think I'm in an ideal position. They can send in people by this motor-launch business, and I can go round anywhere with the transmitter and send all the dope over to Germany.'

'But Rantzau knows that your set is under control.'

'Not the new one, no. I've got a free hand. It's a wonderful scheme.'

Tar rolled his eyes. 'Just like all the other wonderful schemes the Doctor puts up which never come off. It might be an excellent plan from his point of view, but not from ours. He must think the whole of British intelligence are saps.'

'Well, he hasn't a very good impression of your people, no.'

'You've had plenty of time to think about all this, Snowy. Do you still maintain you told Dicketts that the game was blown before he went into Germany?'

'Gospel.'

'Well, we prefer to believe Dick. On its worst construction, you knowingly sent a friend to his death.'

Owens shook his head. 'I did nothing of the kind. Döbler knows it, and Döbler wasn't tight. He heard every word of it.'

'So who was tight? You?'

'We both were, I suppose.'

'Was that not a highly treacherous act?' pressed Masterman. 'You not telling Dicketts?'

'I'm positive I told him.'

'Definitely?'

'One hundred per cent.'

A year earlier, Robertson had experienced the same feelings of revulsion and personal affront when Snow played fast and loose with McCarthy's neck. Unlike his predecessors, Peal and Hinchley-Cooke, Tar strove always to extend the human touch towards Owens, only to have his fingers burned time and again. As yet, however, MI5 knew nothing of Owens' dealings with Germany over radar, and did not consider Agent Snow to be a major traitor. For now, the last salient issue to be resolved was Snow's allegation that Rantzau had accused him of operating under British control. Owens, in turn, had confessed without demur.

'You exercised the poorest judgement in giving in so easily,' Robertson said pleasantly. 'It might merely have been a routine question meant to catch you out.'

'I don't know about that. See, this has happened before. The first time he had proof in black and white.'

'Proof of what?'

'He had a letter from my wife back in August of thirty-nine. Two letters, if I remember correctly.'

'You had no reason to suppose Rantzau actually knew anything about the transmissions. Yet you gave it away at once.'

'Definitely a slip on my part, yes.'

'A slip with disastrous consequences. Surely you see that a person who's capable of making such a big mistake isn't much use to us?'

'Then let Dicketts carry on.'

'But you've already told us Dick's a double-crosser. A very dangerous man, so you said. Think it over very carefully, Arthur.'

'Yes. I see.'

'Just as I don't see that we need to meet in person again,' Tar said brusquely, rising to his feet. 'If you've anything more to add by all means put it in writing.'

On this frostiest of notes the embattled head of B1A left the room, leaving Owens to wonder whether prison lay in store, or Camp 020. Instead the diminutive traitor was driven back to Addlestone, where Lily also gave him the cold shoulder, and Ronnie Reed buzzed a brief final message to Wohldorf. *'Impossible to carry on. Will call you 11.30 to see if any further instructions. If not am going to pack up and hide gear.'*

Wohldorf told Colonel Johnny to make his own arrangements, and resume transmissions whenever he could. In the meantime an operator would continue to listen for him on even days.

Good night, old boy.

So, cheerio.

With this forlorn exchange ended the extraordinary career of double agent Snow, formerly Hitler's chief spy in England and now a candidate for the gallows. 'There was general agreement that it might be necessary to remove Owens from the country,' Masterman minuted after the Twenty Committee met to discuss the closure of the case. 'Or, alternatively, to shut him up.'

Much to the surprise of all concerned, Walter Dicketts vowed to defend Owens against charges under the 1940 Act. 'Celery made a very revealing remark,' declared John Marriott, who visited Dick in Guildford to confirm that enquiries into

'Major Blake' and his dining arrangements were being quietly dropped. 'He maintained that all he had said about Lisbon was absolutely true, and that Owens was lying – but that he would take it very much to heart if the Little Man got into trouble as a result.'

Truly, it seemed, there was honour amongst thieves. In Tripoli, Ritter learned of Johnny's downfall a fortnight later. 'Hamburg told me a message had come from Owens to the effect that he was too ill to continue his work. This had an ominous ring, though this time I had left for North Africa and was therefore out of touch with day-to-day developments in the case.'

After waiting in vain for Captain Jack Brown to bring Churchill to his senses, Berlin quietly released the same trial balloon via the Japanese Foreign Office on 29 April. 'The nations called upon to settle world peace are Germany, Japan, the British Empire and the United States,' trumpeted its unofficial organ, the suitably obscure *Japan Times Advertiser*. 'The strongest powers must have the greatest opportunities of developing the world. This is the law of nature, and attempts to maintain the status quo by dominant powers who continue to function only through alliances must break down.'

London, the seat of the dominant power in question, offered no formal response. Instead, Churchill telegraphed an admirably undiplomatic reply during a stirring speech on the fall of Greece. 'No prudent and far-seeing man can doubt that the eventual and total defeat of Hitler and Mussolini is certain. There are less than 70,000,000 malignant Huns, some of whom are curable and others killable, most of whom are already engaged in holding down Austrians, Czechs, Poles and the many other ancient races they now bully and pillage. The people of the British Empire and of the United States number nearly 200,000,000 . . . They are determined that the cause of freedom shall not be trampled on, nor the tide of world progress turned backward by the criminal dictators.'

Malignant Huns, trampling bullies, killable criminal dictators. The Reich had wasted time and money on Walter Dicketts and his sly sponsor Snow; the Duke of Hamilton, a gentleman supposedly, had not even troubled to reply. How, now, might increasingly twitchy Nazi feelers reach out to the sizeable peace lobby that surely existed in Britain?

Like Dicketts, Wulf Schmidt was also left in limbo by the fall of Snow. The double agent codenamed Tate by MI5, and Leonhardt by the Abwehr, still resided with Tar Robertson and his family at Round Bush House, but was compromised by the £100 sent by Owens to Radlett in February. In a bid to test his continued credibility, the Dane was instructed to buzz Wohldorf with yet another urgent request for funds. 'If Tate is not helped at once he must throw up the sponge,' reasoned Masterman, glumly contemplating a double-cross doomsday. 'We shall only be able to decide what is to be done according to the Doctor's reply.'

Rantzau, however, was in Tripoli with Rommel, and temporarily indisposed. In his absence Hamburg suggested dropping an interim payment from Gartenfeld's Heinkel-111, with more to follow via Watford post office. MI5 got as far as instructing the RAF to avoid shooting down Luftwaffe intruders over Hertfordshire on the night in question, then backtracked when the money bomb plan was suddenly abandoned. Now Schmidt would receive £500 via a parachute courier.

'We have bought two bloodhounds and their keeper,' noted Guy Liddell, keen to avoid a repeat of previous errors. 'They will be available to all regions for tracking down parachutists.'

Robertson was already on the scent. Wohldorf warned Schmidt to expect a visit from 'the man from the Phoenix', a notorious Hamburg club frequented by agents in training during 1940. Schmidt professed ignorance, though fortunately the human reference library at Camp 020 still contained Josef Jakobs, the V-man dropped near Ramsey in January, who duly obliged with a detailed description of the Phoenix friend, since codenamed ROBOTER ('robot') by his Abwehr controllers at Stelle X.

The mastermind behind the revised money-drop scheme was none other than Nikolaus Ritter, still in North Africa but determined to protect his friend Schmidt, as well as his own backside. 'I arranged for the next agent dispatched to England to contact Leonhardt to make a routine payment, and to report what the situation really was.' If Schmidt was still reliable, a satisfactory report would come back. 'But if he were controlled, Roboter would be arrested, and the British faced with the choice of allowing him to return to Germany immediately, as instructed, or keep him and thereby acknowledge Leonhardt's true position. Either way, I should know where I stood.'

Viewed objectively, the intricate plan hatched by Ritter to test Schmidt stood no more chance of success than Jan Willem Ter Braak's mission to Cambridge, which had ended in starvation and suicide. The 'robot' assigned this unenviable task was Karel Richter, a Sudeten German who had served in the Czech air force before a spell as a mechanic on transatlantic liners. 'Schmidt is our master pearl,' Ritter promised Richter, mixing his metaphors in fine style. 'If he is false, then the whole string is false.'

For eighteen months the fate of the double-cross system on either side had hinged on an intemperate Welsh fantasist with false teeth and delusions of grandeur. Now it depended on a former banana farmer from South Jutland with an unmerited Iron Cross and a love of profanity.

Götz von Berlichingen.

For the Twenty Committee, the imminent arrival of 'the man from the Phoenix' seemed to confirm that Agent Snow was innocent of treason, and had lied about exposure in Lisbon. Masterman conjectured that Owens was a burned-out case, and with Britain undefeated desired a comfortable retirement with a foot in both camps. Although this confidence was entirely misplaced, the Little Man could at least be spared the rope – if not prison. On the morning of Monday, 21 April, nine days after Agent Snow's final transmission to Wohldorf, Masterman placed a call to the Chief Constable of Surrey, requesting immediate service of the 18B Order drawn up a whole year earlier. A police superintendent named Curry drove from Weybridge to Addlestone directly and placed Owens under formal arrest. Without further ado, the redundant triple agent was then conveyed a hundred miles north to Stafford Gaol.

A good kick in the pants, as Ritter might say.

No record exists of the reaction of Lily Bade to their forced separation. Perhaps the scene at the safe house on Spinney Hill was highly emotional, marked by bitter tears and desperate pleas. More likely, the revelation that Owens was suffering from a sexually transmitted disease meant that his departure from Homefields fell short of a fond farewell.

Owens arrived at Stafford still bearing identity papers in the name of Thomas Wilson. 'He is a man who has done some work for us,' MI5 informed the governor, remaining purposefully vague, 'but we are very dissatisfied with certain things he has done lately, and are unable to trust him. We wish to be informed of any requests for visits, or any petition he may make to any government department. Otherwise we wish him to be treated as an ordinary prisoner.'

Conditions at Stafford were far from ordinary. A grim, sprawling fortress built at the end of the nineteenth century, the prison had been taken over by the War Office in 1914 to serve as a military gaol, then left empty after 1923 when falling crime rates rendered it surplus to requirements. Thanks to Defence Regulation 18B, the sudden round-up of hostiles and aliens in May 1940 created an acute shortage of secure accommodation.

To help cope with the surge in demand a large wing at Stafford called the Crescent was hastily reopened, despite the fact that the building was now semi-derelict and imbued with a cold, dank atmosphere, smelling of mildew and gas.

It was a long way from Homefields, and double suites in luxurious foreign hotels. 'Big iron staircases, bare, and railings everywhere,' recalled one 18B inmate, without affection. 'No two cells were the same shape or size. In fact I think it must have warped from the damp and age.'

Hitler's chief spy in England was soon joined behind bars by a far more important Nazi emissary. Shortly after sunset on Saturday, 10 May, the pilot of a Messerschmitt-110 twin-engined fighter baled out of his aircraft over Eaglesham, eight miles south of Glasgow, jumping low in fading light and cracking an ankle. Challenged by a ploughman armed wielding a hay-fork, the lone airman identified himself as Hauptmann Alfred Horn and asked to be transported to Dungavel House, eleven miles distant, where he wished to talk to the Duke of Hamilton. Horn was instead handed over to the local Home Guard, who detained him in a scout hut. Only after the prisoner was delivered to Maryhill Barracks in Glasgow did it become clear that Alfred Horn was in fact Rudolf Hess, Hitler's Deputy Führer.

The arrival of the Nazi number two in Scotland represented a last desperate bid to conclude peace with Britain ahead of Operation Barbarossa, the German assault on the Soviet Union. Let down by Dicketts, Snow and the Duke of Hamilton, then goaded sorely by Churchill, Hess had contrived to fly a thousand miles from the Messerschmitt works airfield at Augsberg, coming within an ace of landing at Dungavel, the Hamilton family estate in the Scottish Borders, which boasted a small private landing strip. As well as displaying impressive skills as an aviator, Hess arrived backed by shock and awe. That same night the Luftwaffe delivered a devastating raid on London, with 500 aircraft pounding the capital in relays for hours, killing 1,400 people and rendering another 12,000 homeless. Göring's savage attack marked the end of eight months of Blitz on London. These were the politics of pressure, the psychology behind them all too clear.

Unsurprisingly, the Deputy Führer's flying visit met with no more success than Walter Dicketts' ignominious crash landing at Whitchurch. Informed of his arrival during the screening of a Marx Brothers film at Chequers, Churchill dismissed the event as lacking 'any serious importance', then took the prompt and highly symbolic step of imprisoning Hess in the Tower of London. When Hess failed to return to Germany he was swiftly disowned by Hitler, who blamed his friend's adventure on a fit of temporary insanity, thereby confirming the *realpolitik* around 'loss of face' articulated to Dicketts by Nazi intermediaries in Hamburg and Berlin.

Whether Hitler sanctioned the Hess peace mission remains mired in controversy. Certainly Guy Liddell denied all knowledge. 'Today's sensational news is the arrival of Rudolf Hess,' he rejoiced in his diary, before reviewing Haushofer's letter and the mooted treff in Lisbon. 'The Air Ministry eventually decided not to send Hamilton. Hess may have come with some kind of peace offer. The Germans may have thought they could only convince us of their sincerity by sending a man of high standing. The statement about Hess being mad would merely have been put out to cover up the fact that they are putting out peace feelers.'

Lord Swinton, in charge of the Security Executive, waxed incandescent, and fired off a furious letter to David Petrie, the new Director-General of MI5. Mercifully unaware of Dicketts and his sealed packages from Hjalmar Schacht, Swinton expressed 'outrage' at having been kept in the dark about the Haushofer-Hamilton letter. His ire mattered little, since the Hess initiative was deemed of 'no particular point' by MI5, and his flight conceivably a reverse Venlo encouraged by ingenious rivals at MI6. However, within weeks Churchill's sidelined security overlord would threaten to bring down the entire XX system just as surely as renegade Agent Snow, while at the same time triggering one of the most ignoble episodes in British penal history.

Forty-eight hours after Hess landed in Scotland, Karel Richter was dropped over Hertfordshire by Hauptmann Gartenfeld, landing in a field near London Colney. Just five miles separated Roboter's drop zone from Round Bush House near Radlett, where Wulf Schmidt (aka Tate) still lived with the Robertson family, along with a wireless operator named Russell Lee. This close proximity was entirely deliberate, yet Richter struggled to cover even this short distance. The young Sudetenlander spoke imperfect English, mixing his Vs and Ws, and carried flawed papers based on serials provided by Snow. After hiding in woodland for an entire day, Richter set out on foot along the A405, where a passing lorry driver asked for directions and grew suspicious on receiving an incoherent reply. Prompt intervention by a War Reserve constable ensured that the dubious foreigner carrying £551 and $1400 in cash was soon in custody at Camp 020.

'Richter arrived in reasonably good health and an unreasonable frame of mind,' recorded Tin-Eye Stephens. 'He showed no anxiety to make a confession. But when Josef Jakobs, carefully groomed for his reluctant role, was brought into the room for confrontation, Richter slipped and began gradually to break.'

Ritter's master pearl was worthless paste, his Iron Cross tin plate. On 14 May Richter returned to London Colney under guard and retrieved his equipment from a hedge. The expedition was recorded in a remarkable sequence of photographs, later released to the Imperial War Museum, the informality of which belied the gravity of Roboter's predicament. Back behind bars at Latchmere House, Richter admitted that his 'principal purpose' in coming to England was to deliver £400 and a wireless crystal to Leonhardt. Although he obstinately refused to be turned as an XX agent, Roboter also confirmed that he was to 'discover whether Schmidt was under control and whether the messages he was sending were authentic.'

Richter declined to cooperate fully with B1A, but let slip that he meant to meet Schmidt outside a barber shop at the Regent Palace Hotel, with the Tate Gallery (where else?) in reserve. *'What is delaying the man with the money you promised?'* Leonhardt buzzed Wohldorf angrily when Roboter failed to show. *'I am beginning to think that you are full of shit.'*

Soon after, Schmidt received £200 in a complicated drop involving a Number 16 bus and an Oriental gentleman holding a copy of *The Times*, subsequently identified as an assistant naval attaché at the Japanese embassy. 'The incident was unimportant,' remarked Masterman, 'but the difficulties of securing these early payments were not without value. A real agent would have grave difficulties to overcome, and these tiresome hitches and obstacles can only have served to confirm the Germans in their belief in the case.'

Interrogated by Allied intelligence officers five years later, Ritter appeared to have been driven stark raving mad by the heat and dust of the North African desert. 'About the middle of May I was informed that Roboter had landed safely, but that so far no message had come from him.' This Ritter took to be an encouraging sign. 'Were the British in control of Leonhardt's set, it is incredible that they should have taken the risk of making no move with Roboter in view of his instructions to report on Leonhardt. I therefore felt tolerably certain that Schmidt was safe.'

Lucid or not, such skewed logic could hardly have been predicted by the Twenty Committee, yet it suited their purpose perfectly well. Three months later Ritter's irrational faith in

Leonhardt was confirmed by the Yugoslav playboy Duško Popov, alias double agent Tricycle, whose lucrative Plan Midas netted £20,000 intended to fund future Abwehr operations in Britain. Every last penny was meant for potty-mouthed Iron Cross winner Wulf Schmidt.

Humdinger.

While Roboter remained under lock and key at Camp 020, Agent Snow languished in Stafford Gaol. Hopeful that three weeks in clink might serve to encourage Owens to give a more truthful account of his Lisbon adventure with Dicketts, Robertson and Masterman paid him a visit on 16 May. To their dismay Owens stuck by his previous statement, insisting that Rantzau had blown his cover and that Celery had flipped. 'Long incarceration,' rued Masterman, 'never brought him to change his story.'

Despite lingering doubts, Walter Dicketts was sent back to Portugal at the end of May. With his peace initiative overshadowed by Hess, Agent Celery now hoped to persuade the former Hitler Youth footballer George Sessler to defect in return for a cash lump sum and free onward passage to America. For Dicketts, there was also the promise of Lotti Schade, the Mata Hari hoofer from the Arcadia cabaret, patiently waiting in her cosy Berlin apartment. And if he failed to penetrate Germany again, there was always poor Marcelle Quenall, the ash-blonde Belgian at the Hotel Franco . . .

The mission washed out. Through Hans Ruser, the flag-flying diplomatic aide, Dicketts learned that Sessler was in fact a loyal Nazi. Meanwhile Ruser, whose own loyalties were hopelessly confused, was genuinely keen to defect, and would eventually do so in 1943. Seeking to establish his anti-Nazi credentials, Ruser warned Celery that the Abwehr were wise to what was fast becoming a labyrinthine quadruple cross. Discretion being the better part of valour, Dicketts fled from Lisbon without returning to Germany.

'Our manoeuvres in Hamburg were less successful than I hoped,' Ritter warned his perplexed successor, Doctor Schneider. 'Dicketts is probably a British agent of high standing, whose loyalty we did not succeed in buying and who probably reported on Owens. In these circumstances it seems more than likely our whole previous view of Johnny's case has been mistaken.'

With these few words Doctor Rantzau washed his hands of an ambitious, ambiguous XX sting that had cost the lives of so many luckless Lena agents, then lured the Deputy Führer on a flight of fancy. Small wonder that his memoirs would be characteristically careless with the truth.

Remarkably, MI6 expressed interest in re-employing Dicketts for further operations abroad, including missions to Brazil and Occupied France. However, a reference drafted by Robertson was decidedly lukewarm. 'The information which Celery managed to obtain from Germany was not in any sense of the word useful from a military point of view. I would add that it is open to doubt whether he did not go a very long way towards becoming a proper German agent. This possibility cannot be ruled out.'

Meanwhile Lord Swinton moved to hang more spies. After choosing to deliberately ignore decrees from the Security Executive that all deals offered to enemy agents required prior approval, MI5 had offered unauthorised inducements to Josef Jakobs and Karel Richter. Jakobs lent a hand in breaking Richter, who in turn made certain admissions, thus allowing B1A to salvage the crucial case of Tate. Neither V-man had been able to carry out any useful work for Germany, and in the opinion of most on the Twenty Committee they deserved no worse punishment than detention at Camp 020 or 020R until hostilities ceased.

There was also the obvious security risk in putting enemy agents on trial, even in camera. Despite informed advice to the contrary, Swinton remained unconvinced, preferring to adhere to the rigid diktat imposed in 1940 that 'in all suitable cases' enemy spies should be brought to trial. 'I have given my undertaking,' the intransigent peer warned in June, 'that any spy no longer required for intelligence purposes shall be brought to justice if the case against him will lie. The right man to decide is the Director of Public Prosecutions, and we should certainly have the insurance of his opinion and advice in every case.'

Like Swinton, the DPP understood little of the exigencies of double-cross work, and the outcome edged uncomfortably close to state murder. Following a military court martial convened at the beginning of August, Josef Jakobs was sentenced to death by firing squad at the Tower of London, the first execution performed there since 1916. Still limping heavily on account of his broken ankle, Jakobs was allowed to face death while seated in a brown Windsor chair, thoughtfully placed at the far end of the miniature rifle range below the Constable Tower.

Eight Scots Guards aimed their rifles at a small circle of white lint pinned above his heart. According to Tin-Eye Stephens, Jakob's last words on Earth were a polite request to shoot straight.

Still able-bodied, Karel Richter proved rather less docile. Tried in camera at the Old Bailey in October, Roboter was convicted under the Treachery Act and sentenced to death. After an appeal was summarily dismissed, Albert Pierrepoint travelled to Wandsworth to assess Richter's physical build, calmly calculating the drop required as the prisoner walked in the exercise yard. Shortly before eight o'clock on the morning of 10 December the hangman and his assistant stood ready outside the condemned cell, confident of executing the Nazi spy with practised efficiency. On the far side of the door the prisoner would be pinioned with lightning speed, then propelled into the adjoining execution chamber and placed on the trap. There a white linen hood would be placed over his head, followed by the noose around his neck.

From his initial entry into the condemned cell to the brute pull of the trapdoor lever, Pierrepoint reckoned to take no more than twenty seconds. His personal best was just seven.

Richter, however, was far from quiescent, as the hangman recalled in his ghosted memoir *Executioner Pierrepoint*. 'He was standing at the far side of the table, glowering at the open door, eyes staring, very blue and dangerous. His big fists were clenched. Before I could reach him he heaved away the nearest prison officer and dived like a bullock at the stone wall. His head cracked against the masonry. It may have been his intention to stun himself so that he was hanged unconscious. I do not know. My first impression was quite irrelevant. It was the flurry of robes of the Catholic priest as he tried to get out of the way of the battle which followed.'

Four warders were required to subdue Richter, whose mortal flailings even split the leather strap used to pinion his hands behind his back. Worse was to follow in the chamber itself. 'A strap was quickly fastened round his ankles, the cap and noose were adjusted, and still he fought for life. Just as I was crossing to the lever, he jumped with bound feet. The drop opened, he plunged down, and I saw with horror that the noose was slipping. It would have come right up over his head had it not caught roughly at a point halfway up the hood.'

Untidily, the noose hooked just below Richter's nose – a truly ghastly end. With the rope still swaying gently, Pierrepoint descended into the pit with the prison medical officer, who pronounced it a clean, instantaneous death. 'He sounded surprised, and I did not blame him. I was surprised myself, and very relieved.'

Rather than seven short seconds, the killing of Karel Richter had dragged on for seventeen agonising minutes. Gösta Caroli (aka Summer) and Kurt Goose (aka Gander), whose brief double-cross careers had also come to an end, were truly lucky to escape with their lives.

So too was Agent Snow.

14

Sins of the Father

Despite having evaded the hangman's rope, Arthur Owens remained highly strung, and found life behind bars at Stafford barely tolerable. MI5 inquisitors aside, his visitors were strictly limited and correspondence was restricted to two short letters each week. Only his son Bob kept in regular contact, and on a single occasion made the long journey up from Surrey. From Lily Bade there was no word at all. Anxious to smuggle out an uncensored letter to the mother of his child, Owens bribed a crooked warder with a five-pound note.

Still there came no reply.

The fact that Germany remained odds-on favourite to win what had now become a Second World War only added to his burden of woe. On 22 June Hitler launched Operation Barbarossa, hurling 4,000 tanks and four million troops across the western borders of the Soviet Union, pushing halfway to Moscow by the end of July. Once the scourge of Bolshevism was erased from the map, the British Isles could be invaded at leisure and the warmonger Churchill chased into the sea, at long last making Nazi Germany master of all Europe.

Humdinger.

Except that invasion would mean a visit to Stafford by Mr Mills' Circus. Owens understood the implications of Plan Hegira only too well, and made a point of warning a fellow inmate named Dirk Boon that the military would put a bullet through the head of each and every prisoner. Boon, a Dutch fascist who had served time at Camp 020, initially swallowed Snow's claims to be 'the most important German spy in England' and readily agreed to pool resources in a bid to escape. For £20 the same crooked warder provided a small hacksaw blade, and allowed Owens to take a soap impression of a master key. Boon then fashioned a cardboard positive, from which the warder would arrange to cut a duplicate. Having gained their liberty, the pair planned to make for the German legation in Dublin, after which Owens would make arrangements for a U-boat to take his Dutch sidekick back to the Netherlands.

'The warder had complained of his pay and conditions,' found a subsequent enquiry. 'He was in want of money and asked both Owens and Boon to help find him a better job after the war.'

Boon, however, was less naive, and soon came to realise that 'Thomas Wilson' was nothing more than an avaricious traitor. 'He had gone into the spy business simply to make money, was in no sense an idealist, and alleged he could make about £20,000 in a year.' Owens also boasted of having a secret American bank account, and let slip that he expected to be shipped to Canada because his continued presence on British soil terrified MI5. Correctly deducing that Wilson was untrustworthy, and likely to desert him on the far side of the prison wall, Boon reported the plot to the governor.

At the same time, Snow Junior attempted to spring his father from gaol by staging a stunt of his own. Now aged twenty-one, Robert Owens was still employed by the fire service at Chertsey and engaged to Lavinia Cantello, an attractive girl of Italian descent whose family lived nearby. At the beginning of August Bob wrote to offer his services as a secret agent, rashly promising Tar Robertson that he was able to 'gain entrance and exit into occupied countries' at will. Almost certainly Snow Junior was acting on instructions handed down by his father, whom he closely resembled in almost every respect. Grilled by Tar and Masterman at the War Office, he claimed to have been inveigled by a stranger in an Italian restaurant on Frith Street and invited to spy for Germany. 'Snow Junior was most evasive throughout,' observed Masterman, 'producing his account of the incident piece by piece and most unconvincingly. He proposed that he should be sent to Lisbon by plane, taking a man who could speak fluent French, and bring back information.'

Robertson dismissed Bob Owens out of hand, accusing him of lacking scruples or talent. Somewhat piqued, Bob fell to bragging about his sketching excursions to fighter airfields at Biggin Hill and Kenley during the summer of 1939, and posting plans to Hamburg. Suddenly MI5 took him very seriously indeed. 'We now have to decide whether he should be locked up,' wrote Guy Liddell with satisfaction. 'Snow's son is a frightful little worm.'

Kein glas bier.

Two weeks later, the idiot scion was served with an 18B Order as he clocked off the night watch at Chertsey. 'This does not surprise me,' he told Inspector Curry, the same detective who had lifted his father in April. 'I was expecting it.'

Bob Owens was conveyed to Brixton. After supervising the arrest in person Robertson drove over to Addlestone, where Lily Bade still occupied Homefields and herself remained liable to arrest under Plan Hegira. 'She was very anxious to know for how long Snow Junior would be detained. I said I was unable to tell her. She did not seem to worry, and offered no comment apart from the fact that she asked what he had been up to.'

Still Lily resisted all contact with fallen Agent Snow. Would Lavinia Cantello show greater devotion when it came to Snow Junior?

This rapid reversal of fortune continued in Stafford. After Dirk Boon betrayed their escape plan in August, Owens received another visit from Robertson and Masterman, followed by a stiff boarding from the governor. The various punishments imposed included seven long months in solitary confinement, and a complete loss of privileges which extended even to basic tonsorial care. 'I was forbidden a haircut for ten months until my hair was down to my shoulders,' Owens complained later, following a welcome transfer to Dartmoor. 'I was made the laughing stock of all the prisoners.'

Another good kick in the pants.

Ritter, too, found his career locked in a vertiginous downward spiral. Attempts by his new special unit to insert agents into Cairo met with no more success than Operation Lena, after which Ritter fell out with his chief North African adviser, and broke an arm while ditching a Junkers-88 in the Mediterranean. After a lengthy stay in hospital Ritter landed a cushy posting to Rio de Janeiro, only to see the offer withdrawn following newspaper coverage of the sensational trial of American spy William Sebold in September 1941. 'Nikolaus Adolf Fritz Ritter is named as a co-conspirator in the indictment,' trumpeted the *New York Times*. 'A Gestapo agent, he is identified by Sebold as the man who persuaded him to become a German spy during a visit in 1939.'

Three months later the United States entered the war, effectively ending Doctor Rantzau's inglorious Abwehr career. Determined to retain his rank, and a smart Luftwaffe uniform, Ritter retrained as an anti-aircraft officer, serving in Sicily and Italy with the elite Hermann Göring Division, then returning to Germany to command flak defences in Hamburg and Hanover. Sadly, his astonishing facility for skewed analysis meant that the civilian population of these cities paid a price even higher than that met by the V-men sacrificed in Operation Lena. 'Ritter was the commanding officer for the anti-aircraft defences at Hanover on the occasion of the last saturation raid,' a bemused MI5 interrogator noted two years later. 'That night he studied very carefully the reports received from radar and ground observers, and formed the view that the various small-scale diversionary attacks in progress in other parts of Germany represented our main effort for the night. He therefore gave orders for the defence of Hanover to stand down. Precisely six minutes later some 1,500 bombers arrived over the town with results that are still visible.'

The good doctor, it was noted, had run true to form. MI5 later calculated that the Abwehr had paid over at least £13,850 to Arthur Owens, worth more than a million pounds in terms of earnings today. 'Although Snow's career ended more or less disastrously his case was by no means unprofitable,' maintained Masterman. 'At the beginning of the war he gave us information which formed the basis of our knowledge of the Hamburg stelle, which was of considerable value when that office was the one principally concerned with work against this country. Similarly through McCarthy and latterly Dicketts he provided valuable information about the German organisation in Lisbon.'

The Selfridge's shopper Mathilde Krafft might have been the only Nazi agent whose detection was solely attributable to Owens, yet the planting of false papers on almost every incoming V-man between September 1940 and May 1941 made most of them much easier to break at Camp 020 and flip for double-cross work by B1A. 'The part which Owens played in these early cases shows that he was then regarded as the lynchpin of the Abwehr organisation in England,' Masterman concluded. 'Consequently we were able to form an impression of their methods which have been of incomparable value since.'

Unfortunately plans to resume controlled transmissions as Snow were abandoned after it was discovered that the last code issued to Owens in Lisbon, based on an obscure Penguin paperback, had been mislaid. In the final analysis much of the Little Man's value to the British war effort was inadvertent, after the failure of Operation Lena cost Ritter his job at Stelle X, to be replaced by new case officers with little or no inkling that their agents and networks were rotten to the core.

For the 18B detainee known as Thomas Wilson there would be no immediate reward. Despite submitting regular petitions to the Home Office, Snow Junior was denied permission to join his father at Stafford or Dartmoor and instead served his time on the Isle of Man. Long estranged both from Arthur and Bob, Patricia Owens completed her studies at the Royal Academy of Dramatic Arts, and by 1943 had landed her first movie role in *Miss London Ltd*, a comedy vehicle starring Arthur Askey. As the war entered its fourth year the contrasting fortunes of the fallen spies and the rising starlet could hardly have been more pronounced.

At the same time the tide was turning in favour of the Allies. Following the humiliating surrender of the German Sixth Army at Stalingrad in February 1943, and the rout of the Afrika Korps, British and American forces embarked on the liberation of Europe, landing first in Sicily, then gaining a toehold on the boot of Italy. With the eventual defeat of the Axis powers inevitable by the close of the year, the great majority of prisoners interned in Britain under 18B were released from custody, a process which culminated in the release of dilettante fascist Sir Oswald Mosley shortly before Christmas, provoking a storm of protest and demonstrations countrywide.

Snows Senior and Junior remained firmly under lock and key. Owens was furious, and broke two years of silence with an indignant letter to Tar Robertson. 'I am not worried about the loss of my liberty,' fibbed the former Colonel Johnny. 'But I am worried that I am unable to help my mother country in these difficult times. I have done a considerable lot for this country and your department, although perhaps not seeing eye to eye in our methods in arriving at a given point. However, since Mosley is now released, together with Sir Barry Domvile, I must frankly say I am consumed with rage to have to waste my time here when I can be doing useful work.'

After two miserable years in Stafford and Dartmoor, countries had come to count after all.

Yet much of the useful work had already been done. The Allied success in Sicily owed much to Operation Mincemeat, a macabre deception scheme which drew on elements rehearsed in 1940 through Agent Snow. In order to convince the Germans that the Allies would land in Greece and Sardinia rather than Sicily during the summer of 1943, the Twenty Committee lit upon the idea of tipping a dead British officer into the sea off the Spanish coast, apparently the victim of a plane crash, and still handcuffed to a briefcase containing plans for an attack on Greece. In truth these documents were convincing forgeries, and the corpse of 'Major William Martin' that of an insane Welsh vagrant named Glyndwr Michael, who had committed suicide by swallowing rat poison laced with phosphorus.

Some within the British intelligence community might have preferred to use the corpse of another unstable Welshman, still rattling the bars of his cage on the special wing at Dartmoor. Lingering resentments notwithstanding, Operation Mincemeat owed no small debt to rogue Agent Snow. The falsification of death certificates for Glyndwr Michael and 'Major Martin' followed the precedent set by the inconvenient suicide of William Rolph in May 1940, and was undertaken by the very same coroner, William Bentley Purchase. As for the central strategic deception, causing enemy troops to be diverted elsewhere, this echoed Snow's false dope on landings at Trondheim during the Norwegian campaign. The crucial difference was that in May 1943 Operation Mincemeat was swallowed whole: German reinforcements were directed to Greece, Sardinia and Corsica, thus laying the ground for the successful Allied assault on Sicily, which was taken in just five weeks.

For Robertson, Masterman and the Twenty Committee this grisly stunt by 'the man who never was' embodied signal success. Where a live electrical engineer from Pontardawe had failed, a dead tramp from nearby Aberbargoed delivered famous victory.

A humdinger, in fact.

Owens knew nothing of Operation Mincemeat, and a visit by Masterman to the bleak wilds of Dartmoor in December gave the Little Man scant cause for celebration. 'I told Snow that you were entirely unable to consider his request to be interned in the company of his son,' he informed Robertson, who still declined to communicate with Owens direct. 'On the other hand, I said I knew you wished to recommend his release as soon as you felt it was safe to do so, which might or might not be accepted. Snow expressed the liveliest gratitude for this information.'

Wisely abandoning rants about Oswald Mosley, Owens adopted an obsequious tone in his next note to Tar. 'After being for three years in the closest contact with Germans and other foreigners, I have a very good insight into their mentality and outlook. I trust that you will be able to obtain something for me to do. Once again I thank you sincerely for your kindness, and take this opportunity of wishing yourself, Mrs Robertson and your daughter all the very best for Xmas and the New Year.'

Tellingly, Owens signed off with a simple letter T. Since fellow inmates on the special wing at Dartmoor included a sprinkling of Nazi undesirables transferred from Camp 020, it was safer to remain Thomas Wilson. Impecunious warders might, after all, be susceptible to bribes . . .

At Peel Camp on the Isle of Man, Snow Junior also came round to a better way of thinking. Blaming his earlier confession about sketching Fighter Command airfields on an ill-conceived 'sense of adventure', Bob also now admitted that his story of the German agent on Frith Street was cut from whole cloth. Despite these revelations, the intertwined cases of Snow and Snow Junior continued to divide opinion within

MI5. 'Tar is rather in favour of the release of the Little Man and his son,' mused Guy Liddell. 'Personally I am against this.'

The softer line taken by Robertson was due in part to the defection of Hans Ruser, the flag-flying diplomat befriended by Walter Dicketts in Lisbon. Ruser finally reached London in November 1943 via MI6, and was debriefed at Camp 020 with a view to undertaking double-cross work in Spain. Though the impression he had formed of Owens in Lisbon was distinctly unfavourable ('he drank a lot of brandy, and looked like a very poor class of merchant seaman'), Ruser maintained that Agent Celery had shot his own fox. 'It was all a big tangle,' swore Ruser. 'Dicketts told me one day, after a certain amount of drink, that he was a member of the British Secret Service – but that they must not know he was going on his mission to Berlin, as they had not sanctioned it.'

Dicketts, like Lily, was long since retired from the spy game. 'Celery has apparently disappeared,' jotted Liddell in February 1944. 'Masterman tells me that there is a warning out for his arrest for embezzlement.'

Dick Moreton was back in business. Or was it Squadron Leader Norman? Or Major Richard Blake?

By now the case of Owens – father and son – had begun to elicit sympathy from senior figures at the Home Office. 'My own inclination is to believe Owens Junior when he says he was lying,' Sir Alexander Maxwell wrote to Sir David Petrie, still in post as Director-General of MI5. 'He is obviously a most unreliable person, but the risk of him attempting to give information to the enemy or engaging in sabotage seems remote. It would help the Home Secretary to come to a decision if the Security Service would kindly arrange for some fuller statement to be given as to the specific reasons on which your recommendation for continued detention is based.'

The reason, quite simply, was D-Day. Thanks to a network of two dozen reliable double-cross agents such as Tate, Tricycle,

Zigzag and the Spaniard Juan Pujol Garcia, codenamed Garbo, the Twenty Committee now aimed to convince the German High Command that the Second Front would open not through Normandy but the Pas de Calais. Codenamed Fortitude, this bold strategic deception would be achieved by drip-feeding the enemy a false order of battle, including an imaginary First US Army Group (FUSAG) based in the south-east of England and under the notional command of firebrand General George Patton. This, it was hoped, would bottle up vital German reserves far to the north of the real landing beaches, including several crack Panzer divisions which might otherwise throw the Allies back into the sea.

'In wartime,' Churchill told Stalin at the Tehran Conference, 'truth is so precious that she should always be attended by a bodyguard of lies.'

So important was Fortitude that the head of MI5 attended the Home Office in person to explain why Snow and Snow Junior should remain behind bars until the bridgehead in Normandy was secure. 'We cannot accept the responsibility of having these two individuals at large and uncontrolled at a time of such great security importance,' Petrie told Maxwell. 'Special agents are being used extensively for deception purposes, and although the general theory and practice is well known it would be undesirable that this type of activity should be underlined at the present moment.'

One such special agent was Wulf Schmidt, the Iron Cross winner codenamed Tate by B1A and Leonhardt by the Abwehr. During one fallow period in 1943 the profane Dane received just fourteen messages from Wohldorf and came perilously close to being shut down. *'You never let me know what you think of my work,'* Schmidt carped in an effort to buck up his controllers. *'An occasional pat on the back would be welcome. After all, I am only human.'* Notionally employed on a farm near Radlett – and therefore far removed from the phantom American divisions in

Kent – in the spring of 1944 Leonhardt put over to Hamburg that his employer had loaned him to a friend at Wye who needed help with the harvest. Verisimilitude demanded that Schmidt should actually relocate his transmitter to Kent, where an imaginary railway clerk at Ashford betrayed imaginary FUSAG movement orders, and observed 20,000 imaginary Canadian troops in Dover.

'Tate's reports from Wye were so much appreciated,' crowed MI5, 'that one Abwehr official, as we learned subsequently, was of the opinion that they could "even decide the outcome of the war".' It is no coincidence that Tar Robertson was awarded an OBE in the Birthday Honours List for June 1944.

The bodyguard of lies interposed via Operation Fortitude was undoubtedly the high-water mark of the entire Allied double-cross system and would continue to fool the enemy until August. Placing this achievement in context, John Masterman, a keen sportsman, was careful to acknowledge the colossal influence of Little Man Snow, MI5's troublesome alpha agent. 'Running a team of double agents is very like running a club cricket side. Older players lose their form and are gradually replaced by newcomers. Well-established veterans unaccountably fail to make runs, whereas youngsters whose style at first appears crude and untutored make large scores. If in the double-cross world Garbo was the Bradman of the later years, then Snow was the W. G. Grace of the early period.'

Indeed, by July 1944 Arthur Owens was back on the crease, acting as a stool pigeon on the special wing, intent on working his ticket. In his new role Snow blew the whistle on illicit communications between Dartmoor and the Isle of Man, which again threatened to compromise Tate and Summer and would lead to the dismissal of the camp commander. Snow also informed on the Norwegian agent Tor Glad (aka Jeff), already judged unreliable by B1A, and now said to be 'building up a stock of information concerning MI5 which he intends to broadcast after the war'. According to Owens, the rogue Scandinavian threatened to slit his, Owens', throat. Robertson, however, had heard it all before.

There were other glimpses of vintage Snow. During the early hours of 13 June the first V1 flying bomb to fall on London rattled over the weald of Kent before its noisy ramjet engine cut out over Bethnal Green, dropping the warhead on Grove Road and killing six civilians, two of them children. Within a fortnight German rocketeers had launched more than 2,000 of these primitive cruise missiles, killing 1,600 people, seriously wounding 4,500 more and damaging 200,000 homes. Renewed threats by Hitler to reduce London to a 'garden of ruins' no longer rang hollow. Wrenching his attention from the plight of Snow and Snow Junior, the Home Secretary warned of a 'serious deterioration' in civilian morale. Churchill in turn demanded robust offensive action, urging the Chiefs of Staff to obliterate the cunningly concealed launch sites in Northern France and 'drench the cities of the Ruhr' with poison gas.

Having bided his time, Owens chose this moment to divulge that the Doodlebugs themselves might carry chemical warheads. Referring back to his encounter with the four sinister scientists in Hamburg on the eve of war, Owens now warned of the lethal 'acid vapour' with 'extraordinary corrosive powers' that was capable of melting skin and disintegrating metals. Hints about deadly new chemical agents had also been dropped in Lisbon in 1941. Once again, a junior officer traipsed down to Dartmoor. 'This substance was so dangerous that the Germans have not hitherto had any effective means of using it. Snow argues that the conception of the rocket has altered the whole position, and is convinced that the V1 is a combination of the rocket and this vapour.'

Within MI5, Snow's latest dubious revelation raised the dread spectre of Zeppelin shells. 'This story may be five per cent true,' guessed Helenus Milmo, a newcomer to B Division and later a

High Court judge. 'I doubt if it is more, and have no idea where this five per cent lies.'

Five per cent, or one hundred per cent? Milmo knew nothing of the sinister scheme to poison British reservoirs in 1940, or that Ritter had prized Snow's skills as a chemist. The lethal vapour described by Owens conceivably nodded towards Tabun and Sarin, two deadly nerve agents developed in Nazi laboratories, both of which might have been delivered by V1 and V2 missiles, together with deadly bacteria and radioactive waste. Thankfully London was spared these horrors, and Owens' warnings about new forms of frightfulness were never put to the test. As always in the mysterious, unverifiable world of rogue Agent Snow, there was no way of separating the signal from the noise, or the real dope from the stunts and the spoofs.

For the Twenty Committee, the flying-bomb menace posed a very different problem. Within days of the opening barrage the Abwehr began to buzz urgent requests for details of V1 damage, pressing agents such as Tate, Garbo and Zigzag for arrival times and points of impact. Since accurate reporting would enable the enemy to improve their aim, MI6 scientist R. V. Jones suggested subtle manipulation of double-cross data fed back to Germany, with the object of ensuring that missiles fell short of central London. Residents of hard-hit southern suburbs such as Wandsworth, Croydon and Dulwich might not have approved but their sacrifice was not in vain. 'Up to fifty per cent more casualties might have been incurred,' reckoned Jones, whose own parents lived in Dulwich. 'Up to 2,750 more killed, and up to 8,000 more seriously injured. Even if only a fifth of these figures is ascribed to the success of our deception, it was clearly worthwhile.'

According to Masterman, the Doodlebug stunt also prolonged the working lives of several XX agents. 'The deception was ample justification for keeping the agents alive after the invasion of France, more particularly as the less important agents were the most useful for this purpose.' By the beginning of September 1944 most of the V1 launch sites in France had been overrun, and the threat much reduced. In ghastly contrast, bungling Nikolaus Ritter had allowed a thousand-plane raid to flatten Hanover. Fate, so it seemed, had delivered payback for Colonel Johnny's betrayal of the radar secret in 1939, and the Luftwaffe's failure to blind Chain Home at the start of the Battle of Britain.

A series of rapid advances during August and September 1944 carried the Allied armies almost to Brussels, prompting optimists to predict once again that the war could be over by Christmas. 'I should very much like to arrange for the release of both Snow and his son before the end of hostilities,' Robertson wrote to the Home Office, offering a philanthropic promise that MI5 would support the redundant agent until he was back on his feet. 'Neither is now considered to be a potential menace to the security of this country, and since his internment in Dartmoor Snow has been of considerable use in furnishing bits of information which he has picked up from his fellow detainees.'

Having partially atoned for his sins, Hitler's chief spy in England finally regained his liberty on the last day of August. John Marriott collected Owens from Dartmoor by car, noting that the Little Man showed 'scarcely any gratitude', emerging from the tall granite gatehouse with no ID card or ration book, and just two pounds ten shillings in his threadbare pockets. 'I had very little conversation with him apart from trivialities,' Marriott added. 'Owens did ask if I knew where Lily was, stating that what he really wanted to know was the whereabouts of the child. I told him, truthfully, that I had no idea of where she was.'

Tar Robertson knew full well. In July 1942 Lily Sophia Bade had married a precision turner named Brian Funnell who worked in a local aircraft factory and took on Jean Louise as his own. Only then was the blushing war bride allowed to leave Homefields, but would remain in Surrey under the watchful eye of the Security Service. Snow would never see his mistress again, nor Jean Louise, the daughter born on Eagle Day in August 1940 as the Luftwaffe opened the birdcage.

With no visible means of support, and nowhere to go, B1A were forced to support Owens for six long months. Released simultaneously with his father, Bob Owens showed greater initiative, setting up home in Kingston and marrying patient Lavinia Cantello at All Saints Church, Norwood, on 21 October. Owens Senior attended the ceremony, acting as a witness under his real name and stating his occupation as 'retired'.

At the B1A office in St James's this was all too apparent, since Owens remained resolutely unemployed, and unemployable. 'Snow has not contrived to find himself a job,' Tar despaired. 'I am satisfied that as long as he feels that we shall look after him, he will be content to drift along without making any effort.'

Attempts to place Owens with an engineering or chemical concern came to nothing, and by the end of January 1945 the accumulated cost of maintaining the former Colonel Johnny had risen to £215. His patience exhausted, Tar ran through the accounts from day one, then sought permission to buy Owens off with a lump-sum payment of £500. 'Snow must stand on his own feet,' he told Guy Liddell, 'but not cast on to the world without means. The intelligence dividend we received from the conduct of his case is impossible to express in terms of money, but it was a large one. In addition his case put into our hands the sum of £13,850 in cash. We do not know with accuracy how much money Owens retained for himself by direct appropriation from the Germans, but the payments and expenses we made amounted to less than £4,000. On a pure financial basis the case has been profitable to us.'

These figures were arbitrary at best, and took no account of funds that might have been paid into a secret American account to which Owens occasionally alluded, or of the large debit column opened by his betrayal of radar in 1940. Despite five years of secrets and lies, Robertson, Masterman and Liddell stayed firm in their belief that Hitler's chief spy in England had passed nothing of value to the other side, and therefore the proposed gratuity of £500 stood approved. It was no humdinger, nor right hot, and hardly compared with the £50,000 offered for a Spitfire in 1939. Yet even a miserly one per cent was better than a poke in the eye, or the disagreeable fate of the sixteen Nazi spies executed under the unyielding provisions of the Treachery Act by the time hostilities ceased.

Idle Arthur Owens was tickled to death.

On the morning of Tuesday, 6 March 1945, as Russian forces bombarded the fortress city of Breslau and American tanks rolled through the shattered suburbs of Cologne, the Little Man reported to Room 055, a forbidding basement deep in the bowels of the War Office. Still personally aggrieved, Tar Robertson did not trouble to attend the final debriefing of Agent Snow and chose instead to delegate the task to Len Burt, a former Scotland Yard detective, and Edward Cussen, recently returned from grilling disgraced *Jeeves and Wooster* author P. G. Wodehouse in Paris.

Cussen handed Owens a copy of the Official Secrets Act, predicating various felonies and misdemeanours: *'I undertake upon my honour to abstain from any disclosure which I recognise will entail the risk of jeopardising the interests of Great Britain, her Allies and the Powers associated with her.'*

Owens signed without demur, for countries did not matter. This formality complete, Burt presented former Agent Snow with a cheque for £500. 'I told Owens that it had been decided to give him a gratuity, which it was hoped would assist to establish himself in some future employment. He appeared particularly pleased and said he did not expect it, and in all circumstances felt that he had been generously treated. He intimated that he intended investing the money.'

Burt followed this golden handshake with a cold shoulder. 'I gave Owens to understand that it was very desirable that he should completely disassociate himself from this department, and pointed out the penalties should he be foolish enough to write his reminiscences.'

The obloquy and odium ran deep. 'I told Owens that if at any time he should want to contact us, which was most unlikely, he should communicate with me personally and no one else.'

Not Tar.

Not Biscuit.

Not Celery.

Not Lily Bade.

Without further ado, Colonel Johnny was escorted to the doors of the War Office and cast out onto the busy Whitehall pavement.

There, in the pale spring sunlight, Snow melted away.

Epilogues

Arthur Owens (aka SNOW aka JOHNNY aka Thomas Wilson) took up with a woman called Hilda White and moved to Great Amwell in Hertfordshire. The former Agent Snow changed his surname to White by deed poll in October 1946; a son, also called Graham, was born in November. In low water by 1948, Owens borrowed £5 from his eldest son Bob and relocated to the Republic of Ireland, later setting up shop in Wexford to sell radios and batteries. Snow's birth name and a version of his dubious wartime career were first made public by *John Bull* magazine in October 1957, though his embarrassment – if any – did not endure, since Hitler's chief spy in England died of myocarditis (cardiac asthma) two months later, on Christmas Eve. Diligent research by Madoc Roberts traced an unmarked grave to plot 57, Section O, in the cemetery at St Ibar, Crosstown, a few miles outside Wexford. It may be noted, however, that Tar Robertson informed intelligence historian Nigel West that 'Mr White' died in Ireland far later, in 1976. And so the mystery continues. In 1992 the BBC broadcast *Snow*, a television drama based on the scant information then available, with Michael Maloney in the title role. Heavily weeded, the official Snow files were released by MI5 to The National Archives in 2001, 35 volumes having shrunk to just 10.

Lily Bade (aka LILY) continued to live at Homefields under MI5 supervision – and the shadow of detention under 18B. In July 1942 she married Brian Funnell, a precision turner at a local aircraft factory, and subsequently lived quietly, dying (as

Lily Butler) in West Ham in 1993. Her daughter with Owens, Jean Louise Pascoe, born in August 1940, is still alive at the time of writing.

Graham 'Bob' Owens (aka SNOW JUNIOR) remained close to his father. Soon after the war the pair developed a fuel additive called Wenite, although this failed to catch on despite continued rationing. Following publication of *The Game of the Foxes* and *The Double-Cross System* Graham Owens wrote to the then Prime Minister, Edward Heath, in a futile effort to restore his father's reputation. Snow Junior died in Portsmouth in 1981.

Patricia Owens went on to become a moderately successful film actress, often playing American characters on account of her Canadian accent. She relocated to Hollywood in 1956, and under contract to 20th Century Fox starred with Vincent Price in science fiction classic *The Fly*. Irene, her mother, briefly joined her in America, but soon wore out her welcome. Pat's movie career failed to catch fire, and by the late 1960s she was day-playing on television serials such as *Lassie* and *Perry Mason*. Briefly married to screenwriter Sy Bartlett, Agent Snow's eldest daughter died in California in August 2000, aged 75. Like her brother Graham, she refused to acknowledge that her father had acted as Hitler's chief spy in England.

Walter Dicketts (aka CELERY aka Jack Brown) returned to Lisbon in May 1941 in an unsuccessful bid to persuade George Sessler to defect. In July he was offered the choice of an assignment in Brazil, or an SO2 mission to France, though it is unclear whether he undertook either. Following yet another financial scrape Dicketts was declared bankrupt in 1947 and imprisoned at HMP Wandsworth. MI5 declined to provide evidence in mitigation at his trial, having no doubt digested information provided by Ritter and Ruser which confirmed that Agent Celery had been flipped in Hamburg in March 1941. Compounding tragedy with irony, in August 1957 Dicketts followed the example of William Rolph by committing suicide with the aid of coal gas. Like Rolph, his death certificate was signed by William Bentley Purchase. Like Owens, he would be partially unmasked by *John Bull*.

Sam McCarthy (aka BISCUIT aka MAC) is known to have been a Canadian named Frank but eludes precise identification. Perhaps Biscuit was a McVitie. In 1951 he was charged with embezzlement at East Grinstead, though the case went unreported. Notwithstanding an 'excess of zeal', McCarthy deserved credit for enabling the Snow show to run beyond May 1940, when others – Tar Robertson included – were inclined to throw in the towel.

Gwilym Williams (aka G.W.) died in 1949 at the age of 62. According to John Humphries in *Spying for Hitler*, the only noteworthy entry in Williams' police record is that he once stopped a runaway horse.

Nikolaus Ritter (aka DR RANTZAU) ended the war as a lieutenant colonel, still in charge of a flak unit despite the Hanover debacle in 1945. Briefly employed by American forces as a translator, in July 1945 he was arrested by a British Field Security section and held at the CSDIC (WEA) detention centre at Bad Nenndorf, where the commandant was Tin-Eye Stephens. There British interrogators noted 'a curious lack of knowledge about his own cases' and made Ritter sweep the officers' mess. 'This was not the time to reveal the truth nor his achievements,' a relative hinted much later. Eventually released from custody in 1947, Ritter returned to Hamburg and scraped a living in various casual jobs, settling on import/export sales, and ended his working life as managing director of a charity. His unpublished memoirs informed *They Spied on England* (1958) and *The Game of the Foxes* (1971), and would eventually appear as *Deckname Dr Rantzau* in 1972. According to his son-in-law, Manfred Blume, the former Doctor Rantzau feared prosecution (or worse), and thus the text omits as much as it covers. Nevertheless, by 1972 Ritter was happy to reveal that which had to remain secret at Bad Nenndorf. 'Our little Johnny played his unremitting and fascinating game out right to the very end. The British are right to claim that Johnny worked for their intelligence service. But what the British did not know was that he did so only with my agreement and encouragement.' The dapper, extrovert Rhinelander passed away in 1974.

Thomas Argyll Robertson (aka TAR) retired from MI5 in 1948 with the rank of colonel, unhappy with the new regime imposed by Sir Percy Sillitoe. In the opinion of John Masterman, his decision 'at the end of the war to leave the service in order to farm was one of the greatest losses which MI5 ever suffered.' Tar farmed 120 acres near Evesham in Worcestershire, but was not best pleased by Masterman's decision to publish *The Double-Cross System* in 1972. He died in 1994, never having been allowed to speak freely about his remarkable double-cross war. 'It was people that counted with Tommy,' his brother-in-law Peter Stormonth Darling told author Geoffrey Elliott. 'They all started equal in his eyes. He saw the best in everyone and rarely disliked anyone, though he could disapprove strongly of other people's actions or words. He was non-judgemental and had a soft spot for the unusual types, including the odd rogue with a bit of charm.'

Wulf Schmidt (aka TATE aka LEONHARDT) buzzed his last message to Wohldorf on 2 May 1945, after four and a half extraordinary years as a XX agent. Granted British citizenship as Harry Williamson, the well-travelled Dane settled in Watford and worked as a photographer on a local newspaper, later becoming a leading breeder of canaries and other caged birds. Four decades after Schmidt received his Iron Cross, several members of his German family believed that he was still working undercover in England, though media coverage surrounding an unpaid Poll Tax bill led to colourful publicity. He succumbed to cancer in October 1992, aged 80, still under the protection of MI5.

Gösta Caroli (aka SUMMER aka NILBERG) was deported to Sweden in 1945 and took a job with a firm of seed merchants near Malmö. Scarred by his wartime experiences his health gradually deteriorated, condemning him to several years in a wheelchair before his death in 1975. The German government had earlier rejected his claim for a disability pension.

Jan Willem Ter Braak lies buried in an unmarked grave at St Mary's, Great Shelford, three miles south of Cambridge. The Hinxton Home for Incurables is but an hour's brisk walk away.

George Hamilton (aka G. C. Hans Hamilton), the wealthy investment banker and company sponsor who brought Snow to London in 1933, introducing him both to NID and the Abwehr, served in combined operations during the Second World War. 'Hamilton should be interviewed and required to give a full account of his dealings with Snow,' proposed an MI5 memo in 1944. 'He may have seen in Snow's position an opportunity for profitable, if rather sharp, business.' Evidently Hamilton was cleared of any wrongdoing, and remained on the army emergency reserve list until 1957. He died in 1960.

Guy Liddell retired from MI5 in 1952, afterwards serving as a security adviser to the Atomic Energy Commission. He had been expected to succeed David Petrie as Director-General of

MI5 but was passed over in favour of Sir Percy Sillitoe, a decision due in part to Liddell's friendships with Guy Burgess, Kim Philby and Anthony Blunt, all three of whom were unmasked as Soviet spies. Liddell died of heart failure in 1958. Codenamed WALLFLOWERS, his unique daily journals remained classified until 2002, when – suitably weeded – they were released to The National Archive.

John Masterman left MI5 in September 1945, though not before writing *The Double-Cross System* as an internal history. One hundred copies were printed, of which 75 were promptly destroyed. Masterman returned to the dreaming spires of Oxford, becoming first Provost of Worcester College, then Vice-Chancellor of the University. He was knighted in 1959. Masterman repeatedly pressed for publication of his official XX history, arguing that confidence in the British secret service had to be restored following the scandal of the Cambridge spy ring. Three successive MI5 DGs declined, after which Masterman arranged to publish *The Double-Cross System* through Yale University Press in 1972. In a remarkable (but pragmatic) volte-face, the British edition was issued through HMSO – with the Crown retaining a royalty of 50 per cent.

Masterman died in 1977. His oft-quoted statement (that 'by means of the double agent system *we actively ran and controlled the German espionage system in this country*') remains largely – but not entirely – true.

Bibliography and Sources

Detailed chapter by chapter source notes for *Double Agent Snow* can be viewed online at:
www.ltmrecordings.com/doubleagentsnownotes.html

Please note: some dialogue cited or referred to in official files has been edited to aid clarity.

Archive Sources

National Archives (London): KV2/444–453 (Snow case); KV2/85–88 (Ritter case); KV2/468 (GW case); KV2/674 (Celery case); KV2/60 (Summer case); KV2/114 (Ter Braak case); KV4/13–15 (Camp 020); KV4/185–196 (unedited Guy Liddell diaries); KV2/1452 (Kieboom and Dungeness spies)

Bundesarchiv-Militärarchiv (Freiburg): RW49/566–567 (Snow/Johnny reports, file copies recovered in 1945 from Bremen stelle)

Books

Allason, Rupert. *The Branch* (Secker & Warburg, 1983)

Andrew, Christopher. *The Defence of the Realm: The Authorised History of MI5* (Allen Lane, 2009)

Baggott, Jim. *Atomic: The First War of Physics* (Icon, 2009)

Best, Sigismund Payne. *The Venlo Incident* (Hutchinson, 1950)

Bower, Tom. *The Perfect English Spy: Sir Dick White and the Secret War 1935–1990* (Heinemann, 1995)

Calder, Angus. *The People's War* (Jonathan Cape, 1969)

Calder, Angus and Sheridan, Dorothy (eds). *Speak For Yourself* (Jonathan Cape, 1984)

Collier, Basil. *The Defence of the United Kingdom* (HMSO, 1957)

Colville, John. *The Fringes of Power Vol. 1* (Hodder and Stoughton, 1985)

Doherty, M. A. *Nazi Wireless Propaganda* (Edinburgh University Press, 2000)

Draper, Christopher. *The Mad Major* (Air Review, 1962)

Elliott, Geoffrey. *Gentleman Spymaster: How Lt. Col. Tommy 'Tar' Robertson Double-crossed the Nazis* (Methuen, 2011)

Farago, Ladislaw. *The Game of the Foxes* (David McKay, 1971)

Fielding, Steve. *Pierrepoint: A Family of Executioners* (Blake, 2008)

Fleming, Peter. *Invasion 1940* (Rupert Hart-Davis, 1957)

Harris, Robert & Paxman, Jeremy. *A Higher Form of Killing* (Chatto & Windus, 1982)

Hayward, James. *Myths and Legends of the Second World War* (Sutton, 2003)

Hinsley, F. H. and Simkins, C. A. G. *British Intelligence in the Second World War Vol. 4* (HMSO, 1990)

Holt, Thaddeus. *The Deceivers* (Weidenfeld & Nicolson, 2004)

Hooper, David. *Official Secrets: The Use and Abuse of the Act* (Secker & Warburg, 1987)

Jeffrey, Keith. *MI6: The History of the Secret Intelligence Service 1909–1949* (Bloomsbury, 2010)

Jones, R. V. *Most Secret War* (Hamish Hamilton, 1978)

Jowitt, The Earl. *Some Were Spies* (Hodder & Stoughton, 1954)

Kahn, David. *Hitler's Spies* (Hodder & Stoughton, 1978)

Kieser, Egbert. *Operation Sea Lion* (Cassell, 1987)

Knickerbocker, H. R. *Is Tomorrow Hitler's?* (Reynal & Hitchcock, 1941)

Lampe, David. *The Last Ditch* (Cassell, 1968)

Lewin, Ronald. *Ultra Goes to War* (Hutchinson, 1978)

Liddell, Guy. *The Guy Liddell Diaries Vol. 1* (Routledge, 2005)

Liddell, Guy. *The Guy Liddell Diaries Vol. 2* (Routledge, 2005)

Longmate, Norman. *How We Lived Then* (Hutchinson, 1971)
Masterman, John. *The Double-Cross System* (Yale, 1972)
Masterman, John. *On the Chariot Wheel* (OUP, 1975)
Miller, Joan. *One Girl's War* (Brandon, 1986)
Ogley, Bob. *Surrey at War* (Froglets, 1995)
Overy, Richard. *1939: Countdown to War* (Allen Lane, 2009)
Pierrepoint, Albert. *Executioner: Pierrepoint* (Harrap, 1974)
Popov, Duško. *Spy Counterspy* (Weidenfeld & Nicolson, 1974)
Richards, Lee. *Whispers of War: Underground Propaganda Rumour-Mongering in the Second World War* (Psywar, 2010)
Ritter, Nikolaus. *Deckname Dr Rantzau* (Hoffmann und Campe, 1972)
Searle, Adrian. *Isle of Wight at War 1939–45* (Dovecote, 2000)
Sebag-Montefiore, Simon. *Dunkirk: Fight to the Last Man* (Viking, 2006)
Simpson, A. W. Brian. *In the Highest Degree Odious* (OUP, 1992)
Stafford, David. *Churchill and Secret Service* (John Murray, 1997)
Stephens, Robin. *Camp 020: MI5 and the Nazi Spies* (PRO, 2000)
Thomson, George. *Blue Pencil Admiral* (Sampson Low, 1947)
Turner, E. S. *The Phoney War on the Home Front* (Michael Joseph, 1961)
West, Nigel. *MI5* (The Bodley Head, 1981)
West, Nigel. *MI6* (Weidenfeld & Nicolson, 1983)
West, Nigel. *Seven Spies Who Changed the World* (Secker & Warburg, 1991)
West, Nigel & Roberts, Madoc. *Snow* (Biteback, 2011)
Whiting, Charles & Peis, Gunter. *They Spied on England* (Odhams, 1958)
Winterbotham, Frederick. *The Ultra Secret* (Weidenfeld & Nicolson, 1974)
Winterbotham, Frederick. *The Ultra Spy* (Macmillan, 1989)
Wood, Derek. *The Narrow Margin* (Hutchinson, 1961)

Articles and Journals

Forth, John. *The Village Policeman: A Spy in the Village* (www.bbc.co.uk/ww2peopleswar/stories/51/a5735351.shtml, 2005)

Kluiters, F. A. C. & Verhoeyen, E. *Hilmar Dierks: An International Spymaster and Mystery Man* (www.nisa-intelligence.nl, 2009)

Ramsey, Winston G. *German Spies in Britain* (After the Battle #11, 1976)

Reed, Ronnie (uncredited). *Technical Problems Affecting Radio Communications by the Double-Cross Agents.* Appendix 3 to Hinsley and Simkins (HMSO, 1990)

John Bull magazine, 26 October 1957 (extract from Whiting & Peis)

Unpublished sources:

Lawrence, Marie. Wartime diary (1939–45, preserved at London Borough of Richmond local studies centre)

Acknowledgements

The author wishes to thank Roger Audis, Nick Austin, Christina Di Prima, Zoe Darani, Michael Dierks, Richard Durack, Stewart Gillies, Sarah Gould, Verity Hambrook, Hannah Lane, Jean Pascoe, Sophie Pigott, Winston Ramsey, Madoc Roberts, Kenneth Rose, Bunny Smedley, Neil R. Storey, Etienne Verhoeyen, Nigel West and Graham White.

The staff at The National Archives, The British Newspaper Library, Surrey History Centre, Morden Library, Stratford Library, Streatham Library, MI5 and the National Policing Improvement Agency.

Special thanks are due to Matthew Hamilton at Aitken Alexander, and to Colin Midson, Carly Cook and Briony Gowlett at Simon & Schuster for commissioning and editing *Double Agent Snow*.

All illustrations are drawn from the author's own collection except snow passport and Jaguar Roadster courtesy of Graham White, Lily Bade courtesy of Jean Pascoe, snow M15 file photo courtesy of Madoc Roberts and Hilmar Dierks courtesy of Michael Dierks.

Acknowledgements

Index

A

Abwehr xiv, 9, 12, 16, 17, 18, 24, 25, 30, 34, 39, 40, 43, 50, 72, 105, 122, 133, 134, 139, 140, 141, 153, 155, 258, 265
Addlestone 174, 181, 188, 190, 192, 205, 225, 241, 245, 257
ADLER, Operation *see* EAGLE, Operation
Admiralty 6, 22, 113, 227
Afrika Korps xi, 198, 260
Air Ministry 17, 22, 31, 32, 36, 58, 72, 93, 97, 99, 150, 198, 227, 247
Amsterdam 52, 88, 99, 186
Anglo-German Fellowship 199, 220
Antwerp 69, 70, 77, 82–4, 96–7, 99, 103, 105, 182, 206
Auerbach 17–8, 35, 56
Austria 23, 214, 220, 242

B

1A xii, 47, 52, 55, 64, 73, 79, 90, 95, 104, 111, 123, 127, 137, 153, 160, 173, 174, 175, 180, 186, 188, 193, 200, 203, 215, 231, 236, 238, 241, 249, 251, 259, 263, 265, 269
Bacteriological warfare 39, 58, 59, 60, 84
Bade, Lily xiii, 33–4, 35, 36, 37–40, 41, 47, 48–9, 52, 53, 55, 60, 61, 67, 71, 73, 75, 76, 79, 138, 142, 144, 146, 151, 152, 153, 174, 189, 190, 191, 193, 200, 203, 204, 206, 208, 219, 222, 234, 237, 241, 245, 255, 257, 268–69, 273–74
Baltic 7, 29, 40, 42, 136
Barbados, SS 107, 109, 113, 116–27, 128, 133, 145, 210
BARBAROSSA, Operation xiv, 165, 217, 246, 255
Barcelona 214, 221

Battle of Britain 140, 149, 165, 199, 268
BBC 45, 46, 159, 165, 188, 200, 273
Beaumont-Nesbitt, Paddy 170, 171
Belgium 9, 22, 47, 64, 68, 77, 81, 83, 85, 95, 100, 105, 128, 130, 221
Berlin 18, 40, 51, 74, 77, 78, 93, 122, 129, 138, 149,183, 189, 199, 200, 209, 212, 222, 223, 225, 229, 242, 247, 250
Best, Sigismund 74, 78, 122
Biggin Hill 20, 35, 45, 257
Birmingham 27, 84, 88, 93, 97, 98, 146, 153, 180
BISCUIT *see* McCarthy, Sam
Black market xv, 92
Blackout xi, 36, 78, 154, 155, 180, 198, 206
Blenheim Palace 173–74
Bletchley Park xiv, 140, 147, 162, 184
Blitz xiv, 25–6, 150, 162–64, 173, 179, 186, 189, 190, 198, 230, 246–47
Blitzkrieg 81, 105, 106, 110, 116
Bloodhounds 243
Blunt, Anthony 173, 278
Bomber Command xiv, 49–50, 75, 82, 183, 218
Boon, Dirk 256–57
Boyle, Archie 95, 120, 199
Brandenburg commando 44, 153, 177, 201
Bristol 2–3, 48, 50, 56, 90, 103, 143, 181, 225
British Union of Fascists 20–21, 27, 50
Brooklands 165
Brown, Jack *see* Dicketts, Walter
Brussels 9, 57, 65, 66, 68, 78, 82, 93, 170, 268
Burgess, Guy 278
Burt, Len 270–1
Burton, Maurice 51, 67, 137, 140, 146, 150, 151, 166, 181, 190, 191, 192

C

Cambridge xiv, 168, 169, 179, 184, 192, 193, 196, 197, 202, 235–36, 244, 277
Camp 020 157, 160, 162, 163, 167, 169, 170, 172, 176, 177, 178, 179, 183, 186, 188, 194, 196, 201, 203, 216, 231, 241, 243, 248, 249, 250, 251, 256, 259, 262, 263
Camp 020R 197, 251
Canada 4, 68, 73, 87, 104, 108, 132, 135, 137, 181, 256
Canaris, Wilhelm 58
Cardiff 11

Caroli, Gösta (aka SUMMER) 153–54, 155, 158–60, 162, 165–67, 168, 172, 177, 179–80, 181, 184, 185, 188, 194, 195–97, 201, 205, 228, 254, 265, 277
CELERY *see* Dicketts, Walter
Chain Home *see* radar
CHARLIE *see* Eschborn, Charles
Chamberlain, Neville 26, 45–6, 95, 105
Chapman, Eddie (aka ZIGZAG) 264, 267
Churchill, Winston v, 59, 105, 122, 129, 136, 137, 141, 142, 163, 173, 178, 192, 200, 246, 247, 248, 255, 264, 266,
Cleethorpes 113, 121, 189
Cocaine 219
Codes 29, 39, 49, 50, 99, 131, 208
Cologne 9, 12, 155, 270
Colville, John 60, 136
Communists 21
Cowgill, Felix 205
CROMWELL alarm 163, 171, 227
Cross, Stanley 191–92
Crosstown 273
Crowcombe 152
Croydon 70, 77, 150, 151, 267
Czechoslovakia 23, 26, 35, 214, 220, 242, 244

D

D-Day 139, 263–65
Daily Herald 90–1, 96
Dargel, Editha 76, 79, 96
Dartmoor gaol 258, 261, 262, 265, 266, 268
Dearden, Harold 179
Death ray 32, 58, 60
Defence Regulation 18B 47, 48, 50, 59, 91, 100, 104, 106, 122, 123, 128, 179, 245, 246, 257
del Pozo, Piernavieja (aka POGO) 182–83, 189, 205
Denmark 47, 50, 79, 96, 98, 100
Dicketts, Walter (aka CELERY) 87–90, 91–6, 97–9, 103, 147, 180–1, 188–89, 190–91, 200, 203–4, 209–12, 213–23, 224, 226, 230–32, 234–35, 240, 241–42, 246, 247, 250, 251, 259, 263, 274–75
Dierks, Hilmar 9, 10, 11, 12, 13–14, 15, 23, 155, 175
Dixon, Richard 169, 184, 196
Döbler, Henri 143, 145, 152, 210, 221
Dolphin Square 65, 109, 110, 163
Draper, Christopher 12, 18, 24, 26, 51

Driffield 50
Drücke, Karl 175, 186
Drugs 170, 209, 219, 230
Dublin 84, 139, 178, 256
Dungeness 155
Dunkirk xii, 129, 132–33, 136
DYNAMO, Operation 132–33

E

Eagle Day *see* EAGLE, Operation
EAGLE, Operation 145, 147–49, 150, 151, 165
Erikson, Vera 175–76
Erprobungsgruppe 210 147–48, 150, 154, 164
Eschborn, Charles (aka CHARLIE) 71, 73, 75, 83, 94, 102, 152, 199, 229
Estoril 143, 208, 210, 213, 232
Expanded Metal Company Limited 4, 5, 13, 18, 30, 31, 40, 239

F

Fallschirmjäger 58, 98, 101, 105, 151, 163
Federal Bureau of Investigation (FBI) 14, 35, 72
Ferrett, Fred 5, 18, 33, 52, 193
Fifth Column 63, 81, 90, 102, 104, 106, 112, 149, 182, 214
Fighter Command 33, 77, 149, 150, 199, 262
Forged papers xiv, 144, 145, 160, 170, 175, 177, 184, 187, 192, 202, 208, 236, 237
FORTITUDE, Operation 264–65
France 24, 25, 29, 41, 47, 51, 53, 56, 64, 81, 92, 102, 105, 110, 116, 128–29, 136, 138, 140, 141, 155, 162, 214, 251, 266
Frost, Malcolm 169, 188
Funnell, Brian 268, 273
FUSAG 264–5

G

G.W. *see* Williams, Gwilym
Gagen, William 29, 37, 47, 48, 54, 55, 61–2, 91, 119, 190
Gartenfeld, Karl 154, 158, 168, 177, 184, 243, 248
GCHQ 51, 52, 53
George VI, King 129, 133
Gestapo 14, 71, 74, 92, 97, 127, 170, 215, 219, 258
Glad, Tor (aka JEFF) 237, 265
Goebbels, Joseph 219, 220, 230
Goose, Kurt (aka GANDER) 153, 177–78, 201, 254
Göring, Hermann xi, 77, 129, 145, 147, 149, 150, 162, 247, 258

Grantham 81, 82, 180, 181
Grimsby 28, 82, 96, 106, 107, 111, 113, 116, 117, 119, 120, 124, 133, 189

H

Halifax, Lord 101
Hamburg 9, 10, 12, 14, 16, 22, 24, 28, 30, 31, 35, 37, 42, 49, 53, 75, 79, 106, 138, 159, 166, 170, 174, 189, 198, 205, 206, 209, 215, 217, 218, 219, 222, 225, 226, 242, 243, 247, 251, 258, 266, 275
Hamilton, Duke of 199, 200, 217, 243, 246, 247
Hamilton, George 4, 5, 6, 10, 31, 41, 277
Hanover 259
Harker, Jasper 99, 111, 123, 137, 191
Haushofer, Albrecht 199, 200, 217, 247
Hegira, Plan 193–94, 255, 257
Hess, Rudolf 200, 217, 246–47, 250, 251
High Wycombe 166–67, 168
Hinchley-Cooke, Edward 12, 18, 21, 24, 26, 28, 30, 40, 121, 127, 157, 240
Hinxton 180, 184, 188, 189, 194, 195, 277
Hitler, Adolf xi, xiv, 5, 12, 20, 23, 35, 41, 44, 45, 53, 55, 59–60, 64, 74, 84, 92, 101, 115, 119, 129, 136, 138, 139, 142, 146, 158, 160, 163, 183, 200, 214, 217, 223, 225, 230, 242, 247, 255
Home Guard 141, 149, 153, 159, 163, 168, 171, 184, 246
Homefields xiv, 174, 186, 189, 192, 193, 200, 208, 210, 219, 223, 237, 245, 246, 257
Hornchurch 45, 150
Horsfall, Eugene 83
Horsfall, Jock 169, 173, 225, 226, 227
Hussein, Obed 103, 139

I

Infrared 198–99, 201, 211
Invasion scares 136, 140–42, 158, 163, 171–72, 217, 227
IP Club 110, 114, 121, 129–31, 189, 227
Ireland 64, 78, 83, 84, 85, 139, 140, 141, 183, 204, 212, 256, 273
Irish Republican Army 27, 36, 83, 84, 85
Isle of Man 260, 262, 265

J

Jakobs, Josef 201–2, 243, 248, 251, 252
Jan Mayen Island 188, 198
Japan Times Advertiser 242
JOHNNY *see* Owens, Arthur
Joint Intelligence Committee 102, 163
Jones, R.V. 60, 75, 267
Jowitt, William 176, 185–6
Joyce, William 42, 65, 91

K

Kell, Vernon 44, 99, 111, 137
Kenley 20, 35, 77, 257
Kent, Tyler 143
Kiel 7, 13, 15, 49, 50, 127
Kilburg, George (aka DRAGONFLY) 197
King, John 27, 131
Kingston 49, 53, 54, 55, 59, 61, 66, 75, 150, 165, 269
Knight, Maxwell 65, 104, 109, 143, 163, 170, 227
Krafft, Mathilde 75–6, 79, 83, 96, 123, 259

L

Lamp, Operation 116–27, 229, 234, 259
Latchmere House *see* Camp 020
Lawrence, Marie 164
LENA, Operation 139, 143, 144, 149, 153, 160, 167, 170, 175, 177, 183, 184, 197, 207, 208, 236, 237, 251, 258, 259
LEONHARDT *see* Schmidt, Wulf
Liddell, Guy
  on Abwehr competence 141, 201–2
  capturing parachute agents 153, 160, 243
  character 43
  execution of spies 59, 178–9
  on del Pozo 183
  fake explosions 103
  Fifth Column 43, 50, 63–4, 81–2
  on Goose 178
  on Harker 137
  on Hess 247
  infrared 198
  invasion threat 129, 171
  Operation Lamp 113
  on McCarthy 104, 146
  peace initiatives 53, 65, 81, 199
  retirement 277–78
  on Romney Marsh spies 157
  on Snow 64, 73, 79, 82, 99, 104, 110, 181
  final collapse of Snow case 223–24 247, 257, 263, 269, 270, 277
  on Swinton 178–9, 188

on Ter Braak 236
and Twenty Committee 168

on Venlo 74
war diary 43
on Williams 182–83
Lielow 182
Lisbon xiii, 137, 142, 168, 181, 184, 187, 188, 197, 203, 205, 208, 221, 231, 242, 244, 247, 250, 257, 259, 263, 274
Liverpool 78, 84, 146, 147, 203
Llandudno 193
LOBSTER, Operation 139
Lody, Carl 51
London Colney 248
Luftwaffe xi, 25, 32, 39, 46, 60, 61, 77, 81, 106, 125, 126, 129, 140, 141, 145, 147, 149, 150, 154, 162, 164, 178, 186, 193, 197, 243, 246, 258, 269
Lydd 156, 185
Lympne 82, 83, 148

M

McCarthy, Sam (aka BISCUIT) 104–5, 107–9, 111–15, 116–121, 137–38, 142, 143–45, 147, 150, 151–52, 158, 166–67, 168, 170, 174–75, 176, 181–82, 183, 188, 189, 193, 196, 198–99, 201, 205, 259, 275
Manston 148
Marlborough, The (public house) 87, 88, 89, 105, 153, 158, 188
Marriott, John 183, 241, 268
Martin, William 133, 261
Masterman, John 88, 168, 179, 192, 202, 230, 236, 238–41, 244, 245, 250, 257, 259, 262, 265, 267, 270, 276, 278
Maxwell, Alexander 263
Meier, Carl 155–58, 185–86, 191
MI5 12, 19, 21, 24, 25, 27, 38, 42, 43–4, 46, 47, 51, 55, 59, 63–4, 70, 85, 90, 91, 97, 99, 100, 106, 107, 108, 110, 114, 117, 122, 126, 129, 134, 137, 140, 141, 142, 144, 145, 155, 160, 165, 168, 169, 170, 172, 175, 177, 179, 181, 182, 183, 186, 187, 189, 200, 206, 216, 217, 220, 223, 227, 231, 235, 236, 240, 243, 247, 255, 256, 257, 258, 265, 277
MI6 6, 7, 9, 11, 13, 18, 30, 60, 64, 73, 74, 79, 88, 91, 110, 137, 140, 163, 168, 171, 179, 180, 187, 191, 200, 205, 208, 223, 227, 245, 248, 251, 267

Michael, Glyndwr 261
Micheldever 46
Microphotography 71, 76, 81, 94, 199
Midas, Plan 197, 250
Milch, Erhard 33
Miller, Joan 143, 163
Milmo, Helenus 266–67
MINCEMEAT, Operation 133, 261–62
Morden 19, 31, 35, 36, 47
Morse code 29, 49, 51, 67, 91, 126
Mosley, Sir Oswald 20–1, 44, 48, 65, 261, 262
Mumbles 3, 5
Munich Crisis 23–4, 26, 147
Mussolini, Benito 21, 136, 178, 197, 242
Myner, Alex 35, 36–8, 42, 47, 48–9, 99, 176

N

Naval Intelligence Division 6, 11
Netherlands 9, 29, 42, 47, 55, 64, 74, 78, 100, 104, 105, 106, 107, 184, 196, 227, 256
New York 5, 14, 35, 144, 172, 258
NILBERG *see* Caroli, Gösta
Norbiton 54, 59, 60, 61, 67, 76, 184
North Weald 150
Northolt 15, 20, 70
Norway 98, 100, 101–03, 175, 237, 261

O

Official Secrets Act 13, 22, 270
Old Bailey 158, 176, 185, 186, 252
Oslo Report 74–5, 79
Ostend 22–3, 42, 51, 71
Oster, Hans 64
Otter, The (public house) 188, 237
Owens, Arthur (aka SNOW)
 air raids (fear of) 36, 146, 164, 174, 190
 Antwerp treffs 68–71, 78–9, 82–4, 96
 appearance 11–2, 15, 37, 258, 263
 arrested in 1941 245
 background 1–2, 3
 and Battle of Britain 150, 151
 betrayed by wife 40–1, 42
 bugged by MI5 77, 79, 90, 181
 and Canada 4
 character flaws 4, 5, 230, 237–38
 as chemist 3, 39, 69, 267
 coded letters 10, 14, 17, 20
 and Cromwell alert 163
 death 273

defection to Germany 19, 219
meets Dicketts 87–90, 91–6, 98–9
reunited with Dicketts 188–89
betrays Dicketts 206, 213
confrontation with Dicketts 231–32
drinking 15, 29, 35, 36, 43, 67, 92, 95, 190, 204, 209, 212, 218, 234
earnings 9, 10, 16, 20, 52, 57, 71, 72, 84, 108, 151, 174–75, 182, 189, 207, 223, 228, 239, 256, 259, 269
false teeth 17, 71, 204, 222
fieldcraft 7, 16, 17, 41, 188, 208, 229
and First World War 2–3
Hamburg treffs 28–9, 34–5, 37–40
and Plan Hegira 193–94, 255
and Hess 246
admiration for Hitler and Germany 32, 67, 92–3
at Homefields 174
and infrared 198–99
interrogation (strength under) 127, 206
as inventor 4–5, 6
JOHNNY codename 10, 15
and Krafft 75
Operation Lamp 111, 112–15, 116–29
laziness 14, 46, 218
mission to Lisbon in 1941 205–226
Lisbon debrief 227–32
and McCarthy 105, 108, 118–9, 145, 150, 152–53, 158
marriage 3, 36
mental health 123, 200, 232, 234, 237
attitude of MI5 towards 18–9, 86–7, 238, 244
first controlled transmission for MI5 51–2
concludes deal with MI5 53
removed from active duty by MI5 in 1940 134–35
retirement 273
returns to active MI5 duty in 1940 158
final debriefing by MI5 238–41
ultimate value to MI5 55, 259
recruited by MI6 6
dismissed by MI6 13
nerves and paranoia 61, 63, 68, 69, 193, 206, 225, 237
and Norwegian campaign 102–3
outbreak of war 42, 45–6
and peace initiatives 223, 243
poor health 124, 127, 208, 215, 226, 229, 234, 237, 242

radar betrayal 32–3, 57–8, 96, 147, 149
betrays Robertson 111
meets Rolph 85
betrays Rolph 131–32
Rotterdam treff 56–9
and Operation Sealion 138–39, 141, 144, 150
secret communication channel with Germany 118, 122, 126, 142, 190–91
slang usage 5, 11
SNOW codename 6
spendthrift nature 4, 5, 16, 18, 19, 66, 191
Stafford and Dartmoor imprisonment 257–58, 260, 262–63, 265, 268
Stafford escape attempt in 1941 255–56
and Summer 166–67
talkative nature 7, 31, 105, 203–4, 238
first transmitter 24, 28–9, 30–1
first transmissions to Germany 42–3
final transmission 241
treachery motives 8, 10, 40, 93
and V weapons 266–67
in Wandsworth 1939 47–54
meets Williams 66
undermines Williams 72, 77–8
winter reconnaissance tour 1940 81–2
womanising 15, 22, 33–4, 212, 215, 225
Owens Battery Equipment Company 6, 8, 19
Owens, Graham (aka SNOW JUNIOR) 3, 19, 22, 35, 40, 124, 190, 193, 255, 256–57, 261, 262, 266, 269, 273, 274
Owens, Irene 3, 5, 19, 22, 23, 33–4, 36, 38, 40–1, 42, 68, 151, 240, 274
Owens, Patricia 4, 5, 19, 22, 151, 260, 274

P

Peace initiatives 21, 24, 26, 53, 58, 84, 139, 142, 149, 199, 217, 220, 224, 230–31, 233, 242–43, 246–47
Peal, Edward 6, 7, 9, 10, 11, 13, 18, 26, 127, 240
Petrie, David 247, 263, 264, 277
Philby, Kim 278
Phoney War xiii, 62, 64, 65, 84, 98, 100, 105, 120
Pieper, Erwin 7, 8, 10, 13, 23, 41
Pierrepoint, Albert 186, 252–53
Plaid Cymru 57, 104
Plan 1 197

PMS2 130
Poison gas 24, 39, 46, 60, 65, 266, 267
Poland 26, 41, 44, 45, 47, 53, 56, 102, 214, 220, 242
Police Gazette 88, 97
Pollitt, Harry 44
Pons, Sjord 155–58, 185–86
Pontardawe 2, 3, 4, 5, 176, 262
Popov, Dusko (aka TRICYCLE) 187, 197, 250, 263
Post Office 30, 46, 63
Psychology 56, 143, 179–80
Pujol, Juan (aka GARBO) 187, 264, 265, 267
Pullman Court 16, 18, 19, 76
Purchase, William Bentley 133, 261, 275

Q

Q-ships 124

R

Radar 32–3, 50, 57–8, 59, 71, 75, 96, 110, 147–48, 150, 162, 163, 198, 240, 268, 270
Radio Security Service 53, 64
Radlett 185, 202, 228, 243, 248, 264
Reed, Ronnie 165–66, 178, 200, 210, 222, 225, 241
Richmond 67, 76, 79, 80, 95, 97, 104, 108, 111, 131, 146, 151, 157, 163, 164
Richter, Karel 244, 248–49, 251, 252–53
Ritter, Nikolaus (aka Dr Rantzau)
- and America 14–15, 258
- Antwerp treff 68–71, 78–9
- background 14
- character 14–5, 34, 37, 144, 211
- and Dicketts 211–12, 216, 251
- double-crosses MI5 38, 73, 140, 221, 276
- and FBI 258
- leaves Abwehr 258–59, 268
- leaves Stelle X 198, 259
- and Operation Lena 153–54
- Lisbon treff 206–12, 223
- and McCarthy 137, 144
- memoirs 251, 276
- MI5 plans to kidnap 112–13, 120, 122, 124–26, 183
- North Sea treff 78 100, 117–26, 145, 189
- retirement 275–76
- Rotterdam treff 56–8
- and Operation Sealion 139
- slang usage 245
- and Snow 15–16, 20, 23, 138
- blackmails Snow 127, 207
- collapse of Snow case 216, 242, 249, 251
- criticism of Snow 144

Ritter, Nikolaus – *continued*
praise for Snow 17,18, 39, 66, 144, 218
and Summer 154, 167
and Tate 160, 168, 206, 228, 244, 249
and Ter Braak 184
Robertson, Joan 86, 185, 248, 262
Robertson, Thomas (aka Tar)
background and character 26–7, 28, 276
and Dicketts 95, 97–9, 180, 188–89, 190–91, 200, 205, 251
and Plan Hegira 194
and Hess 200
Jan Mayen Island 188, 198
and John King 27–8
Operation Lamp 106–7, 111, 112, 120, 122–23, 124
Lisbon debriefing 227–32
and McCarthy 105, 108, 150, 152, 158
and OBE 265
as radio specialist 30–1
retirement 273, 276
and Rolph 85, 128–32
and Round Bush House 185, 195, 202, 243, 248
confidence in Snow 68, 99
disillusion with Snow xi, 49, 52, 73, 76, 79, 86–7, 95, 109, 121, 134–35, 137, 189, 231, 234, 240, 241
final interview with Snow 238–41
later dealings with Snow 250, 262, 263, 266, 268, 269, 270
and Snow Junior 256–57
and Stewart 84
and Summer 160–1, 167
Rolph, William 85, 89, 91, 102–3, 104, 110–11, 119, 121, 123, 126, 128–32, 135, 183, 188, 189, 191, 227, 261, 275
Romney Marsh 155–58, 162, 163, 172, 176, 185–86, 191
Rotterdam 55, 56–7, 65, 66, 106
Round Bush House 185, 194, 195, 202, 243, 248
Royal Air Force 12, 17, 19, 35, 49, 57, 64, 65, 70, 81, 82, 92, 105, 110, 117, 125, 140, 145, 146, 147, 150, 164, 165, 168, 189, 198, 200, 218, 224, 243
Royal Flying Corps 2
Ruser, Hans 213, 214, 225, 250, 263, 274
Russians in England 51, 101
Ryde, Michael 61–2, 63

S

Sackville Street 85, 86, 91, 93–4, 102, 104, 110, 119,

120, 124, 128–32, 134, 139, 142, 191
Sas, Gijsbertus 64, 74
Schacht, Hjalmar 220, 223, 230, 247
Schmidt, Wulf (aka TATE) xiii, 153, 160, 167, 168–71, 172, 181, 185, 193, 194, 197, 202, 206, 207, 216, 228, 243, 244, 248, 249, 250, 251, 263, 264–65, 267, 276
Schneider, Doctor 37, 219, 251
Scotland, Alexander 169–71
Scotland Yard 31, 42, 47, 62, 97
SEALION, Operation 138–39, 141, 142, 144, 165, 171, 225
Secret weapons 39, 59, 60, 205, 206
Security Executive 178, 251
Seebold, William 258
Selfridges 75–6, 259
Sessler, George 215, 218, 219, 221, 250, 274
SHARK, Operation 217, 227
Short-wave 24, 28, 53–4, 90
Short Brothers 18, 70, 77, 165
Sibs 171, 198
SICHELSCHNITT, Operation 105, 106
Sicherheitsdienst 74
Sillitoe, Percy 276, 278
Simon, Walter 28
Sintra 205, 224, 225
Sloane Avenue 5, 8, 11, 76
SNOW *see* Owens, Arthur
SNOW JUNIOR *see* Owens, Graham
Snuffbox, Plan 47, 48
Spain 140, 182, 183, 187, 226
Special Branch 11, 19, 21, 29, 31, 34, 37, 41, 42, 47, 54, 55–6, 61, 63, 71, 86, 91, 97, 123, 190
Spitfire 36, 66, 77, 104, 122, 140, 200, 270
Stafford prison 245–46, 250, 255, 257–58, 261
Stalin, Josef 41, 44, 136, 264
Stalingrad 260
Stelle X *see* Hamburg
Stephens, Robin ('Tin-Eye') 157, 160, 170, 179, 186, 194, 197, 203, 248, 252, 275
Stettin 29, 30
Stevens, Richard 74, 78, 122
Stewart, Samuel 83–5, 123, 176, 197
Stopford, Richman 61–2, 71–2, 75–6, 106, 124, 127, 128–32, 137, 138, 208, 215, 223
Stratford 5, 33, 52, 193
SUMMER *see* Caroli, Gösta
Sunday Graphic 90
Surbiton 37, 42, 45, 47, 53

Surrey xv, 61, 151, 174, 181, 191, 245, 255
Swansea 3, 57, 65, 71, 72, 96
Swinton, Ernest 178–79, 181, 188, 200, 247–48, 251–52
Sylt 125

T

TATE *see* Schmidt, Wulf
Ter Braak, Jan Willem xiv, 184, 187, 192, 202, 235–36, 244, 277
Thames House 7, 21
Tommy guns 58, 141, 171
Tower of London 51, 247, 252
Treachery Act 122, 127, 132, 145, 158, 170, 172, 178, 185, 270
Tripoli 198, 242, 243
Turkey 187
Twenty Committee 168, 172, 187, 200, 202, 229, 230, 238, 241, 244, 249, 251, 261, 264, 267

U

U-boats xiv, 18, 56, 57, 64, 69, 72, 78, 90, 101, 113, 125, 204, 207, 256
Ultra xiv, 163
Underground Propaganda Committee 171

V

V weapons 266–68
van den Kieboom, Charles 155–58, 185–86, 192
Vatican 64
Venlo Incident 73–4, 78, 96, 183, 230, 248
Ventnor 147–8
Verisimilitude 54, 77, 81, 85, 109, 140, 166, 182, 197, 202, 203, 265
Veronal 209, 215, 219
Victoria station 30, 36, 71, 83, 95, 176
Virgiels, Louisa 34
von Klitzing, Irmgard 15–6, 34–5, 138, 218

W

Waldberg, José 155–58, 162, 172, 185–86, 191
Walti, Werner 176
Wandsworth prison 47–8, 50, 54, 252, 267, 274
Waterloo station 47, 75
Weather reports 39, 49, 61, 62, 78, 132
Weber-Drohl, Ernst 85
Welsh nationalism 1, 17, 54–5, 57, 59, 65, 67, 69, 104
West Ham 33, 52, 55
West, Nigel 170, 273

Whitchurch xii, 143, 205, 224, 226, 231, 247
White, Dick 238
Wilhelmshaven 49, 75
Williams, Gwilym (aka G.W.) 65–8, 71–2, 77–8, 96, 99, 103, 146, 182–83, 193, 229, 275
Williams, 'Hellfire' 21
Wilson, Thomas *see* Owens, Arthur
Winter weather 80–1, 96
Wireless Branch 187
Wireless Committee 71, 77, 78, 146, 149, 168
Witzke, Lothar 69, 70, 144, 182
Wohldorf 39, 42, 45, 51, 52, 54, 62, 77, 79, 80, 104, 105, 106, 107, 128, 138, 140, 146, 151, 164, 165, 166, 167, 171,182, 185, 187, 197, 199, 241, 243, 245
Wormwood Scrubs 43–4, 54, 60, 109, 137, 173

Z

Zeppelin 1, 9, 14, 25, 32, 33, 114, 126, 154, 199, 237, 266

A Note on the Author

James Hayward's previous books include *The Bodies on the Beach*, *Shadowplayers* and *Myths and Legends of the Second World War*. As a solicitor he worked on the Bloody Sunday Inquiry, and as a historian has collaborated with organisations including the BBC, ITV, Channel 4, Imperial War Museum and National Army Museum. He lives in Norfolk and is the proud owner (and very occasional rider) of a vintage 1938 autocycle.

under observation, and the watchers should drop him at once if they think that they have been spotted by him.

Below is a description of as supplied by

Very short and slight; thin brown hair; clean shaven; rather thin and bony face; small, almost transparent and ill-shaped ears, disproportionately small for size of man; curious brown eyes set wide apart and slightly oblique, which gives him a somewhat shifty look; wears brown felt hat, pepper and salt overcoat. Usually wears brown shoes or boots. Very small bony hands stained from cigarette smoking; typical Welsh "underfed" Cardiff type. Speaks fairly correct English without pronounced accent; soft-spoken and lacks assurance in manner. Often wears white or light necktie.

S.7.
15.10.36.

Agent Snow in a contemporary photograph held on file by the Security Service, MI5. 'Typical Welsh underfed "Cardiff" type', according to hostile watchers from the Special Branch

Arthur Owens' passport photograph from 1948. By then Hitler's former chief spy in England was living in Ireland as Arthur White

Lily Bade and her daughter Jean, a portrait taken not long after Owens was arrested in April 1941

Owens (left) pictured with one of his several families, and beloved Jaguar Roadster

Pullman Court, the modernist development on Streatham Hill completed in 1936

Thomas 'Tar' Robertson, Snow's long suffering case officer at MI5. Early mistakes made with Owens would ensure that the double-cross system functioned effectively after 1941

Edward Hinchley-Cooke, Snow's first handler at MI5 in 1937, and later an interrogator at Camp 020

Snow's first German transmitter, delivered to Victoria station in January 1939. Some in the Abwehr referred to these early sets as *klamotten* ('junk')

Maxwell Knight, the MI5 counter-subversion specialist who brought agents G.W. and Biscuit to the Snow case during the Phoney War period (West)

John Masterman, chairman of the Twenty Committee. An Oxford history don in peacetime, Masterman was also a first class cricketer

Nikolaus Ritter, Owens' Abwehr case officer from 1937 onwards, known to MI5 only as 'Doktor Rantzau' when this candidate portrait was added to the Snow file

Hilmar Dierks, the Abwehr veteran who recruited Owens as a German spy as early as 1936. Here he inspects wrecked shipping at Dunkirk

A sketch map of RAF Odiham prepared by Owens circa 1938. His betrayal of radar to Germany was far more damaging

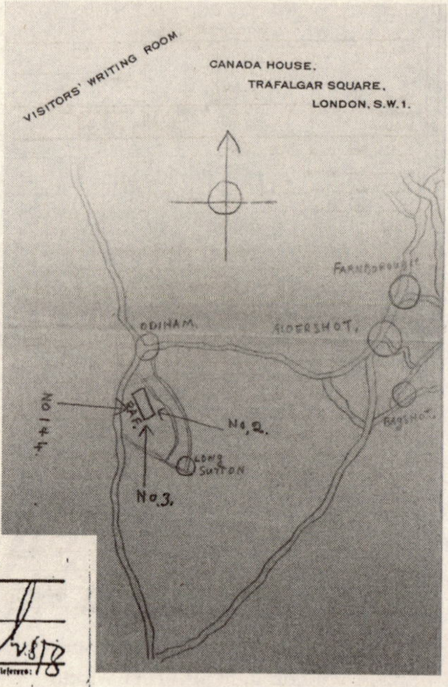

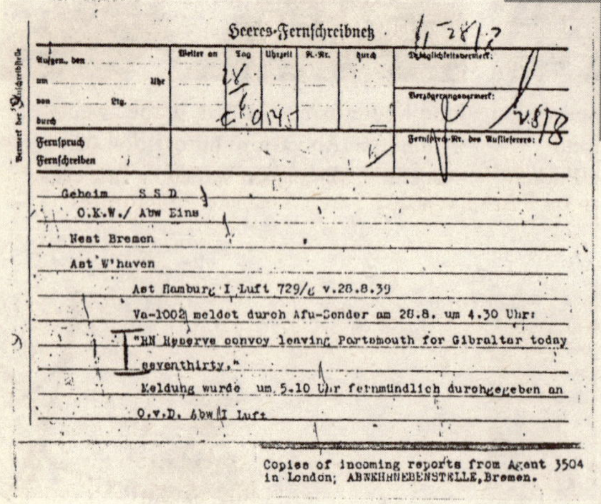
Heeres-Fernschreibnetz

Geheim S S D

O.K.W./ Abw Eins

Nest Bremen

Ast W'haven

Ast Hamburg I Luft 729/g v.28.8.39

Va-1002 meldet durch Afu-Sender am 28.8. um 4.30 Uhr:

"RN Reserve convoy leaving Portsmouth for Gibraltar today seventhirty."

Meldung wurde um 5.10 Uhr fernmündlich durchgegeben an O.v.D. Abw I Luft

Copies of incoming reports from Agent 3504 in London; ABWEHRNEBENSTELLE, Bremen.

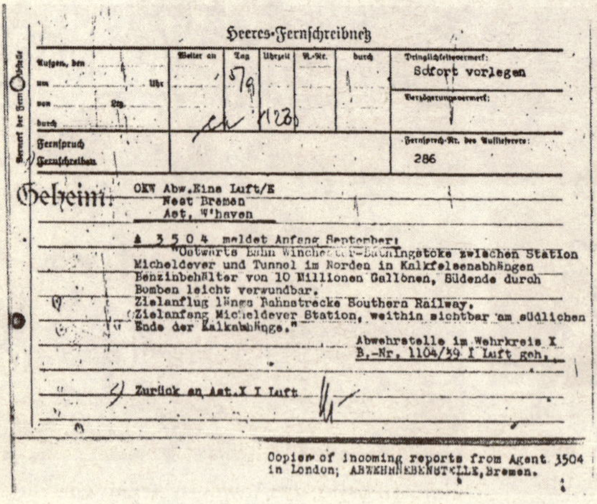
Heeres-Fernschreibnetz

Sofort vorlegen

286

Geheim: OKW Abw.Eins Luft/E
Nest Bremen
Ast, W'haven

A 3 5 0 4 meldet Anfang September:
"Ostwärts Bahn Winchester-Basingstoke zwischen Station Micheldever und Tunnel im Norden in Kalkfelsenabhängen Benzinbehälter von 10 Millionen Gallonen, Südende durch Bomben leicht verwundbar.
Zielanflug längs Bahnstrecke Southern Railway.
Zielanfang Micheldever Station, weithin sichtbar am südlichen Ende der Kalkabhänge."

Abwehrstelle im Wehrkreis X
B.-Nr. 1104/39 I Luft geh.

Zurück an Ast.X I Luft

Copies of incoming reports from Agent 3504 in London; ABWEHRNEBENSTELLE, Bremen.

Abwehr transcripts of signals buzzed by Owens between 28 August and 3 September 1939, none of which were controlled by MI5

Gwilym Williams (aka G.W.), the former Swansea policeman recruited as Snow's first MI5 sidekick in October 1939

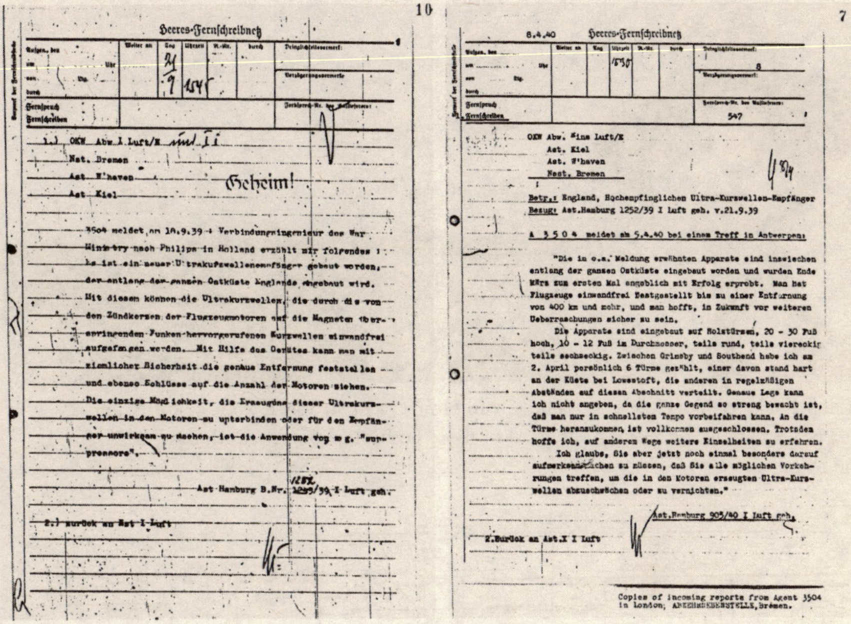

10

Heeres-Fernschreibnetz

Tag 21.9 Uhrzeit 1545

Fernspruch Fernschreiben

1.) OKW Abw. I Luft/E und I i

Nst. Bremen

Ast N'haven

Ast Kiel

Geheim!

3504 meldet am 18.9.39 : Verbindungsingenieur des War Ministry nach Philips in Holland erzählt mir folgendes : Es ist ein neuer Ultrakurzwellenempfänger gebaut worden, der entlang der ganzen Ostküste Englands angebaut wird. Mit diesem können die Ultrakurzwellen, die durch die von den Zündkerzen der Flugzeugmotoren auf die Magneten überspringenden Funken hervorgerufenen Kurzwellen einwandfrei aufgefangen werden. Mit Hilfe des Gerätes kann man mit ziemlicher Sicherheit die genaue Entfernung feststellen und ebenso Schlüsse auf die Anzahl der Motoren ziehen. Die einzige Möglichkeit, die Erzeugung dieser Ultrakurzwellen in den Motoren zu unterbinden oder für den Empfänger unwirksam zu machen, ist die Anwendung von sog. "suppressors".

Ast Hamburg B.Nr. 1252/39 I Luft geh.

2.) zurück an Ast I Luft

7

8.4.40 Heeres-Fernschreibnetz

Uhrzeit 1530

8

Fernspruch Fernschreiben

547

OKW Abw. Eins Luft/E

Ast. Kiel

Ast. W'haven

Nest. Bremen

Betr.: England, Hochempfinglichen Ultra-Kurzwellen-Empfänger

Bezug: Ast.Hamburg 1252/39 I Luft geh. v.21.9.39

A 3 5 0 4 meldet am 5.4.40 bei einem Treff in Antwerpen:

"Die in o.a. Meldung erwähnten Apparate sind inzwischen entlang der ganzen Ostküste eingebaut worden und wurden Ende März zum ersten Mal angeblich mit Erfolg erprobt. Man hat Flugzeuge einwandfrei festgestellt bis zu einer Entfernung von 400 km und mehr, und man hofft, in Zukunft vor weiteren Ueberraschungen sicher zu sein.

Die Apparate sind eingebaut auf Holztürmen, 20 - 30 Fuß hoch, 10 - 12 Fuß im Durchmesser, teils rund, teils viereckig teils sechseckig. Zwischen Grimsby und Southend habe ich am 2. April persönlich 6 Türme gezählt, einer davon stand hart an der Küste bei Lowestoft, die anderen in regelmäßigen Abständen auf diesen Abschnitt verteilt. Genaue Lage kann ich nicht angeben, da die ganze Gegend so streng bewacht ist, daß man nur in schnellstem Tempo vorbeifahren kann. An die Türme heranzukommen ist vollkommen ausgeschlossen. Trotzdem hoffe ich, auf anderem Wege weitere Einzelheiten zu erfahren.

Ich glaube, Sie aber jetzt noch einmal besonders darauf aufmerksam machen zu müssen, daß Sie alle möglichen Vorkehrungen treffen, um die in den Motoren erzeugten Ultra-Kurzwellen abzuschwächen oder zu vernichten."

Ast.Hamburg 903/40 I Luft geh.

2.Zurück an Ast.X I Luft

Copies of incoming reports from Agent 3504 in London; ABWEHRNEBENSTELLE, Bremen.

Abwehr reports on two of Snow's crucial betrayals of radar, made during *treffs* in Rotterdam on 18 September 1939 and Antwerp on 5 April 1940. MI5 were unable to monitor his personal meetings with Ritter

In May 1940 Owens set out to meet Ritter on a Grimsby steam trawler, the SS *Barbados*. Snow's MI5 file contains this image of a very similar vessel

Ritter flew out to the abortive North Sea rendezvous in a large Dornier 18 flying boat, which boasted a range of 2000 miles and an endurance of 12 hours

Walter Dicketts (aka Celery) in a pre-war mugshot from the *Police Gazette*

The Chain Home radar station at Poling near Arundel, typical of those positioned on the south coast of England

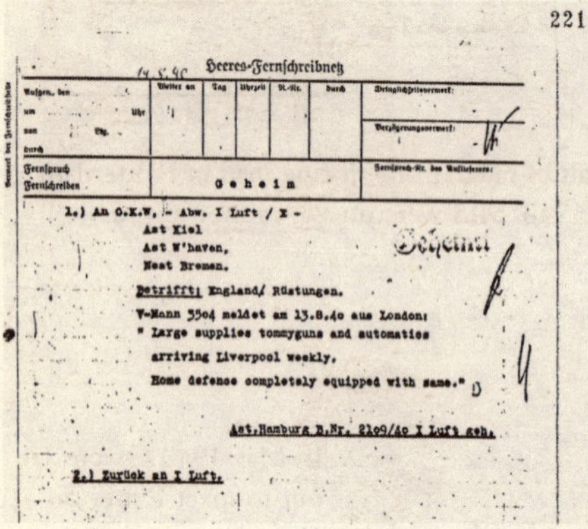

221

14.8.40 Heeres-Fernschreibnetz

Fernspruch
Fernschreiben Geheim

1.) An O.K.W. - Abw. I Luft / E -
Ast Kiel
Ast W'haven,
Nest Bremen.

Geheim!

Betrifft: England/ Rüstungen.

V-Mann 3504 meldet am 13.8.40 aus London:
" Large supplies tommyguns and automatics arriving Liverpool weekly.
Home defense completely equipped with same."

Ast.Hamburg B.Nr. 2109/40 I Luft geh.

2.) Zurück an I Luft.

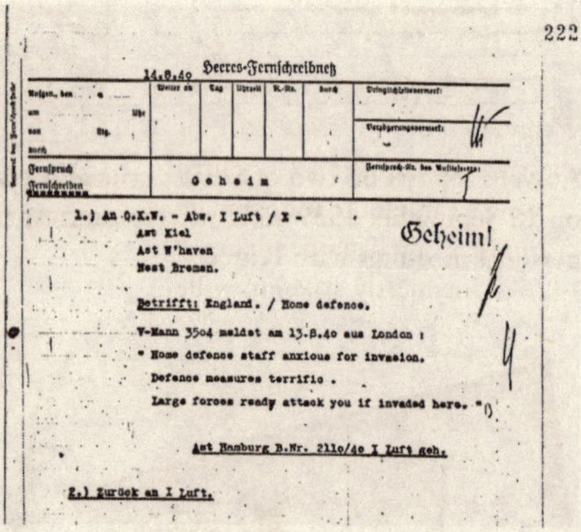

222

14.8.40 Heeres-Fernschreibnetz

Fernspruch
Fernschreiben Geheim

1.) An O.K.W. - Abw. I Luft / E -
Ast Kiel
Ast W'haven
Nest Bremen.

Geheim!

Betrifft: England. / Home defence.

V-Mann 3504 meldet am 13.8.40 aus London :
" Home defence staff anxious for invasion.
Defence measures terrific .
Large forces ready attack you if invaded here. "

Ast Hamburg B.Nr. 2110/40 I Luft geh.

2.) Zurück an I Luft.

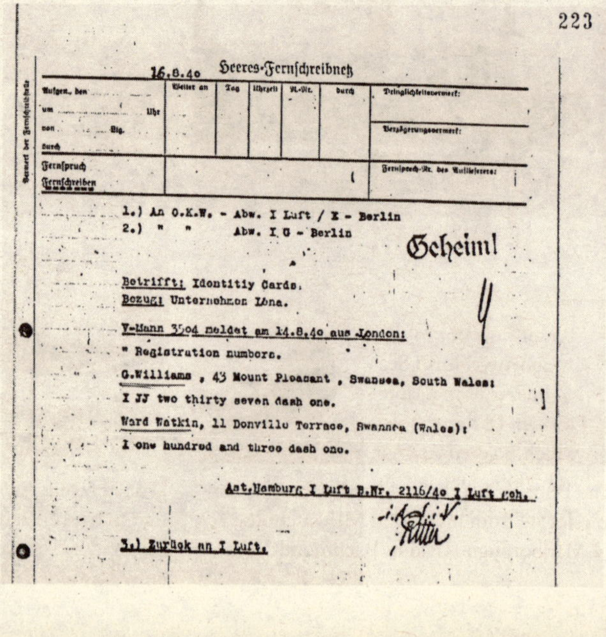

223

16.8.40 Heeres-Fernschreibnetz

1.) An O.K.W. - Abw. I Luft / E - Berlin
2.) " " Abw. I G - Berlin

Geheim!

Betrifft: Identitiy Cards.
Bezug: Unternehmen Lena.

V-Mann 3504 meldet am 14.8.40 aus London:
" Registration numbers.
G.Williams , 43 Mount Pleasant , Swansea, South Wales:
I JJ two thirty seven dash one.
Ward Watkin, 11 Donville Terrace, Swansea (Wales):
I one hundred and three dash one.

Ast.Hamburg I Luft B.Nr. 2116/40 I Luft geh.

i.A. i.V.

3.) Zurück an I Luft.

Abwehr transcripts of three controlled signals buzzed by Snow on 13 and 14 August 1940, two of which seek to deter invasion, and one providing ID serials for incoming German spies

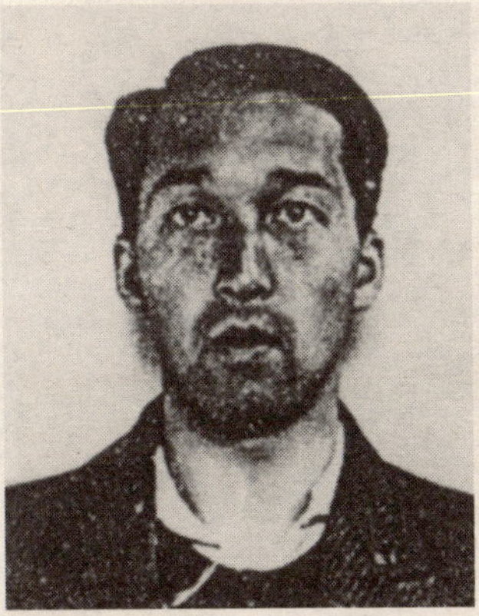

Charles van der Kieboom, one of the hapless invasion spies captured in Kent on 3 September 1940

WELL, WHO HAD THE RADIO SET, ANYWAY?

You remember those German Spies they caught? You remember their radio set? It seems to have changed hands a lot. All the papers show it in the hands of someone different.

TWO German spies came to England with a little radio set. By day, they planned to hide in woods and quarries. By night, they hoped to transmit valuable information to Germany through the little radio set. They believed they would soon be released by Nazi troops. They believed their task would be short. The first was wrong. The second was right. They were quickly caught, convicted, executed. But what happened to the little radio set? Almost every London daily paper photographed it. We reproduce these photographs on this page. Each one shows the set in the possession of someone different.

What we want to know is, who *did* have the radio set, anyway?

The Daily Express *Showed an Officer Playing With It*

"This neat little [illegible] radio transmitting set—being demonstrated in London—was found in the possession of two German spies," said the "Express."

The Daily Telegraph *Showed an N.C.O. With It*

"The transmitting set found in possession of two enemy agents," was the "Telegraph" caption.

The Daily Mirror

All the [illegible] got was a mysterious hand. Whose could it be?

The DAILY HERALD

got theirs just as this mysterious gentleman made off with the set.

The News Chronicle

snapped this young man with the set before he could get rid of it.

The Daily Sketch *Version of the Story*

"Nazi spies executed. This was their radio," said the "Daily Sketch." And they show it in the possession of a pretty girl.

10 PICTURE POST

Kieboom's wireless set revealed in the *Picture Post* for 28 December 1940. Three weeks earlier, the unfortunate Eurasian spy had been hanged inexpertly at Pentonville

The Blitz on London eventually forced Snow to relocate from his second MI5 safehouse at 14 Marlborough Road in Richmond

Wulf Schmidt (aka Tate) and his suitcase transmitter. Codenamed Leonhardt by the Abwehr, and a favourite of Ritter, in 1941 he was awarded an unmerited Iron Cross

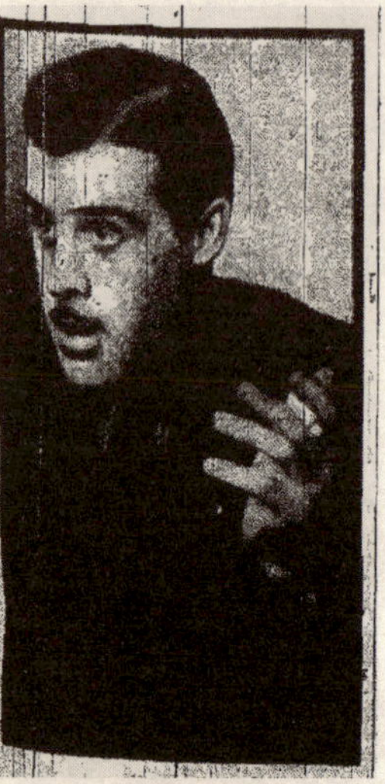

Spanish (not very) secret agent Piernavieja del Pozo, pictured in the *Daily Express* on 7 November 1940

The body of Jan Willem Ter Braak, as discovered in a Cambridge air raid shelter on April Fools' Day 1941

Rudolf Hess with Messerschmitt 110 twin-engined fighter at Augsburg. On 10 May 1941 the Deputy Führer arrived in Scotland hoping to broker peace ahead of Operation Barbarossa, the German assault on Russia. Six weeks earlier Owens and Dicketts had returned from Lisbon with the very same mission

Karel Richter (aka Roboter) retrieves his parachute and equipment from a field near London Colney in May 1941. The officers on the left of the picture are Tin-Eye Stephens and Edward Hinchley-Cooke